WOMEN at the HELM

by
Jeannine Talley

published by
Mother Courage Press

The pen and ink illustrations throughout the book are by the author.
Cover photo by George Hoffman.
Back cover photo of the author by Jeanne Arnold.

19.95 PB

Library of Congress catalog card number 89-63620
ISBN 0-941300-16-1 (cloth edition)
ISBN 0-941300-15-3 (trade paperback)

Mother Courage Press
1533 Illinois Street
Racine, WI 53405

To my mother for encouraging independence
and
Jo and Janet for their continued support.

Acknowledgments

As every writer knows it is nigh impossible to remember everyone who has contributed to and influenced the writing of a book. Much of the credit in this case must go to people who assisted with various details concerning caring for *Banshee*. Often relieving me of these pressures. At the head of this list must go Hilton and Melva Ward for giving tons of technical advice and help in locating the right people and places in New Zealand to deal with a multitude of boat projects and for housing a good portion of *Banshee's* equipment while Joy and I blissfully trotted off as vagabonds to roam the countryside. Enid and Bert Emtage aided in so many concrete and emotional ways in boat projects and making us feel at home that to list everything would take pages. Likewise, Joyce and Jim Irving saw to our safety and comfort on so many occasions it would be impossible to recall them all. These very special friends and many others greatly enriched our time in New Zealand.

The primary person who has taken on the major responsibility for the technical aspects of this voyage—everything from mucking out the bilge to soldering the tiniest wire—is my partner Joy. She has been generous in recognizing my need to have ample time and space to write. This also means that often she undertakes more than her share of the maintenance of our craft.

Several friends have at times read and commented upon my efforts. Joyce and Jim read through some of the early chapters. I appreciate Joyce's attention to spelling and grammar, but I especially treasure her esthetic and creative suggestions. Early on in my efforts, Fay Marie Ainsworth-Hughs read and expertly commented on chapters that I originally conceived of as separate magazine articles.

My special thanks must also go to Joy who has not only lived with me through the entire process of writing a book, but has read and reread every chapter and its revisions, offering—against her protestations of being *un*literary— some of the soundest and wisest comments.

I cannot say enough about my publishers, Barbara Lindquist and Jeanne Arnold of Mother Courage Press. They acted above and beyond the call of duty when they came to New Zealand to finalize arrangements for taking on this book and signing a contract. I shall forever be indebted to them for making the second part of my dream come true.

January 3, 1990
Mooloolaba, Australia

Contents

Prologue

Often the most important day comes and goes unnoticed, without fanfare, fireworks, or bouquets. Who can say when an important decision has been made? Does it come all at once, consciously, or does it float at the subconscious level of the brain mixing indiscriminately with trivia? I honestly don't know when I decided I wanted to sail around the world on my own sailboat. It didn't just happen one day because I had read a book about it. No, it wasn't that kind of thing at all. It was an idea that grew in my mind with almost the same kind of force that caused my infant bones to elongate and harden into their adult form.

To be sure, my desire to sail around the world stems to some extent from my love of adventure and my curiosity about all kinds of things. Still, it is also something deeper, perhaps something akin to destiny. Even on an unconscious level, I have always been attracted to boats—all kinds—and to the sea.

The idea of seeing the world from the deck of a small sailing vessel goes back a long time. One day stands out in particular, a day when something profound happened inside. I was three or four years old, sitting on the floor of the front porch. In keeping with houses of the 1930s, this one had a wood floor, freshly painted porch gray. I remember gazing with wonder at the milky white moon hanging on a colorbook blue sky. The wonder of it, the vastness, kindled an awareness of the world and myself. What this event meant for me was that nothing I wanted to do ever seemed out of my reach. No dream was too wild or inaccessible.

Some dreams thrive even without substance. My dream of sailing did. I never sailed a boat until in my early thirties, yet for all those years I knew I would. I could taste the salt on my lips and feel the surge of the deck; I could see the sails full, their whiteness gleaming in the sun. I could hear the wooden blocks creaking rhythmically as the wind fingered the rigging. The oceans of the world called to me in a series of images, smells, physical sensations. The ocean—serene, grandiose, frightening—was an entity mirroring my own soul. My mind could not separate romance from reality. It could only respond to something enormous that pulled at me with magnetic power.

1

Most of the time when I was growing up—and even as an adult, I wasn't prone to talking about my ideas. Girls weren't supposed to be adventurous. I kept my desires and dreams to myself. I suppose I didn't discuss these things because I was afraid someone would burst my bubble. Instinctively I sensed that a negative response would knock the edge off, somehow deplete my energy and rob me of something essential. As a girl and as a woman I have needed every ounce of courage to attempt to live down the idea that I couldn't do something simply because I was female. Like other women I have spent much energy trying to shrug off, to banish such baseless condemnations of my sex. Self-doubt, born of such origins, hangs around like heavy smoke, smoldering, before the fire bursts out in angry hot flames.

If you are a tomboy, at some point—usually around puberty when family and friends are trying to talk you into wearing frilly dresses—you begin to ask yourself, what is wrong with me? People think I'm strange, maybe even a little crazy, because I want to do something with my life. When they would say to me, "When you get married and have children . . ." I could feel dread heavy as lead sink to the bottom of my stomach. Inwardly shuddering, I would say silently, like a litany, *I don't want to get married, to end my life in oblivion!* I pushed myself back from the abyss, clinging tenaciously to those wispy straws that waved back and forth in my confused young head.

How many scientists, musicians, writers, doctors, professors, carpenters—creative human beings—have been lost because girls are discouraged from pursuing their interests? This senseless prejudice, plaguing us from birth to grave, may ultimately do more to contribute to the decline of the human race than anything. Perhaps it already has!

My salvation was in being a tomboy. I learned independence and above all, defiance. Even silent defiance is a powerful weapon because it enabled me to turn a deaf ear to pronouncements that "if you aren't a man, you can't . . ." In spite of self-doubts I plodded on and on with dogged determination. Being a tomboy gave me mental and emotional strength just as it increased my physical strength and prowess. I learned how to use my body, a skill that many women lack. Totally rejecting dolls and girl toys, I took to the trees. Those wondrous living giants offered their limbs to climb, to swing from, to sit upon and look down upon the world and dream glorious dreams. Fields of tall grass invited running, chasing butterflies, turkeys, footballs. Shooting a bow and arrow improved my hand-eye coordination; skating and bike riding taught me grace and balance. Best of all, these activities opened the world to me, taught me to relish, to cherish the freedom to discover.

For three decades my dream of sailing around the world lay dormant. I had been academically occupied—completing a doctorate and teaching folklore and mythology at UCLA, working my way up the ladder of success and respectability. One day it hit me: I'm craving physical activity. I don't play tennis anymore, don't swim, don't hike. I sit behind a desk in the office, in the library, at home. I'm approaching 35 and I haven't learned to sail yet. All my life I've lived in Florida or California within a stone's throw of the ocean, but I've never even been in a sailboat!

Within a week I was enrolled in two sailing classes. Five years later I bought my first sailboat, a 25-foot sloop. Realizing there were other women like myself who wanted to learn to sail, but to learn in a supportive, non-threatening environment, I started a business offering such services—Seaworthy Women. We gave sailing instruction for women and undertook weekend or week-long cruises to nearby islands. I was spending a lot of time sailing and loving every minute.

My dream was turning into reality—almost. I had been sailing for ten years and had owned three boats. I had learned coastal and celestial navigation, had taken a course in diesel engine repair, did my own diesel maintenance on a Perkins 40-horse power engine. Boats, as I had rapidly discovered, present the opportunity to learn a number of trades: carpenter, electrician, plumber, rigger, engine mechanic, sail maker. As a good friend once said, "This is a labor intensive boat." These many avocations are in addition to mastering general boat handling under sail, under power anchoring, heavy weather sailing and rescue techniques should anyone fall overboard. Like everything in life, sailing is something one continues to learn from experience, from reading and from talking with others. No matter how long you do it, you can never know everything.

In ten years I had made considerable progress toward releasing the dormant dream from its silk-lined cocoon. But I still needed more time to think, to plan before spreading my wings in sweet freedom.

3

My experiences with Seaworthy Women had made me desirous of founding an international sailing organization for women. It was a concept I discussed constantly with friends and acquaintances and with Ellen Power, my partner in Seaworthy Women. Finally in 1980, at the National NOW Convention which was held in Los Angeles, we launched the organization—Women at the Helm— with a booth selling t-shirts and memberships. We also managed to get good coverage in sailing magazines and this publicity brought in a considerable number of women members.

One of the major goals of WATH was to put together a circumnavigation with an all-woman crew. To involve as many women as possible, we conceived of having different crews for each leg of the voyage. In all we expected the voyage to last three years.

Our other stated objectives were 1) to advance the status and independence of women on the water; 2) to encourage the learning of sailing and navigation; 3) to expand knowledge of the physical world and its changes, including meteorology and marine biology; 4) to promote the safeguarding of marine life and the protection of ocean and inland waters; 5) to link women of different cultures through voyaging and 6) to establish a strong network of women worldwide who share an interest in sailing and who will work toward these objectives.

To help promote all these goals, WATH published a quality quarterly newsletter. We were hoping to begin the circumnavigation in March 1982.

Initially we had a good response, gaining members from almost every state and a few from foreign countries with Canada leading the list. Locally we had potlucks, work meetings and got several local women with boats to volunteer day sails and instruction in racing. At the activity level, the turnout was disappointing. Almost no one took advantage of these free events. Few wanted to help write and produce the newsletter. After two years of shouldering the major organizational responsibilities—in addition to working half time as an editor and operating Seaworthy Women—I was finding myself greatly overworked. It was disillusioning. Together with these complications were financial difficulties which I was left to cover with my own personal funds. Ellen, although a co-founder, dropped out completely. The financial burden left me with no choice but to officially fold WATH.

It was a sad day for me. I was not used to failure.

What went wrong? Why did WATH fail? In retrospect two reasons stand out. First, the program of launching a circumnavigation in two years was unrealistic. Many logistical problems of scheduling passages and bringing in new crews for each leg was virtually impossible, though at the time I had no way of knowing that. In short the plan was overambitious. The second reason was that I miscalculated the need or desire for such an organization. Perhaps it was a concept ahead of its time, and I returned to my own dreams.

Not only did I intend to sail the world's oceans, I wanted to write about these adventures. Since I was not able to introduce other women to the actual experience of ocean sailing as I originally wanted, it is even more important to share my experience with them through a book. Perhaps in this way Joy's and my endeavors will help to dispel the trite but well-ingrained notion that women lack the strength to meet the demands of long distance ocean voyaging. Several women have circumnavigated the world as solo sailors, providing even greater proof that tremendous physical strength is not a criterion for long distance voyaging.

Sailing in modern rigged yachts does not require gargantuan physical prowess. Joy is 5 feet 7 inches tall and her weight throughout our four-year voyage has varied between 125 and 140. I am 5 feet 4 inches tall and my weight has also gone up and down in the same range as Joy's. Boats can easily be rigged to give the sailor mechanical advantage thereby greatly reducing the need for exceptional muscle power. Of course, exercising, regardless of the sport, will develop and tune one's muscles. While the two of us may be more "muscular" than the average woman, it is a result of our active lifestyle rather than natural endowment.

Perhaps the most frequent question we are asked is, "Aren't you afraid?" The other side of the coin, a statement that we also hear is, "My, you are brave." Neither of us considers ourselves brave for doing something we dearly love. My usual response is that my life is at less risk on the sea than it is driving on a Los Angeles freeway. People always seem to reject the truth of that statement. What people are really referring to, I believe, is fear. They want to know if we are afraid and if not, how have we conquered that fear? Most often fear derives from the unknown, therefore fear vanishes once we learn how to deal with the situations which arouse fear. The surest way to dispense with fear is to have confidence in yourself, to believe that whatever occurs, you will be able to cope with it. Fear begins to evaporate as we gain knowledge, understanding, experience and learn self-trust.

Perhaps a few women who read this book will be encouraged to seek out their dreams of ocean voyaging or weekend sailing. No doubt the majority will not be so motivated in this direction. I hope, however, they will be able to see our account as a metaphor: that women can succeed in all kinds of adventures, professions or occupations. The main thing is to pursue your dreams, work to achieve whatever it is you desire by preparing yourself intellectually, physically, spiritually—in short—in every way that you can. One day, when you are ready (even though you may not at first realize it) the door will open. You have but to step forward over the threshold.

Chapter 1

In the Beginning

Romance about the sea is powerful, heady stuff. If one made a survey of people randomly selected at any American street corner and asked if they would like to sail around the world on a sailboat, probably 90 to 95 percent would respond "yes" without a single moment's hesitation. The idea conjures up curvy, white sand beaches, swaying coconut palms, blue-green lagoons, lazy days lounging around on an immaculate deck—sipping an aphrodisiac while engrossed in a titillating novel—and nights dining by candle-light in some cozy café with the muffled sounds of native music adding just the right touch of exotic flavor. Paradise lost is rapidly regained in this imaginary flash. In this rash moment, puritanical inhibitions are cast aside to allow forbidden, carnal desires to become purified in this back-to-the-beginning-of-life innocence.

Yes, most of us are dreamers. Who wouldn't like to sail off into the sunset leaving the traumas of congested urban life behind? But, believe it or not, when one is really serious about finding a companion to sail off into the sunset with, it's another matter. When you are a woman and you want your companion to be a woman, your chances are considerably diminished. This situation has every-thing to do with the way we have been raised.

In this area, I had a couple of false starts—women who bought the dream but fled from the reality of cruising on a small sailboat. Twice burned, I had slumped into a skeptical sea-blue funk. Maybe after all I would be making this wonderful voyage on my own.

Early in 1982, one telephone call changed the direction of my life. When the call came I wasn't even home. The answering machine took the message for me—a name, number and time to call. I returned the call. The mysterious caller had a short first name, but an impossible (save for my expertise in German) surname—Joy Lauffenburger! (Much to my relief and hers, she was then in the process of legally changing it back to her maiden name—Smith, after a long stormy marriage and a painful divorce.) All this aside, it turns out that Joy and I had several things in common. She also owned her own boat and ran a sailboat chartering service. Joy wanted to meet other women sailors so she called to ask about Seaworthy Women. After I explained the nature of my enterprise, Joy suggested that I might be able to use her services for some of our cruises. (It was an unusual idea, but not without interest to me.) I countered that perhaps we could meet sometime for more discussion. Joy offered her boat as a meeting place and we agreed on a time.

On the appointed day, Joy called—to cancel. Her house had been burglarized and she had to deal with police and the insurance company. We set another date, February 23. That was the beginning, low-keyed at first. Joy and I became friends and eventually partners when we merged our two charter businesses. Certainly we talked about sailing around the world from the first day we met. As one of my good friends put it to Joy, "I bet you didn't know Jeannine five minutes before she mentioned intending to sail around the world!" We discussed circumnavigating but it was about a year before we committed ourselves to the project.

The question foremost on our minds and a frequent subject of discussion was which boat to take. I still owned a 31-foot Mariner ketch purchased in 1978. *Esperanza* was a beautifully appointed wood boat. For me, after searching hard for six months for a good cruising boat, it was love at first sight when I laid eyes on *Esperanza*. For five years *Esperanza* and I had shared many wonderful experiences. No matter what the conditions, she took care of me. In return I cared for her, varnished her bright work, painted her topsides, polished her metal. I had sailed her to Mexico for one month with three other women. For five summers *Esperanza* and I had shared many wonderful sails with other women to Anacapa, Santa Cruz, Santa Barbara and Catalina Island. I knew her from her bilges to the top of her two gleaming wooden masts.

If it sounds as if I'm speaking of an animate being with a personality, it's because I am. All boats have a spirit, and if you love them, they become a part of you. Sometimes, just to show other people that she had a personality, I would play Strauss waltzes for *Esperanza* while she was sailing. Every time it would change her whole movement and cadence. It was as if suddenly she picked up her skirts, lightened her step and began to glide like a Viennese grand dame. Oh she was proud, beautiful, graceful with her soft rolling, and spoke to us with gentle creaks and moans. Once, as she was nosing along with her bow splashing through the swells, a whale—no doubt attracted to her beauty—surfaced along side and swam in tandem with her. I had always suspected that boats had something in common with wombs. *Esperanza* proved it to be so. Being on her and inside her was like being reborn!

Joy's boat *Banshee*, a 34-foot cutter rigged sloop, was designed by Halsey Herreshoff and built in Bristol, Rhode Island. As most serious sailors know, Halsey comes from a very famous family of several generations of boat designers and builders. In fact it was Nathaniel Herreshoff who built one of the early American boats raced in the America's Cup. Joy had owned *Banshee* for twelve years, had sailed her twice across the Pacific—once to New Zealand, once to Tonga—and later to British Columbia and back to Los Angeles.

We discussed the merits of each of our boats to decide which vessel we should take. Two factors favoring *Banshee* were her additional space and her fiberglass construction. Wooden boats fair well in cool waters, but in the tropics, the wood can too easily become riddled by toredo worms if just a bit of protective bottom paint is scratched off, leaving bare wood. But, I countered, wooden boats have been sailing around the world for centuries, fiberglass for only three decades. In the end the argument boiled down to space. The boat was going to be our home for five to ten years, maybe longer. We needed as much room as possible. Three feet doesn't sound like much space but on a sailboat three feet makes an enormous difference. So, reluctantly I said a mournful farewell to my waltzing *Esperanza*. I sold her and I bought a half share in *Banshee*.

Thus it came to be that *Banshee* was my fourth boat. The name is Irish. The ancient Celts called their gods and goddesses *síde* which became *shee* in modern Irish. A *ben síde* is a goddess while in Irish folklore a "banshee" is a female spirit whose wail presages a death in the family. Not, one would think, a very auspicious name for a boat! But, as Joy explains it, she chose the name not for its Irish meaning but because her mother used to refer to Joy and her brother as "screaming banshees." Frequently we Americans take the liberty to change traditions and language as if there had never been anything before us. As you may well imagine, I was most relieved to learn *Banshee's* name derived from American rather than Irish tradition—not that I'm superstitious . . .

Once we had decided to go sailing off over the horizon, we told friends and family of our intentions. At first they tended to ignore it. After all we weren't wealthy. How could we just sell everything we owned and—in our 40s—quit our jobs and sail away? That's irresponsible. "What about your retirement?" some asked. Both of us knew something essential. If we waited until everything was perfect, until we had every cent in the bank, we'd never go! It's that simple. On land, and especially living in the USA—bless the old stars and stripes for teaching me about freedom, we live our lives according to a formula of protecting ourselves against any eventuality. We become insurance poor. The more you own the more you have to protect and the longer you have to work to pay for the insurance.

Another idea or concept has an ironclad grasp on those of us growing up American or European: we are what we do. Our whole life or identity centers around what kind of work we do. (For women it has historically been an identity derived from their husbands.) For those of us saddled with the protestant work ethic, life consists of working 8 to 5 with an annual two-week vacation. Seldom, if ever, do we stop to consider that most inhabitants of this planet do not work at a job or occupation as we Westerners do. What we think of as normal is not at all normal for 75 to 80 percent of the world's population. As usual, *normal* is relative.

Much of civilization is artificial. Take insurance, for example. Insurance is an attempt to keep an eventuality from affecting us, if it should happen. Air conditioning is an example of creating an artificial environment. There appears to be an almost immutable law that the more "civilized" we become, the more we tend to live our lives for the sake of security. For this sense of security we pay dearly, too, often dying without having lived. Perhaps it's a kind of survival of the Christian ethic to put everything aside for later, the life hereafter. Unfortunately *later* too often comes sooner than later.

Because of such longings for security, many people found it difficult to comprehend how we could just leave everything behind. But *everything* is ahead—sights, adventures, people, learning, living—all of that is ahead of us. How can we ever know who we are if our identity is no more than what we do and how much we earn?

Our responses to their objections were simply: our expenses

won't be much; our boat will be paid for; we won't need insurance—can't get it anyway for a 34-foot boat with only two people on board. When we need more money, we can work. We have skills and varied abilities. Ultimately it's a matter of trusting yourself. I've done this kind of thing two other times. Once when I went to Europe alone with a return freighter ticket, a little money and destination unknown. Another time, I left Florida with my meager belongings and drove my car to California. I had no job, little money and only one friend who had invited me but who, upon my arrival, ditched me. Within one month I had a permanent, full time job that I liked at UCLA and my own apartment.

Once we had committed ourselves to long distance voyaging we had to get down to the nitty gritty, to prepare *Banshee* for cruising. We also had to establish a workable budget so we could afford to prepare the boat and still have money saved up for the voyage. We could earn more along the way as many cruisers do.

I had anticipated that the majority of cruising people would be retired. To my surprise most of them are under 40, not retired, and determined to see the world and enjoy life while in good health. Some cruise with their families. Some go alone; some go with crew, but, with only one exception, and aside from singlehanders, we are the only boat we have encountered with an all-women crew. Based on these statistics one might conclude that we are a rare breed. I would have to agree. But rather than think we are something of an endangered species, I would hope that the scale is moving in the other direction. More and more women are sailing independently and the number should continue to increase.

Why do we want to see the world from the deck of a small yacht? An important reason is because it is something we are doing ourselves. If we traveled by commercial plane or ship, we wouldn't have a feeling of accomplishment or challenge. Our mode of travel allows us a very flexible schedule. If something comes up in a place we're visiting and we want to stay, we can. Quite honestly, the sense of accomplishment is probably the most rewarding aspect of making ocean passages. We spent 34 days sailing from La Paz, Baja California to Atuona on the island of Hiva Oa in the Marquesas. There's no way for me to compare this 34 days with the same length of time on land. For a moment let's compare going to the Marquesas by commercial flight versus sailing. By plane we would have left from Los Angeles International Airport, gone from a bustling urban center in a moderate climate and arrived in a slow-paced, sparsely populated tropical environment all in a few hours. On a plane there is nothing in between, not enough time to bridge two worlds at opposite ends of the human and natural spectrum.

On a small boat the passage of time is both internal and external. Day by day, hour after hour you travel through your head, through a myriad of feelings and thoughts, experiencing continuous subtle changes. The sun, moon, stars, wind and seas soon establish a natural rhythm and a sense of the reality of the physical world. Suddenly the planet becomes alive. The distance between La Paz and Atuona is more than the view of one international airport to another and then a short hop by prop plane to a strange, remote island rising steeply out of the sea. By contrast the lapse of time in a sea voyage definitely conveys the great geographic distance between La Paz and Atuona.

Curiously enough the ocean has various features which impressed me much as geographical features of a landscape might. Contrary to what many people think, the sea is not monotonously the same day after day. Some excerpts from my journal convey a sense of what happens during a long blue-water passage.

> *Where does one's time go on a sailboat? Just living, eating, sleeping, cleaning the boat and one's self, making repairs, reading. Everything takes more energy and time. Constantly moving to compensate for the boat's motion makes each chore more arduous and requires patience; a sense of humor helps immensely. Aside from such activities, one has lots of time to think, but it's not just time, it's also a kind of freedom from the many, many distractions one encounters on land. There's also the psychological aspect of space and distance. The ocean goes on and on, its size incomprehensible to me until I try to compare the distance we've sailed with driving my car from California to Florida. The nearest land for days has been over a thousand miles distant. We're alone. Really alone. Whatever happens, it's up to us to deal with it.*

There it is, or at least part of what it is—independence, self-reliance, freedom. At sea one faces immediate reality, both nature and one's self. In the Western world we have invented thousands of diversions. We can live our whole lives avoiding reality, if we choose. At sea there is no place to hide and no way to avoid what one really feels.

Chapter 2

Putting the Ark in Order

Outside, *Banshee* looked like a patchwork quilt. Some areas of her deck still showed her faded and worn paint while other places sparkled with new pearl gray and crisp, white trim. On old fiberglass boats, painting amounts to far more than cosmetic improvement. After ten or fifteen years of weathering, the gel coat on fiberglass starts to break down and become porous. Eventually, if not remedied, moisture penetrates the fiberglass itself, causing delamination. One of the major jobs facing us in Marina del Rey before we could begin our voyage was the repainting of *Banshee's* exterior with a linear polyurethane paint. The end product results in a superior exterior, which, unlike the original gel coat, never needs waxing and remains shiny and new looking. The process of painting with this chemical wonder, however, is another story. First of all the LP paint is a two-part affair. It doesn't like moisture or extremes in temperature. Anyone who has spent time on the coast of California will know that more often than not the days tend to be damp. Often the dampness starts moving inland around two P.M. It was exactly this kind of weather that caused our shiny paint to turn dull. Finally we learned to stop painting early in the day and the paint stayed shiny.

Inside, other problems awaited or rather demanded our attention. Half the cabin sole (boat talk for floor) had been cut out so we could remove an original stainless steel water tank that had started leaking like a sieve. At the same time we had this massive cavity in the cabin sole, we also removed a cabinet housing the ice box. We wanted to put in a refrigerator and needed to insulate right down to the hull.

During the three years of preparation, Joy and I continued working—she in real estate and teaching and I as an editor at the Oriental Healing Arts Institute. We also continued sailboat chartering and instruction up until about three months before beginning our cruise.

When well-wishing friends dropped by to see how our outfitting was progressing, chaos awaited their curious inspection. Valiantly they struggled to say something supportive, failing to find anything to compliment. I'm sure they thought we were wrecking a perfectly good boat and spending a lot of hard earned money to do so. I must admit that often during our three-year period of renovation I thought building a boat would have been easier and perhaps even quicker.

To insulate properly for the refrigerator, we tried to measure the angles and dimensions for fitting solid polyurethane foam. We glued together slabs of pea-colored foam and then carved off extraneous areas. Once the cabinet had been refitted, it was time to install the compressor in a cool dry place on the opposite side of the boat. The tricky part was running fifteen feet of copper tubing without bending it. We recruited a dock neighbor—a power boater—who was sure there would never be enough room to run all the tubing. Perched like ballet dancers, Jerry and I weaved back and forth supporting the precious tubing and countering Joy's movements as she snaked the copper through the foam insulation, under the quarter berth, across the engine room and finally bent it—gingerly—and pushed it through a hole in the bulkhead so it could be joined to the compressor.

Another snaky job was replacing all the original salt water and fresh water hoses—almost 200 feet in all. This job had something in common with the original water tank—tank and hoses were laid in the bilge when the boat was built, then the fiberglass interliner was set down on top. After years of sailing, the interliner had shifted, trapping hoses, electrical wires and water tank. One can only conclude that boat designers and builders are either optimists or pessimists. Either they think hoses, wires and tanks are indestructible or they build boats to last only ten years. Tugging on stiff, trapped hoses encased in slippery black globs of bilge grease was a memorable experience. It took Joy and I exactly three weekends working full time to extract old hoses and run new ones.

The three-year restoration was done on a part time basis. Because *Banshee* was still being chartered out, restoration jobs had to be carefully scheduled. Other major repairs or changes included replacing all the plexiglass windows and glass ports and rebedding and refastening them. Every single deck fitting had to be removed and rebedded in an effort to prevent leaks. Toward the end of our restoration, new equipment began arriving and had to be installed. Among these were a satellite navigation system, an electric windlass, a ham radio, an antique barograph, a whole new set of sails and an autopilot—to name just a few items. For a source of alternative energy, we installed a wind generator, which we named Frieda after a Dutch friend. Frieda's three blades, standing ten feet or so above the stern deck, attracted a great deal of attention. People wanted to know why anyone would put a windmill on a boat! Complete strangers wandered down to the dock to ask about Frieda. Usually the questions led to further inquiries about our intended voyage. Most of these conversations went pleasantly, but one man we found particularly boorish. He was no sailor himself but he had the gall to ask if either of us "girls" could navigate? I still don't quite understand why some men find it so incredible that women can navigate. The first time I sailed to Mexico, the immigration officer seemed most astounded to learn I was captain of the boat. With complete amazement in his eyes and voice he said, "You didn't get lost?" I had to laugh at that and responded, "No, I didn't get lost. I'm here!" Strange. I just can't imagine anyone putting this question to a man.

To return to Frieda. Frieda's input went directly to a single generator. We also had a tow propeller that turns in the water at the end of a long line that could be switched to the generator, literally churning out amps which are stored in batteries. We didn't want to be bothered with switching the connection to the generator from wind to water all the time, so we bought two generators. Joy installed them, permanently wiring them into *Banshee's* batteries. Another tremendous job Joy tackled alone was rewiring the entire boat. After this feat she was graduated to the laudable position of chief electrician!

In rigging the boat we paid particular attention to setting things up so that either one of us could singlehand *Banshee*, if we had to. We also made it possible to hoist and lower all sails (except the spinnaker) from the cockpit. To do so, we put downhauls on each halyard. We arranged it so we can also reef from the cockpit rather than going on deck. By doing all these things we made the operation of the boat in heavy weather easier and safer because we have minimized the need to go on deck and risk falling overboard.

In 1984, within just a few months of our planned departure, we lost both of our fathers. Joy's father died in May after a prolonged illness and mine suffered a sudden fatal heart attack in December.

Both of us received small inheritances which helped pay off *Banshee's* mortgage and assisted in buying certain pieces of equipment. The financial benefits did not mean that we need never work again, only that we would not have to spend all our time working and we would have a bit more financial security to begin our voyage.

Our goal was to depart sometime between December, 1984, and February, 1985. Needless to say we were running behind schedule. In January we hauled out in the boat yard. We pulled the mast, removed and inspected all the hardware, painted the mast and boom, painted the hull and antifouled the bottom. In February we had a massive garage sale, ridding ourselves of an apartment full of things that couldn't go on *Banshee*. We sold both our cars. Now down to the wire, we scurried about frantically trying to round up all the items on our endless lists: engine parts, all sorts of hardware, sail cloth, lines, various kinds of fasteners, head (toilet) parts, batteries for everything on board and light bulbs for all light fixtures; glues, epoxies, paint, varnish, not to mention all the provisions—beans, rice, wheat, other whole grains, nuts, fruits, home canned meats and fresh vegetables.

As the time for departure neared, each of us woke up many times at night remembering additional things we needed to add to our list. As each key on my key chain disappeared, the reality of departure began to sink in. Finally a friend set a date for a dock party and invited our friends. It had to be postponed for two weeks. At last the day of the party came. We had planned to spend the morning getting everything shipshape, but alas, there was a plumbing failure in the galley sink. By the time I drove all over Los Angeles searching for the part and finally located it, the party had started. To boot—I had purchased the wrong part! Finally, at about ten that night we repaired the sink and fell into bed exhausted. It was becoming more apparent each day that in order to get any rest we were going to have to leave. It was nearing the end of March. If we didn't leave soon, we'd be committed to spending the hurricane season in Mexico. Neither of us wanted to do that. We were eager to visit the Pacific islands. Also, we'd given notice to the marina. Come April 1 we'd have no place to dock our boat.

We decided to leave on Friday, March 29, 1985. No one knows better than I the old superstition that one should never begin a voyage on Friday. Not that I'm superstitious, but why tempt fate? We rationalized that if we went to Catalina Island and stayed for a few days, we wouldn't be leaving on Friday. So, early Friday morning a few of our close friends gathered dockside to drink champagne and wish us a final farewell. As we raced down Marina del Rey's main channel under sail, a small craft warning flag flapped furiously from the flagpole in front of the Coast Guard station. Our friends had driven ahead by car to the jetty and stood there waving and clicking their cameras as we flew past. In response to their waves and shouts, we released several balloons that rapidly arose, shrinking to mere specks.

Soon we too were dwindling in size to our friends ashore as the fresh wind filled our sails. We were gliding along on the tail of an Alaskan storm that had brought snow to the mountains behind Los Angeles. It was a scene from the Alps, the distant snow golden and white against a deep blue sky. What a day for departure. Los Angeles had never looked so beautiful. For a moment I felt like crying—until I turned seaward. The thrill of the sea—the wind gusting 30 knots and white caps bouncing off the hull—caught me and filled me with a sense of excitement and anticipation. Once we hit the open sea, spray flew in a silvery shower as the bow rhythmically lifted up and down over the swells. We donned our foul weather gear, still white and smelling new. Billowy clouds scudded overhead as if to race with us. The boat parted the green water, scattering the sailor's metaphoric "white horses" at our bow.

Despite her heavy load and lower waterline, *Banshee* leapt through the seas, sharing our exuberance to be underway at last, sailing toward the unknown. About five hours later we rounded Catalina's West End. The back side of the island greeted us with confused and breaking seas. For another hour or so we bounced around until reaching the calm waters of Cat Harbor. By 1930 hours, as darkness closed in, we set the 35-pound CQR anchor. We straightened up the lines and packed away sails. With chilled bodies and cold hands, we went below, glad for the warmth and dryness in which to prepare dinner. Looking up at the sky rapidly filling with stars, I realized it was going to take some time to adjust to this kind of freedom! Saying goodbye to my friends and a city that had been home for twenty years left me feeling sad and somewhat empty.

Chapter 3

Sailing South of the Border

After resting for several days at Catalina and doing some minor boat tasks, we got underway for real. Nightfall found us ghosting along in the midst of incoming and outgoing traffic for Long Beach/ San Pedro Harbor. Light, fickle winds made us work to keep the sails full. At about 2030, I sighted a big freighter closing on us. But its navigation lights were confusing. Joy raised them on Channel 16 on the VHF to ask if they could see us. In answer to her question, "Where are you headed?", the operator responded, "Up your ass!" It was an ambiguous response but when the ship lit up like a Christmas tree, we took the operator's words as intended good humor. Just to be safe, we changed course, tacking clear.

Having settled that situation to our satisfaction, Joy tucked herself into a berth, leaving things in my hands from 2100 to midnight. The night was cold and damp, but I barely noticed. It was so good to be there fulfilling my dream, and I was captivated by the scene before me. Amazing how much light the half moon cast. The sea looked like a crumpled sheet of gold foil. Wondrous.

The next day, off San Diego by mid-afternoon, several whales escorted us, cavorting for at least half an hour within our view. Not long after they had disappeared, we spied a rather large, black object moving towards us but not on a collision course. We finally figured out we were seeing a US Navy submarine.

It was time to decide whether to sail through the night or alter course slightly and anchor overnight at one of the Coronados. We decided a detour to the islands would be nice and would give us a full night's sleep. Since we'd not cleared into Mexico yet, we'd not be able to go ashore. We consulted the *Baja Sea Guide* which noted a small secure anchorage on the eastern side of South Coronado, the biggest of this island group.

A good hour before sunset we dropped our sails and powered into the cove. The island was steep, rising about 300 feet above the sea. Several buildings on top comprise the military housing for men left to tend the lighthouse. Moorings for small boats dotted the cove, but we found clear water toward the center of the anchorage and set the hook in 24 feet. We settled back to have a drink and enjoy the magnificent scenery. A few goats grazed on the stubby hillside and two roosters on top of the hill did a ritual combat dance, tails spread out and wings flapping. From recent rains, vibrant wildflowers had sprung to life, announcing the arrival of another desert spring. Their brilliant yellow contrasted sharply with the earth tones of the windswept hills.

After a tasty dinner of turkey curry on brown rice topped with peanuts and chutney, it was off to bed. The Santa Ana winds, dry and warm from the inland desert, had made the evening pleasantly warm. We decided to sleep outside in the cockpit so we could enjoy the star-filled sky. Exhaustion from the previous night's passage soon sent us off to dreamland, oblivious of everything.

In perfect weather we left South Coronado early in the morning, trying to escape the rude invasion of biting kelp flies. Three hours later we were still swatting them as they clung everywhere on the boat. We made it to Ensenada, our Mexican port of entry.

Before leaving L.A. we had already discussed how we would deal with the question of who is captain. Although we each have different areas in which we excel, both of us have captained our own vessels for years. Neither of us felt it was fair for one of us to be captain permanently. We decided to alternate. Generally we would change captains each time we left a country. Since I had already cruised to Mexico, we agreed I would be captain there and Joy would become captain in French Polynesia.

If left up to us, we would not even have a "captain" because on board we make decisions jointly. However, for the sake of entering a country, everyone on board must have a position. When clearing customs and immigration, yachts are treated just the same as commercial vessels. In many instances this treatment verges on the comical because most of the rules simply do not apply to small private yachts sailed by a couple or a family. The other point we both adamantly agreed upon was that we would never have a "first mate." The term to us is synonymous to the "little wife" who functions exclusively on board as the ignominious galley slave. The person who is not captain assumes the title of "navigator," a term we each feel comfortable with.

In reality, while functioning as co-captains, we each tend to do those chores and jobs we feel most competent with. Joy deals with most technical matters, I assist. While sailing, I function more as the sailing master but we both handle sails, though Joy tends to do more of the deck work than I. When maneuvering the boat in tight places, it seems I always end up at the wheel. So, while we do have tasks that each of us gravitates toward naturally, we do not operate in a hierarchy that designates one job as higher ranking than another. Running *Banshee* is a partnership.

Our arrival and clearance with the port officials, running back and forth between Immigration and the Port Captain's Office, brought back fond memories of seven years previously when I had cleared here on *Esperanza*. Nothing had changed in the interim except, perhaps, the town was more crowded. Blankets, baskets, carvings, brightly colored paper flowers—native crafts intended for tourists—crammed the tiny stores lining both sides of the street. Ensenada Harbor was still filthy. My previous visit had taught me to take a mooring for a nominal fee rather than anchoring to avoid a two or three hour clean up of dreck from the bottom of the harbor that bonds itself to your anchor and chain. Despite the rundown harbor, Ensenada has its charms. Located right on the town, the harbor affords a bird's eye view of street life, a blend of lilting Spanish calls, honking horns from a steady stream of bucking and stalling vehicles, strains of Mexican music and the colorful clothing of pedestrians. Joy and I delighted in eating our favorite Mexican dishes at several different shoreside restaurants. Before leaving, we made sure we brought on an ample supply of handmade tortillas.

Our first visitors came to see us in Ensenada. David Fein, a young friend of Joy's who had helped her run her charter business, came with his friend Dave. Ever since hearing our plans to make the voyage, David had been after us to let him crew with us from Mexico to the Marquesas. Finally in Ensenada we told him he could join us in La Paz to make the crossing.

Eager to be on our way, we didn't stay long in Ensenada. Our first stop, the Todos Santos Islands, was only nine miles away. I had grown to like one of these small uninhabited islands during my previous visit because of the abundance of wildflowers, sea birds, sea lions and seals. I was not disappointed the second time. We walked the flower-covered hills, enjoying the view of the sea from the craggy steep shore, and dinghied around the rocks to view seals close up.

Working down to the wire as we had, meant we had not had the opportunity to try much of our new equipment before we left. Because it was new, we were unaccustomed to its operation. Consequently, we had some hilarious episodes—at least in retrospect. One such event occurred when we took up anchor at Todos Santos. Joy stepped on the switch for the electric windlass. Zip. In no time, 75 feet or so of chain clicked up over the gypsy and dropped through the deck into the chain locker. Then, the windlass just stopped. Joy stepped on the switch, but nothing happened. We must be on a rock. We waited momentarily, giving the wind time to shift the boat. Then I powered slightly forward, having a new direction on the anchor. Finally after successive maneuvers of this type—all unsuccessful—we simply pulled the chain in by hand, letting it pile up on deck. Only when I went below to help pull it through the hawse pipe did I discover the problem: two large fenders we stowed in the chain locker prevented the chain from falling into place. Now that's something a landlubber would do!

A few days later we were underway once again, this time bound for San Martín, a small volcanic island inhabited by Mexican fishermen. Here we had our first serious flirtation with disaster. We were anchored several days, during which time some bad weather and moderately strong winds came up. The little bight where we anchored was filled with lobster traps. We had carefully anchored well clear of them. In the blow, however, the anchor dragged and we blew down on one of the traps. We didn't want the line to become wrapped around our propeller, but we had to run the engine to hoist the anchor and relocate ourselves. Thus I cut the lobster line and the trap floated away from us. On shore the fishermen were watching and soon one was in his *panga* powering out to catch the drifting trap. Joy and I felt terrible. By now we had re-anchored and decided to give the fisherman a new line. He came along side and we apologized, Joy making an effort to communicate with him in Spanish. The man was very gracious, wished us well, and adamantly refused our line. Absolutely not. He would not take our line.

When anchoring the second time, we did not put down adequate scope because we had decided to leave after setting everything in order. Momentarily I went below. When I came back up on deck, I noticed we had drifted precariously close to a rocky reef lying astern. I yelled loudly to Joy who immediately bounded up on deck after flipping on the depth sounder. We were in 11 feet of water! We draw 6 feet 7 inches. Fortunately with the electric windlass we pulled the anchor up rapidly and powered out into deeper water on a course away from the island. As quickly as possible we had the sails hoisted and engine off. The cold morning dampness cut through my heavy wool sweater coloring my mood to conform with that of the choppy gray seas and the murky low sky. The coast around San Martín is awash with numerous rocks and shoals. We had carefully plotted a course clear of these hazards, first going almost due west and then turning south onto a direct course for Cedros Island. Just near a point in the open water where we intended to turn south, I suddenly spotted a clump of kelp and a rather large rock momentarily awash just off our port beam. The adrenaline surged and my heart jumped into my throat. I yelled to Joy what I had seen. I was on the wheel so she quickly reached below and started the engine. I threw the wheel hard to starboard and we both kept our eyes glued to the area where I had seen the rock. Nothing. Then we both saw it at once, a whale right there on the surface! As if to confirm our identification, it spouted, lying there no more than 20 feet from our beam. We could see the barnacles on its back. Probably the creature had been asleep. Either we nudged it or the engine noise woke it. The sight was spectacular but frightening. All that mass was just a little too close for comfort.

Unfortunately it continued to be one of those days. All the way down the coast we had been trying to get the old Aires windvane to steer. The vane had been stored for several years in the garage, but Joy swore it worked. Before leaving Marina del Rey, a friend had joined us for a sail one day to try the vane. There was almost no wind, but the guy assured us the vane was okay, just too little wind for it to steer. In the meantime we got involved in other tasks and never tried the self-steering gear until we finally left. Periodically while sailing down the coast we tried the vane. This day we tried it again, to no avail. It was steering very erratically, first in one direction and then in the other, swinging back and forth in a 50-60 degree arc. Each of us thought that maybe we were operating it incorrectly or else something was drastically wrong. We couldn't find anything wrong and nothing we did made any difference. Feeling angry and thwarted again, we gave up in disgust and put on the autopilot. We would have preferred the windvane simply

23

because it doesn't require electricity to run. It steers by the force of the wind pressing on its vane. Nonetheless, we were thankful to have the autopilot. The sail to Cedros was overnight and it's very tiring to have to steer continuously day and night. Normally at sea we don't touch the wheel for days because the windvane does all the work.

The windvane was not the only problem. My journal all too vividly recalls other difficulties that day:

> *It was also about this time that 'Kinky' (the tow generator) had stopped turning after hooking into a large piece of kelp for the third time! This becomes a real nuisance because each time the towline is brought out of the water it must be disconnected from the generator and the reverse end thrown into the water and the entire line fed out into the water to unkink the line. (Hence the name* Kinky.*)*

> *We had decided to begin our watch at 7 P.M. Therefore we would have an early dinner. I started dinner about 4:40 in the pressure cooker. Just the time it was done, we noticed the wind had strengthened. We doused the headsail and reefed the main. The wind was gusting to 28 knots. By the time we completed the reef and hoisted the staysail it was 7:30. Dinner was cold and had to be reheated.*

The following day dawned gray and remained that way. Gradually the wind slackened but, out of simple inertia, we left the reef in the main until quite late in the day. Arriving at Cedros was like stepping into a new world. It was about 4 P.M. when we rounded the north end of the island. Suddenly, just as if we had moved through a door, we were out of the cold fog being thawed out by warm sunlight. Simultaneously the wind came blasting out of the hills at a brisk 25 knots, laying us over on our ear and whipping the deep blue sea into frothy whitecaps.

Cedros presented two highlights. First was meeting Gloria and Edie, the owners of a Bowman 49-foot sailboat, and their two women crew. Seeing only women on board, Joy and I decided to dinghy over. The two women on deck said they were crew and that the owners were dying to meet us! All of us were equally surprised to met another boat with all women crew. To celebrate, we were invited to breakfast on board the Bowman. Much to our disappointment Gloria and Edie were sailing north to San Francisco the next day on their way home after having cruised for some weeks in Mexico.

The second treat on Cedros was going ashore to visit the fur seals hauled up on shore sunning. Creeping along in a half crouch, I approached one silvery brown seal. I noticed how coarse its whiskers and how catlike the face. But there the resemblance ended. Here was 800, maybe 1,000 pounds of animal looking more like a giant slug than a cuddly mammal. Tentatively I reached out and stroked the sun-dried fur. I thought I detected a slight twitch and something resembling a sigh, but nothing more. I petted and it slept on.

Another overnight sail and we reached Bahia San Juanito, a secluded fishing village 87 miles north of Magdelena Bay. We had barely anchored as the only boat there when a pelican swooped down, glided to a landing beside our bow. Shortly it swam up to our beam and began clapping its beak back and forth. Most unusual behavior for a pelican, but the message was all too clear. We had no fish so we tossed Pelly a small piece of ham. It only sank about two inches before the massive beak scooped up the tidbit. Pelly rolled it around its tongue momentarily as if to taste it. Too strange. It spit it out. Pelly looked as us again and instantly began the beak clapping routine. It was a pointed gesture. By now Joy had brought up a snack of smoked oysters. Oh yes. Brilliant. Pelly would like that, surely. Wrong. The bird refused the delicacy outright. Then, to our great surprise, the giant bird awkwardly lifted itself from the water, its wings beating hard, soared upward, circled *Banshee*, then landed on the boom! Still it eyed us with its "feed me" look, snapping its beak again. We didn't want to encourage Pelly to remain on its newfound perch, fearing it might leave a runny calling card on our mainsail and deck. Finally, Pelly gave up, took off and never returned during our two and half day stay.

Early the next morning two fishermen from the village came and offered to take us ashore. This was a thoughtful gesture because the surf was too big for a landing in our little dinghy. Grabbing our shoes, we thankfully jumped into their *panga*. A big grin engulfed Ben's face as he gunned the Yamaha 45, leaving a rooster tail behind. The surf was considerable but he only cut the motor at the last minute before beaching the craft. We leapt ashore just barely retreating before the next wave thundered onto the beach. Ben and Antonio rolled out a very rusted chassis. Pulling and tugging and using the surf to assist, they muscled the heavy plywood boat onto the makeshift trailer and maneuvered it above the high tide mark. We climbed the sloping rocky hillside behind the two men, chatting back and forth, half Spanish, half English.

A number of dilapidated dwellings built from odds and ends of house trailers and scrap wood lined the dirt roads that cut straight across the flat, hardened desert floor. Here and there some families had taken great pride in hanging a hand carved sign with the family name by the entrance. One better constructed house of adobe was especially eye-catching. It had been painted a light purple with decorative flourishes in yellow and light green. Antonio led us up the dusty road to the general store. We exchanged a few pleasant-ries with the man and woman inside. A heavy kind of silence one feels in the company of strangers not quite knowing what to say was there amid the dusty packages and cans set on dusty, sagging shelves. No fresh produce was in sight, but several cartons of eggs stood by the entrance. As if to authenticate their freshness, a chicken scratched around on the dirt floor nearby. Aside from fresh vegetables, we only needed beer but there was none here. We told Antonio and he motioned us to follow him. *Cerveza* was in another building. He went to get the owner to open up for us. A pleasant faced, plumpish older woman appeared with keys and waved us in behind her. We picked up a case, inquired the price and paid her. She was quite talkative, but at the rapid speed I could only understand about every fifth word. It was enough to comprehend her sentiments. She thought it most unusual and "valiant" for two women to sail the ocean. She, she assured us with a smile, got very seasick.

While walking through the village, we happened upon a man feeding his trained golden eagle. The regal bird delicately took a couple bits of entrails put before him. Its appetite satisfied, it jumped up onto its perch in a tree. With the owner's permission I took their picture, the man beside his bird, beaming with pride. Young boys kept coming up, first approaching the bird with make believe bravery—all a show for us, no doubt—but at the last moment, squealing and hastily retracting their hands.

As we walked back along the road to the sea, I noticed how many of these poor dwellings sported TV antennas. Television and outboards were the only signs of the twentieth century in this remote village. Otherwise their lives continue much as they have for decades—most of the tiny homes surrounded by their fenced-in vegetable gardens, intermixed with flowers and the tallest hollyhocks in the world. Drying on some of the fences were strips of turtle meat from someone's recent catch.

Ben and Antonio took us back to *Banshee* and gave us some fish and lobster for dinner. We talked with them over a beer and learned that few yachts visit their village. Probably for this reason we were getting such a royal welcome. The two men had greeted us, invited us to their village and would look out for us as long as we stayed.

Early the following morning, Ben came back to ask if we wanted any shrimp from the shrimper that had pulled into the bay that morning. Shrimp! You bet! He motioned us into his *panga* and off we sped to the shrimp boat. The captain sent a man down into the hold. He returned with a large basket filled with fresh shrimp.

Except for the need to move on, we would have enjoyed spending more time with these friendly people. Before the final leg to Cabo San Lucas we had one more stop: Santa Maria. As it turned out, these last two legs were the most difficult because we had no self-steering. Inadvertently, on the way to San Juanito, Joy had sat on the wires extending from the autopilot control unit, disconnecting them from the sealed unit. Having to steer around the clock, we shortened night watches to two hours.

Santa Maria was windy alley. Through the night the wind howled and whined unabated. At daybreak we raised anchor and raced out of the bay with 15 to 20 knots pushing our poled-out sails. All day we surfed down six to eight foot swells with a reefed main and a poled-out staysail. A glorious sunset lingered through a long twilight that faded into pitch blackness. In the enveloping darkness, it seemed as if ocean and sky united, becoming a black hole filled with wind dragons.

By 1430 the next day we still had 24 miles to go before reaching Cabo San Lucas. Winds had lightened so we turned on the engine, hoping to get to our destination before nightfall. As the sun set we were about two miles off Cabo Falso light and too late to make the harbor. Normally in this situation one simply heaves to in an attempt to stay in the area and not come too close to land. However, we found that the SatNav was going to be giving three good fixes, one after the other. That was as good or better than radar. Why not try it? Joy could stay below constantly plotting our progress as the SatNav gave our position and I could steer. As we neared the outer harbor, Joy called on the radio for contact with someone inside. Assistance came from Milt and Marie Hughs on *Moonchild*. With our strobe flashing, they were able to spot us and determine that our course into the inner harbor was good. To give a beacon, they shone one of their bright lights.

The whole procedure was a bit nerve wracking, but it worked. Thanks to their kindness, we were anchored at 2330, tired but happy. We had reached land's end at the southern extremity of Baja California. We had completed the first thousand miles of our voyage. All the hard work, the three years of preparation, had been worth it.

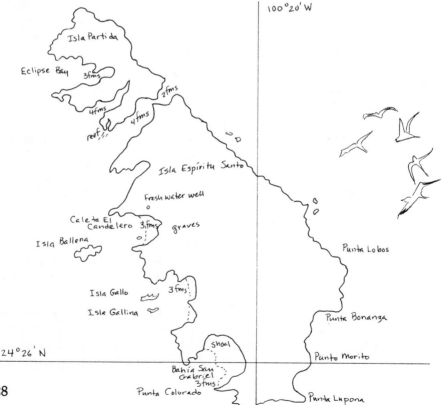

Chapter 4

The Importance of Siesta

After the first day in Cabo San Lucas, Joy and I were stricken with the fatal disease known as "Cabo fever." It is difficult, if not impossible to describe this malady. It has something to do with the desolate beauty of the surrounding mountainous desert and the easy-going inhabitants. The area breathes a tropical softness in the air nicely offset by brilliant splashes of riotous color: lush bougainvillea nodding gently at a cobalt sky and the backdrop of desert hues magically changing with the slant of the sun's rays from deep purple of morning and evening to earth tones of umber and rust at midday. What a lovely blend of desert and tropics. Being at the tip of Baja California, Cabo benefits from the cool moistness of the Pacific Ocean on its west side as well as the dry heat radiating from the Sea of Cortez to the east. The main symptom of "Cabo fever" is the feeling that time has ceased to exist and you are content to stay right where you are.

Our first day was spent taking care of formalities—checking in with Immigration and the Port Captain. Once that was done, our new friends, Milt and Marie, took us on a grand walking tour of the quiet little town. We stocked up on wonderful *pan dulce* from the bakery and a stack of tortillas. From other little stores we obtained a wonderful selection of fresh fruits and vegetables. By then hunger had set in and we headed off to a pleasant restaurant up in the hills with a view of the ocean. Here we lunched on fresh sea bass and traded sea stories.

For the first time we had joined with a community of cruisers. In all there were 50 to 60 yachts in port. Some were anchored in the outer harbor; others, along with us, in the more protected inner harbor. Here we had gone bow to the quay, placing our anchor ashore wedged under a large rock. A second anchor went off our stern, thus preventing the boat from swinging when the wind changed directions. Each morning at 8 A.M. we listened to the local VHF net giving weather forecasts. The net also afforded a chance for people to ask questions about where to get needed gear, propane, diesel fuel and water. We quickly learned how helpful people were. We felt an immediate kind of camaraderie among them. Within the first couple of days I found I had fallen into a kind of routine— chatting with people off other yachts, strolling leisurely down the streets of Cabo and, in general, relaxing.

Evard was a character right out of a novel. He hopped into his dinghy as though he had two regular legs. He didn't. One was wood with a foot with toes! His long matted hair and beard blended into an indistinguishable mass. We met him when we took a propane tank over to the outer anchorage to drop it ashore. Evard had announced on the morning net that he was taking his camper to San José to do a propane run. We made a beach landing just down from the Hacienda Hotel to deliver our tank to him. In the end we had Evard deliver diesel fuel to us in exchange for t-shirts.

In Cabo I was struck by a profound contrast between Cabo San Lucas and Ensenada. Ensenada tries desperately to be what Americans want it to be. Consequently, it is a bastardized town prostituting itself and its people. It also suffers from dire poverty most clearly visible in the number of women and children begging on the streets. There is no sign of such things in Cabo or in San Juanito. In fact, both of these places show healthy signs of pride in themselves and in their towns. One sure measure of a town's pride is cleanliness. On the streets of Cabo, rubbish cans are very much in evidence. Water is drinkable from the tap and we heard of no cautions about eating food here. We ate at several small taco stands and found the food tasty and the places very clean. In Ensenada the streets are littered with rotting garbage and the inhabitants must rely on bottled water for drinking. In addition, Montezuma's re- venge is legendary.

By now we were a month out of Los Angeles and had not listened to any news broadcasts or read any papers or magazines. Occasion- ally I found myself having some twinges of curiosity, but I suspected the same issues dominated the headlines with the Reagan Admini- stration pursuing the same mindless objectives—oblivious to envi- ronmental concerns, and rattling swords about Star Wars. The biggest reason for educating people in Third World nations is so they have some say and some control over the future of our planet. Is this a gap that can be bridged? I felt remote here and at this Land's End, but I realized that no corner of the world is remote from the often whimsical decisions made by major world powers.

I am torn. Should everyone be politicized? Shouldn't people be able to live their lives contentedly, enjoying each day as it comes? I guess I envy what I think I see around me: people who still enjoy the simple pleasures of life. In Cabo life does not appear to revolve around sex scandals, big money and corrupt politics. But I am an outsider. What can I really know? But I must try to understand them. I came on this voyage to experience people who live differently from me. I want to make their experience part of my own reality. Perhaps I'll come to have some balanced view of the world. Perhaps I shall find it or perhaps it only exists within each of us.

We would have liked to remain longer in Cabo, but we had to move on. Hurricane season was drawing closer. Just within the week we spent in Cabo, most of the boats planning a Pacific passage had left. Those spending the hurricane season in Mexico were moving into the Sea of Cortez.

Our friend Alethea flew in from Texas to join us on our short cruise up the Sea of Cortez north to La Paz. We planned to leave Monday morning, only a week after our arrival. Friday night I developed a toothache which had worsened by the following morning. We remembered seeing a dentist office, so off we went. Even though it was Saturday, the office was open. We had a half hour wait in the patio with one broken down love seat, various discarded parts of old engines and four playful kittens. The dentist finally called all three of us into his tiny office. It looked clean. I sat down in his chair and related my symptoms. He examined the area and said he was confident that it was an infection. He wrote a prescription for an antibiotic and an anti-inflammatory and told me to see a dentist in La Paz. Thus my imagined horrible scenes of having my tooth painfully extracted with some rusty pliers was instantly dispelled by his efficient and capable manner. The same day after starting the medication, the pain subsided.

Monday morning at 6:30 we powered out of Cabo toward La Paz. When light southeast winds came at 10:00, we hoisted the spinnaker. With the winds being the reverse of normal, we should have suspected the direction would not hold. It didn't. Around noon the wind momentarily died and then veered 180 degrees, causing the spinnaker to wrap around the forestay.

I could see the whitecaps about half a mile ahead and knew we had to work quickly to get the sail unwrapped and doused before the heavy wind reached us. We managed to get everything under control just in time. The remainder of the day we pounded into heavy seas with reefed main and under power to make Los Frieles before dark. The calmness of the anchorage at Los Frieles was welcome after an afternoon of bashing seas and salt water spray covering our decks with an occasional drenching sea streaming into the cockpit.

Massive granite rocks rising 500 or 600 feet dominate one side of Los Frieles. The remainder of the crescent-shaped bay is an expansive beach. The next day in this natural amphitheater, I was playing my electronic keyboard in the cockpit when some fishermen stopped by. They were surprised to hear my instrument and wanted me to keep playing it. If I had, I don't think they would have left. Finally I stopped. We traded with them for some red snapper for dinner.

Our next stop was Muertos, forty miles up the coast. The depth sounder was not working when we entered so we had to judge the depth by color of the water. We thought we anchored in about 12 feet, but during the night a warm westerly started gusting down the canyons. We let out more chain to have sufficient scope to hold us in stronger winds. Less than an hour later I suddenly was awakened by a thud. Joy and I agreed that the keel had struck bottom. We hurried up on deck. I grabbed a nine-foot boat hook and thrust it over the side. I went into soft sand! Quickly we got the engine going and started bringing in the anchor. I steered us seaward to what I thought was deep enough and we reanchored. Perversely, the depth sounder blinked on after we set. We were in 25 feet, a good depth. We slept peacefully though the wind whistled through the rigging.

After one leisurely paced day eating and shopping in La Paz, we headed out to the nearby islands of Partida and Espiritu Santo. This area is spectacularly beautiful. We stayed in Eclipse Bay, a deep intrusion into magnificently carved sandstone cliffs. Behind the massive, rust-red rocks, we discovered a lagoon and a large dry river bed. The region supports only sparse vegetation—mainly rugged cacti that cling tenaciously to the barren hillside. But there was no lack of live, crawly things. We spotted several varieties of lizards and were serenaded by a chorus of locust that buzzed incessantly in the noon day heat. Of birds we saw tiny colorful hummingbirds and soaring eagles as well as a steady procession of frigates and pelicans fetching their dinners from the placid blue-green sea. Early one morning when it was still calm, we powered out to the seal islands of Partida. While Joy circled around in *Banshee*, Alethea and I rowed the dinghy over to the island that was literally covered with barking and bellowing seals. But even more spectacular and somewhat frightening were the herds of these mammals who dived into the water and swam out to our dinghy, madly cavorting in the water around us. Some even bumped into the bottom of the dinghy. I wasn't sure whether that was accidental or they were trying to overturn us! Wanting Joy to have a chance to experience the seals close up, I changed places with her. Unfortunately, just about the time she and Alethea rowed back to the island, the wind came up, and in combination with the current, it made staying in the dinghy untenable. I powered as close as I dared and got them aboard so we could sail back to La Paz.

Alethea flew out on the same day David was supposed to fly in. But, no sign of him and no way to find out what had gone wrong. He came in the next day and explained the delay. David was bringing in an enormous amount of equipment for us: an Aires windvane, a depth sounder, a new ham radio and plastic fuel cans—to name just a few items. Originally he had planned to drive his truck to Tijuana to catch the flight there. But with all the boat equipment, they wanted him to pay duty. This would have amounted to a considerable sum so he backtracked and started driving to L. A. Somewhere along the way his truck broke down! Undaunted even by this turn of events, he rented a vehicle to get himself and all our gear to L. A. Miraculously he caught a flight out. Once in La Paz, though, customs refused to release the packages to him because they were closed until Monday! So, finally after all these difficulties, he showed up empty handed. Only someone with David's determination would have persisted. All ended well. On Monday the three of us took a taxi to the airport where we waited for a customs man to check through all the boxes. After seeing our boat papers—substantiating we were a yacht in transit—he released everything to us without one *peso* in duty—or bribe!

Now followed one busy day after another. One morning David and I taxied across La Paz to the largest grocery store to do a massive provisioning. It took several dinghy trips to get all the boxes of food out to *Banshee*. After walking to town for a few more purchases and lunch, it was 2:45 and we were dead tired. It was the heat. Although not yet summer, the temperature climbed each day to 100°F. At least Joy and I had been in the heat for about a month, but David didn't have this advantage. He had just come from a temperate climate. We had also learned to walk a little slower in the noon heat (when the Mexicans very wisely were having their *siesta*) but David went hurrying down the street at his North American pace. I really had to laugh when I noticed that anytime from noon to 2 the streets were almost deserted except for the three of us.

Other days were filled with installing all the new gear. Drilling into the stern of the boat while standing in a rocking dinghy and mounting the windvane were severe tests of David's agility and strength. Diesel fueling, filling propane tanks and water tanks took time and energy. Then, finally, with all tasks done, it was time to check out with the officials and get our port clearance. It was May 16—getting late in the season to sail offshore in this part of the world. Just one day before departure, Joy discovered a bolt on the rocker cover had sheered off. David checked with the shipyard and they affirmed they could repair it. We powered over to the yard and Joy and I walked to town to check out. It was an exhausting two-hour walk in the oppressive heat. Afterwards we stopped for lunch one more time at Adrianna's *palapala* where we had delicious tacos.

When we returned, the repair was done, but they wouldn't take a travelers check. I had to return to town. Of course it was still *siesta* and the *Casa de cambio* was closed. Fortunately I remembered *La Perle de la Paz* would be open and they would cash my check. I hurried back. We paid Ramon for his work and shoved off. It was four in the afternoon. We sailed several miles over to a quiet little cove at Pichilique and anchored for the night, hoping to get a good night's sleep before our departure the next day.

Chapter 5

The Milk Run

As I came up on deck I saw the first rays of the sun crawling down the low hillside of Pichilique. No sign of life on the other boats anchored nearby, the sea was placid, throwing back a perfect reflection of earth tones from the landlocked bay. Even this early one could already sense it was going to be a scorcher. Probably another day of 98 to 100 degrees in the Sea of Cortez.

David and Joy came up to secure some last minute things before getting underway. I went below, poured us all a cup of steaming coffee and started preparing breakfast.

Most of our conversation expressed our excitement about finally getting away. It was already May 17—late to be leaving the west coast for a Pacific crossing. Officially the hurricane season starts June 1, but the elements don't adhere to a calendar. In the two previous years, hurricanes had lashed Baja in late May. Usually a tropical disturbance that builds into a full blown hurricane makes up around latitude 10° N. As it gathers momentum, it moves northward. Then it can either swing eastward into mainland Mexico or, if coming far enough north, hit Cabo San Lucas. Sometimes these dreaded storms move westward away from the continent.

Having almost 3,000 miles to sail before landfall, we decided to use our fuel conservatively. We carried about 34 gallons of diesel fuel in our main tank and an additional 15 gallons in jerry cans. We had to wait until 0950 for enough wind to sail. Unfortunately it was blowing out of the south, the direction we were going. This meant tacking, thus adding more miles to our track out of the Sea of Cortez. Good weather held and decent winds kept us sailing along at five knots for several hours.

We decided on a course that would carry us outside Isla Cerralvo in order to have plenty of sea room during the night and avoid putting us between the island and the peninsula. I remembered the story one sailor had told us. Going north to La Paz, he spent 12 windless hours caught in this slot.

Nighttime brought fickle winds—blowing light then gusting. Mildred, the new windvane, was steering. A night watch entailed looking out for traffic at least every twenty minutes and periodically checking our position on the SatNav. If we appeared to be coming too close to the island, it was time to tack. Each of us could usually manage the maneuver alone unless it was blowing too hard. To tack, it was necessary to release the windvane and hand steer. After putting the wheel hard over, we let go the jib sheet and then trimmed the sail in the the new track. This maneuver is accomplished by shagging back and forth between the wheel and the sheet, sometimes using one hand on each. It can be a little awkward at first but with practice it becomes quite smooth. Joy and I rigged *Banshee* so she can be easily handled by one person. With three people to stand watches we had it made. Each of us could get six hours of continuous sleep each night unless an emergency might require more hands on deck.

Finally on the morning of the fourth day we sailed out of the Sea of Cortez. The Pacific stretched out before us. *Banshee* laid over in the 25-knot breeze, her bow rising rhythmically over four to six foot swells. With white foam scudding past, our spirits soared. Now we were really on our way. How long would our crossing take? Would we have any gear failures, meet any storms?

We soon discovered the 100 degree hot and dry desert air we'd become accustomed to in La Paz was a thing of the past. The open Pacific with a water temperature ranging from 56 to 58 degrees brought cool damp weather. When the sun set, we pulled on our jeans and wool shirts and sweaters. Usually our foul weather gear went on top to ward off the soggy night air.

The passage from Baja to the Marquesas is commonly know as the "milk run," meaning an easy passage. "Run" refers to the sailing position—the wind astern and the sails all the way out. Downwind, or running, is usually the preferred position because the boat tends to remain more level than on other points of sail. In order to sail down wind, we needed the northeast trades to push us southwest. Daily we looked for signs of the trades, but the wind continued steady out of the west. This meant we had to beat or close reach, banging into large seas. With the boat in this position, the G-force pulls so hard on one's body, one's energy is squandered just trying to stay balanced. We still didn't have our sea legs. None of us had much spare energy—just enough to eat, sleep, navigate and stand our three-hour watches.

After about a week, Joy and I settled into the routine. We became concerned about David who spent a lot of his off time sleeping. Into the second week at sea, David continued to sleep 12 to 15 hours a day. When we questioned him about it, he said he'd also had problems on land. I thought perhaps it related to his diet. As a vegetarian, I believe he consumed too little protein. Joy and I also ate primarily vegetarian meals on board. We had stocked ample supplies of about ten kinds of dried beans, lentils, brown rice, whole grain wheat and texturized vegetable protein (TVP) made from soybeans. We also made sure that we prepared meals with complimentary proteins. *Diet for a Small Planet* not only explains how to combine foods to insure adequate intake of essential proteins but has delicious recipes. After two weeks of eating with us, David's tiredness vanished.

As the days passed, our desire to find the tradewinds mounted. We were ready for a more comfortable point of sail. On May 23, the seventh day out, I wrote in the ship's log:

> *Tradewind clouds loom overhead, almost within reach. They are puffy, cotton-like daubs. Ahead they look like elongated stratified layers. The low gray ones on the eastern horizon are tinged slightly pink while those to the west are pure white. The wind is abeam, blowing 10-12 knots. Are we in the trades? I think not. This is a transition zone. The seas have calmed and the air temperature is about ten degrees warmer and definitely moister—both signs of the trades. But as yet the winds are not steady. Little gusts zip us along at 5.5 knots and then the wind lightens and our speed reduces to 3-4 knots.*

Three days later, May 26, I wrote in my journal:

> *I feel as if we are just bobbing up and down on the same place in the ocean. The sky with its low, oppressive cloud cover has been with us for three days. The sea is steel gray ... only the SatNav tells us that we are indeed moving and our position plots on the chart show a slow change in latitude*

and longitude. Still no tradewinds. I think we're too close to mainland Mexico and hence in a weather system influenced by the land mass.

We have been eating very well—experimenting with new recipes and creating our own. Nine days out and most of our fresh produce is gone. Still in the bin are white and sweet potatoes, onions, cabbage, a few carrots and several oranges. Now that we have used up most of the fresh vegies, we've started growing sprouts.

On the tenth day we found the trades and our spirits soared. Our speed picked up too. As I read through my journal, I noticed a kind of progression in my thoughts. After the tenth day out I seemed to be more attuned to the environment. On night watches my mind filled with thoughts and reflections on all sorts of things. I had a tremendous desire to write them down but we couldn't spare the power to run a light for anything but navigation. A flashlight was out too because we needed to conserve it for use on our watches. I tried to remember my thoughts and put them on paper the following day. On days when I had the 0400-0700 watch, sunrise, I could see to write in my journal.

On May 28 at 0514 I wrote:

How fascinating to think that we are experiencing the wind and weather patterns of the old sailing ships. I feel a kind of continuity with the human race and with the planet. It's as if nothing ever changes overall, yet, each detail and the combination are unique. Millions of sunrises and sunsets have occurred, each unique. Now the sun glints through a gray cloudbank, its rays spanning out below to the ocean. Above a brilliant yellow swath is bordered by puffy gray clouds tinged peach. Still higher up the sky is pastel blue. The scene resembles a delicately conceived watercolor, but this one changes; is actually alive. The immensity, the panorama strikes me as profound. I have never been so removed from people but I've never felt so connected with time, as if the present encompasses all history, all life happening simultaneously in one single breath.

Several times daily we listened to weather forecasts on the ham radio. These communications are nothing like the ones we have on land. Marine broadcasts give only warnings of gales or hurricanes, providing the coordinates (latitude and longitude) and the direction in which the storm is moving. The weather broadcasts also give information about the Intertropical Convergence Zone (ITCZ), often erroneously called the doldrums. The ITCZ is a region where a low pressure forms between the tradewinds of the northern and southern hemispheres. Because of the earth's rotation, two opposing currents swirl around the equatorial bulge, one flowing east, the other west. Consequently the weather in this area tends to be quite unstable. Winds may be light and variable or alternating with squalls and heavy rains and thunderstorms. Characteristically this "band" extends over an area of approximately 250 miles and moves north or south. We entered the ITCZ on June 1. Unfortunately it moved in the same direction as we, southerly. For this reason we spent days in the ITCZ, locked in its vise-like grip for 400 miles.

The ITCZ was inhospitable. It became a kind of twilight zone. Our entrance was greeted by high winds and heavy rains. The seas were huge. We banged into these walls of water through the first night. With each impact *Banshee* shuddered down to the bottom of her keel. *How much of this kind of punishment can she take,* I wondered?

Finally by the second day, the winds moderated but the rainfall increased. Soon all our towels were wet and many of our clothes because there was no place to dry anything. With all the hatches and ports closed to keep out rain and sea, the inside of the boat was an inferno. Our bodies glistened with sweat. This part of the ocean was a no man's land where winds came from any direction and then shifted. Occasionally the wind was light but periodic squalls whipped up the seas and rattled the sails.

On June 3 as I came down the companionway, my wet feet slipped on the slick cabin sole. The boat lurched and I was thrown into the companionway steps. I felt a terrible incapacitating pain and spasms in the area of my lower back ribs on the right side. Any movement—either the boat's or my own—caused such wrenching pain that I involuntarily screamed out in agony. At first I thought I had done something to a muscle. David massaged my back, which helped, but the pain persisted. By the third day there was no doubt in my mind: I had cracked a couple of ribs. Joy tried taping me up but it only made the pain worse, so she removed the tape immediately.

I didn't know it then, of course, but the pain would continue to recur for three years, set off by damp weather or when I stood or sat in one position too long.

Two days before breaking my ribs, I smoked my last cigarette. Like many smokers I periodically tried to stop, succeeding only for a week or so. Still, I wanted to kick the habit. So, without telling anyone, I planned the sure fire cure. I would run out of cigarettes mid-passage. Without the corner store I was stuck with my decision.

Naturally it was hell and not much better for Joy and David. I kept thinking of places where I might have left half a pack. I continuously asked Joy where she had hidden two or three cigarettes! Several times a day I tore up one area or another of the boat, searching. The broken ribs only added to the agony and distress that goes with nicotine withdrawal.

When I got into Atuona, the temptation to purchase cigarettes was almost overwhelming. But I didn't do it. Four years later I have not smoked a single one.

On June 8 the bad weather was still with us but, in addition, when we plotted a fix on the chart, we found that a 1.8 knot current was carrying us north! We were trying to go south. We turned on the engine. With it full bore, we could only average about 2.5 knots! Normally running at 2,400 RPMs, we would be moving about six knots. The steep seas and the strong wind on the nose relentlessly pushed us back. Without the engine we would have lost ground.

After ten days in the ITCZ, I came to view it as a kind of witches' cauldron where hurricanes were brewing right in our midst. Heavy torrential downpours with winds up to 35 knots were almost continuous. The currents ran through the ocean like a giant river cutting through boulders, spewing foam, building into massive crests that tumbled and spit with a vengeance. Quite dramatic from the deck of a small yacht. It was too wet to remain outside in the cockpit and too hot to stay in the cabin with all the ventilation closed off. Sleeping was difficult; cooking almost impossible. When we finally left the ITCZ, we felt as if we had barely escaped from the grasp of a powerful supernatural force.

By June 13 we had sailed over 2,000 miles but still had 950 to go. Once free of the ITCZ, good southeast trades and a favorable current made our mileage jump to 150 or 160 miles a day! Good when you stop to think that our worst day was only 47 miles.

On June 14 I wrote:

> *The trades are monotonously beautiful, steady. The same day in and out. Clouds stacked on the horizon, blue sky, gentle seas. Up and down, up and down with a hypnotic rock that lulls and dulls my brain. It drains my ambition; sleep is almost too difficult to contemplate. I slip into dreams and doze at the drop of a hat.*

On June 15:

> *Once again proof that one should never become complacent about the ocean. Just after writing about the sameness of the trades, a monstrous rain cloud overtook from behind. The rest of the day and night was squally.*

On June 16 at 0533 hours:

> *A peaceful sunrise. The winds are rising and have throughout the night. Gentle zephyrs nudge us along but with current we made 135 miles yesterday . . . The time is getting close. Less than a week and we should raise land . . . Here comes the sun. A burst of light orange seeping through a bank of gray clouds . . . It's another sunrise, private just for me. Such extravagance. I feel spoiled. Sometimes I think about the complexity—every little swell and each puff of wind relate to the sun, its position and time of day. All things come together inexplicably joined, related to each other but defying explanation. Not a mystery either, just a universe breathing its natural rhythms whether they be soft and gentle or harsh and unforgiving.*

On the final day of the crossing my thoughts turned frequently backwards, filled with nostalgic longing for friends and familiar haunts—Westwood Village, the UCLA campus, Olympic Boulevard, downtown L.A., streets filled with persons of multi-ethnic backgrounds, the sounds of foreign tongues, my favorite restaurants. I contrasted L.A., the 24-hour-a-day metropolis with my present environment of the last 34 days—the open ocean, three thousand stars gleaming in the night sky, the solitary sounds of the sea, the wind, the boat and we three humans. It was not cultural shock but cultural abstinence I was experiencing, and environment conducive to reflection. The cerebral parts of the brain seemed to merge with the sensual ones. Maybe right and left brain were functioning together. I was attuned to the changes of light, darkness, coolness and heat, the waxing and waning of the moon. I could understand "primitive" ritual which grows out of cyclic repetition. Ritual pulls one into the cosmic dance. I was experiencing cultural withdrawal. I was suffering from a feeling of loss of a time past, of an era that had ended. Perhaps a rite of passage would have been in order. In a way it was not unlike leaving childhood and crossing that invisible line into adulthood. I had made my first ocean passage.

Blue-footed booby,
our friend at sea

Chapter 6

Mystical Marquesas

As landfall got closer, each of us seemed to become more agitated and restless. I found myself yearning for the joys awaiting me on land. First off, just to be able to walk about freely and to bathe again in fresh water. Simple things become a real treat after 34 days at sea.

We arrived in Atuona on June 20 just after sunset. We didn't dare risk trying to go into the anchorage in pitch darkness, so we dropped our hook off the island of Hiva Oa in about 40 feet. Joy called on Channel 16 just on the off chance that someone might be in the anchorage. To our surprise we got an answer and within ten minutes Bob and Paula from *Armourel* came out in their dinghy offering to lead us in! We followed them into the harbor. It was too dark to see anything of the surroundings but the rich, fragrant air was unlike anything I had ever smelled. Probably no more than ten minutes after the anchor bit in the three of us crashed.

When I awoke the wonderful scent was still there. I rushed up on deck to have a look. I simply couldn't believe my eyes. Sheets of green. Steep, jagged mountains rose up and up, covered in layers of fertile green. Vines, trees, palms crowded together into a mass of living jade. Heavy full-bodied clouds clung to the tallest peaks, their edges tinted in an array of pastels. The view was magic. It was mystical, almost surrealistic. A fine mist drifted down and within seconds a rainbow formed, one end rising out of the water at the edge of the bay, arching across the highest mountain and dropping into the sea. Then a second rainbow appeared above the original one. I grabbed my camera. If I didn't take a picture I would never believe it was real. Deeply I breathed in the sweet, spicy scent. It reminded me of cinnamon and ginger.

By the time the light rain had stopped, we had finished breakfast and dinghied ashore. It felt so good to walk again, but the exertion in the extreme heat and humidity was almost unbearable. When a driver stopped to offer us a ride into town, we eagerly jumped in, happy not to have to walk the two miles. Our check-in with the Gendarmes went quickly. The only little hitch was that our clearance papers from Mexico showed me as captain but Joy was filling out the French papers with herself as captain. We explained that we take turns being captain!

We stopped at one of the local stores just to see what supplies they had. There was a conspicuous lack of fresh vegetables. Speaking with several other cruisers who had gathered in front of the store to chat and drink beer, we learned that a young Frenchman name Phillip raised vegetables on his land outside the town. We never asked how far to his garden. We left for Phillip's about four in the afternoon, walking two to three miles, mostly uphill, along a rough dirt road. Crowding in from both sides was lush rain forest. Still, everywhere, the wonderful spicy fragrance filled the air, intoxicatingly.

In his nicely terraced garden, Phillip was growing quite a variety of vegetables and even a few herbs, but the size of the vegies was not to be believed. Tiny. Tom Thumb sized. But, when you haven't seen any fresh vegetables for twenty some odd days, anything looks good. We bought some of everything. Loaded down, we staggered along the road in complete blackness. Exhausted and starved we finally got back to the boat. The omelette, chock full of fresh things, tasted wonderful.

At the end of June we sailed to the little island of Fatu Hiva, made famous by Thor Heyerdahl who lived here in 1936. The entry into Hana Vave (Virgin's Bay) is truly dramatic. The massive rock formations on each side of the bay stand guard like giant tikis. These incredible natural boulders lend Hana Vave and the village an air of ancient mystery. Perhaps it was this energy that infected the villagers. What a contrast to the people in Atuona! Whereas those people had been solemn, almost morose and not motivated to do anything, the villagers at Hana Vave were exceedingly friendly and vivacious. Here we found people still maintaining much of their old culture—women making beautiful *tapa* cloth (pounded from the bark of paper mulberry or breadfruit trees) and men doing attractive wood carvings.

Upon arrival we found about ten yachts anchored. Charlotte and Marcell dropped by to welcome us and tell us there would be a church service ashore the next morning at 8:30.

We heard the warning bells at 8:00 and hurried ashore. By the time we arrived the little chapel was crammed full of Marquesans—men, women, children and infants. We stood outside with other yachties and listened attentively to their incredible singing. Perfect harmony, all sung *a capella*. I noticed that 20 or 30 dogs were lying outside beside the church walls, sleeping contentedly as they waited for their families. Chickens busily scratched and clucked on the grounds and an occasional rooster crowed or chased a squawking hen.

After the service, people filed out and eagerly came to greet each of us with a big smile, a handshake and a warm welcome. One older woman spoke at length with one of our group in French. She asked Tina to explain that she made *tapa* and anyone interested in seeing her *tapa* should follow her home

It was a short walk along the river to her four-room house. The only furniture was a double-bed mattress without any bedding, one in each room on the floor. The surprising thing was a giant freezer that operated off a generator. After seeing her *tapa*, Joy and I followed a path up the hill. Every house along the way had a profusion of flowering plants tastefully planted around the dwelling. Such brightly colored flowers contrasted handsomely with the ubiquitous lush green. The path followed a stream lined with coconut palms and banana plants. Several times we spotted small Marquesan horses grazing on the bank. Off to each side of the stream rose steep mountains. I could feel the presence of an enormous amount of power. No wonder people believed in forest spirits. In these majestic environs where vaporous clouds shrouded the peaks, the atmosphere was charged with an electrifying energy! We had come on the walk to see the waterfall, but pesky mosquitoes discouraged further ascent. Disappointed, we turned around and made our way back to the village.

There is no bakery at Hana Vave, but in Omoa, about five miles away by water, there is a bakery that bakes French bread. Our English friends Tim and Heather had told us they took their dinghy over to Omoa and landed there. It is also possible to go by land, if you want to spend the entire day climbing the steep mountain trail. Joy and I opted to go by water. This adventure almost ended in disaster.

We started out early. It was a fine day with light wind. We were in *Nessie*, our hard dinghy, and we powered close to the shoreline where the steep sides drop precipitously into the sea. As we rounded the point off Omoa, we saw the landing where supply boats dock. It was completely awash. No way to land there. The entire bay was turbulent, as evidenced by the pounding surf. Tim and Heather had described the bay just as it appeared to us, but they said they had found a good landing place off to one side. We powered closer inshore to try to locate the landing area but saw only swirling surf dashing into rocks. Four Marquesans were on the beach waving us in, but we decided it was too rough to land. Just as I turned the boat to head back out, I saw that we had gotten inside the surf line! An enormous wave was bearing down on us and we were going to be caught in its curve!

I shouted to Joy, "It's too late! This is it!" Suddenly we were being lifted up in the curl. I felt myself being pushed and pulled under the water. Reflexively I threw my arms around my head to protect it and pulled my legs up, making a tight ball of my body. I hoped the dinghy or the outboard would not pound either of us. The boiling sea dragged me shoreward at an incredible speed. Gradually the force subsided enough that I could pull myself up and attempt to stand. But a split second later another powerful wave pushed me down and tumbled me over the bottom. Finally I was able to stand. I saw Joy behind me and the dinghy floating upside down. The four Marquesan men hurried out to us. We assured them we were okay. They then went to rescue the boat, the outboard—which was tied on—the oars, thongs, two float cushions and gasoline can. In no time they had everything ashore and the outboard fastened onto an outrigger canoe where it could be worked on.

The helpful Marquesans tried. They washed the outboard in fresh water, emptied out the gas from the tank and poured in fresh uncontaminated gas, dried the spark plug, but nothing worked. After about an hour trying this or that we knew the outboard was not going to start.

I insisted that we came here for bread and we were not leaving without it. At this point it was still uncertain *how* or even *if* we were going back to Hana Vave. We walked through the village to the bakery and came back once more to the beach. The surf had not lessened and the young men who'd helped us were gone. Up the beach we saw one older man puttering around on one of the canoes. We approached him and in mixed English and French asked him if there was any way we could launch our dinghy. He faced the ocean and studied it for a long time. Haltingly he told us there was only one place. He pointed down to one end of the bay. To get there we had to portage the dinghy uphill and then down some steps that had been carved into the rocks. We made a second trip to carry the outboard. Meanwhile the old man had called another man over to help launch us.

Looking out from the place we were to launch, we could see the seas roaring and wildly crashing everywhere, but there was a narrow "path" from the landing where we stood leading out past the breakers. We lashed the outboard to the bottom of the dinghy. The man explained that we should have to row very hard and strong to get away. As the stronger rower, that would be my job. We got the oars set up in the oarlocks. The two men quickly placed the boat into the water as they had timed it. Joy jumped in, scrambled to the bow and I hurried behind, clasping the oars in a death grip. The men shoved us away hard, saying, "Alle!" and motioning furiously with their hands waving us to seaward.

I rowed for all I was worth and Joy kept a watch to yell directions. Several times I glanced over my shoulder and saw a mighty swell. My stomach rose with it. I must have voiced my fear because Joy said, "It's all right. Keep rowing!" At any moment I expected another curl to flip us over, but the dinghy rose and fell as the seas bounded past us on both sides.

When finally clear and safe, I was exhausted. I rowed with what remaining strength I had but it was insufficient to propel us past the point where the current was setting us back. It was all I could do to keep us in place. Joy changed places with me and was able to get us past the point. Still, we faced another four hours of hard rowing before getting back to *Banshee*. By then the sun was setting. We told David of our mishap and he and a young Englishman, Bruce, set about taking the outboard apart so they could properly clean it. Joy and I had just enough energy for a quick warm shower and then fell into bed for a full night's sleep. Thanks to Bruce and David, the outboard was working the next day. As for Joy and me, we were feeling stiff in the joints and suffering from blistered palms. After this episode we created a little maxim—"Never power further than you can row back!" We try to adhere to it.

From Fatu Hiva we sailed back to Hiva Oa but anchored on the side of the island opposite Atuona in Hana Menu Bay. At the head of the bay lies an abandoned coconut plantation. Ashore we waited out a heavy downpour in a deteriorating shack with thatch roof. Once the rain stopped we wandered back to an abandoned dwelling that still contained some dishes, an old refrigerator and a primitive stove. Planted around the house were lime and orange trees. Fresh water was even piped into the house from the stream in back. We walked through the jungle and muddy land to the stream. Along its edge we discovered a stone wall that had been built by the ancient Marquesans. The area was heavily planted in bananas, papayas and breadfruit, all growing so thick the sunlight could hardly filter through the tangled canopy. Beautiful rose colored hibiscus grew along the bank. Running the entire length of the stream right down to the ocean was the old stone wall, still in good shape, At one point we came to a lovely small waterfall that dropped into a perfect pool. A delightful place for a fresh water bath except the mosquitoes were eating us alive.

Hana Menu and the deserted coconut plantation was just one more tragic indication that the Marquesans are leaving these islands. I felt saddened to see the place vacant where formerly a vital people had lived. How healthy can it be that throughout the world numerous societies are vanishing from the face of the earth? With them go cultural diversity, languages, religions, belief systems—disappearing forever into oblivion. What are we losing? How dull if the world becomes one gigantic cultural monolith where everyone speaks English and we all fall prey to TV ads and have nothing more exciting in life than the latest soap opera.

It is estimated that in their wide ranging migrations across the Pacific, the Polynesians first settled in the Marquesas around 200 A.D. A mere 200 years ago when Captain James Cook landed in these islands, the Marquesan population numbered around 50,000. A half century later their numbers had dwindled to 5,000, approximately the same number living there today. Most of the inhabitants had succumbed to a host of European-induced diseases—smallpox, tuberculosis, measles and influenza, but some fell victim to blackbirders—slavers.

Today precious little is known about the pre-Christian life of the Polynesians. Christianization put an abrupt end to a tribal life that in every respect revolved around the tribe's religious beliefs. What remains of their original culture are scattered *ahus* (religious platforms), house foundations, agricultural terraces and stone carved tiki statues. Most of these remains are hidden by jungle. Having few accommodations for tourists and inadequate means of transportation, the Marquesas remain largely inaccessible. Ironically this remoteness mirrors their geographic position. Lying the greatest distance from any continent, the Marquesas are the most remote islands on earth. Their location, though, makes them a convenient stopping place for yachts enroute from the Galapagos, Panama, Mexico and the States. Consequently the most frequent visitors are those aboard the 100 to 200 yachts that annually lay over for a few weeks.

Being avidly interested in early cultures, I was quite excited when we came to the island of Nuku Hiva and learned that we could make a one-day excursion into the jungle to see a group of tikis whose images were carved in stone. Joy and I rented a Land Rover and a driver, Taiki, for the day and invited Tim, Heather, Bruce and Nigel—cruising friends we'd just met in Fatu Hiva—to accompany us.

We got an early start, leaving from Frank and Rose Courser's hotel. Once out of Taiohae, the Land Rover was put through its paces, bouncing over the washed-out unpaved road and climbing almost straight up the steep grade. The road, a burnt apricot colored clay, twisted and turned through dense overhanging jungle. For the most difficult areas, Taiki shifted into four-wheel drive and the engine groaned and strained. After rounding one razorback curve where a substantial portion of the road had fallen away in yesterday's torrential rain, the road leveled off. Taiki pulled to the precipitous side and turned off the engine.

Taiki peered at us through the back window and gestured to the view lying below us. We all alighted, glad for the momentary relief from having our teeth shaken loose. We were poised on the edge of the world. Here the verdant mountains fell away to the distant, wide bay and beyond, a placid Pacific Ocean. More than once Taiki stopped, proudly showing us another breath-taking panorama.

Taiki was taking us to an ancient Marquesan sanctuary in the jungle outside Taipivai village. For more than an hour we climbed up the primitive road, moving at a snail's pace. Finally we came to another precipice overlooking a large valley cut through by a broad river that flows right through Taipivai. It was to this valley where

Herman Melville came in 1842 when he deserted the whaling ship. His four-month visit inspired his book *Typee*, a classic on nineteenth century Marquesan life.

It was close to noon when we descended from the heights to the village. A heat-laden stillness hung everywhere. As we crossed the wide and slow-moving river, the smell of rotting vegetation filled the air. Tall, brightly colored crotons and numerous ornamental plants lined the dirt road and crowded around the dwellings. After crossing the river, Taiki turned left and drove to the edge of the village. Here he pulled off the road and stopped.

We got out and Taiki explained that a young boy living in the house just off the road would take us to the tikis. A young woman, a baby clutched to her, came and greeted Taiki in Marquesan. Shyly she nodded to us. After Taiki had communicated what he wanted, she yelled to a young girl who ran off toward the village in search of our guide. Meanwhile Taiki had led us to the back of the house. We stood by an open porch. Puppies and piglets mingled, almost indistinguishable from each other. Off to one side and separate from the dwelling was the traditional Polynesian earth oven. At the back door coconut husks were smouldering, presumably to discourage mosquitoes. Nonetheless they were feasting on our exposed arms and legs undeterred. While waiting Taiki broke off some bananas from a stalk hanging nearby and passed them around.

After about ten minutes a boy of ten or eleven came running up and we set off behind him. It was a narrow trail, muddy and slippery. The sides of the path were marked off by stones laid down by the ancient Marquesans. In every place where the old civilization had lived, walls and walkways have often survived. Sometimes rocks are missing, removed by contemporary Marquesans for their own building purposes.

As we penetrated deeper into the jungle, *nau-naus*—tiny, almost invisible insects—and mosquitoes attacked us relentlessly! With the effort of climbing uphill in the stifling heat and humidity, all of us were soon drenched in sweat and were hyperventilating. Every hundred yards or so our young guide—totally immune to such discomforts—would stop and wait for us to catch up to him.

Perhaps dazed by the heat, my imagination began to work vividly. I could hear the sounds of ancient Marquesan drums and chants accompanying a nocturnal procession on its climb to the sanctuary. Flickering torches cast ominous shadows and jagged shapes over the thick underbrush. I could feel the surge of anticipation among a throng of warriors enroute to a human sacrifice. My heart was beating, gradually speeding up in time with the hypnotic drum beat.

Finally we came to the remains of the *me'ae*—a wall of about three feet, supporting three tikis placed six or seven feet apart. Features of some of them have almost weathered away. When we had photographed and looked for a while, the boy motioned us on. We curved around more heavy growth and came to another area with more stone wall and two tikis, still further on another tiki and part of a wall, both very badly deteriorated and covered over by thick foliage.

Standing there I was filled with conflicting emotions. On the one hand I experienced a deep satisfaction of discovery and in a sense, completion. I had journeyed across the sea by an ancient means of transport under the spread of canvas. At this special moment on a remote island, I had been transported into a timeless past whose culture remained obscure but whose vitality stared out at me from the round-eyed tikis. I felt saddened, too. The wise old tikis still guarding the once sacred area would continue to erode and with them would go forever some vital part of our humanity.

Hibiscus

Chapter 7

The Spirit of Polynesia

Taiohai on the island of Nuku Hiva is the largest and most prosperous village in the Marquesas. We came here for the annual celebration of Bastille Day in mid-July. The week-long celebration includes many sporting competitions as well as a variety of festivities. From islands all around, dancers and singers and a host of musicians gather as do the Marquesan spectators. At night the performers dance, sing and chant, their bodies glistening from applications of coconut oil. Elaborate costumes of green palm fronds and grass skirts decorated with brightly colored flowers set off the dancer's honey colored skin and jet black hair.

An intoxicating scent of tropical flowers hovered in the air. Without a doubt the most spectacular of the dances was the *tamare*, an arousing fertility dance. Enraptured, the audience scarcely breathed. Building from slow undulations to rapid rhythmic thrusts, the dancers, in pairs, erotically gyrated to a bursting climax. The crowd became even more agitated when two men danced the *tamare* with one man assuming the female part even in dress. In our society such a dance would be done as comic pantomime but the Polynesian crowd response would better be described as enthusiastic rather than humorous. Perhaps this is an example of Polynesian acceptance of men who dress as women and choose to live as women.

Incredibly the performances the second night surpassed those of the first. The dance troupes wore more extravagant costumes. Each complex motion of the dancers was executed as a single body! The instrumentalists consisted of eight drummers—two beating on big hourglass drums with skin heads and the remainder on various sized hollowed-out logs which were scraped and scratched—three or four guitarists and one person playing a Marquesan ukulele. The singing sometimes took the form of a round, sometimes in a kind of counterpoint, in octaves, and occasionally in western harmony. Always the voices were robust, the faces animated as their bodies, arms and hands pantomimed the lyrics.

Our stay in the Marquesas was becoming more lengthy than

anticipated. David planned to meet his girl friend in Papeete before we would arrive so he hopped a local supply boat to Tahiti. After having him with us for two months, Joy and I were ready to be on our own again.

Whether from the water, food, or excessive insect bites, Joy developed a severe case of "travelers trots." When she failed to recover after several days, I insisted she go to the clinic at Taiohai. The doctor and medications were totally free. To their credit the French provide good medical care free to everyone on the remote islands and at a nominal cost to city dwellers in Papeete. After an intravenous injection, Joy began to regain both her spirits and strength rapidly.

With Joy well on the road to recovery, we set sail for Rangiroa in the Tuamotus on July 17. Light winds continued until the third day when intermittent squalls began to overtake us. Gradually over the next two days wind velocity increased as did the frequency of squalls.

The *Pacific Pilot* recommends entering the pass at Rangiroa at slack water. The reason: it is the largest atoll in the Tuamotus, so large in fact that the entire island of Tahiti would fit inside with room left over! The pass, by contrast, is a very small opening through which tidal streams can build to a considerable speed or become so rough as to be untenable when the wind blows opposite to the flow of current.

Having arrived in the morning, roughly three hours before slack water, we decided to heave to three to five miles off Avatoru Pass. As we waited, the wind rose to 25-30 knots. When we sailed closer to the pass as the time for slack water approached, immense swells obliterated the pass! As we edged cautiously nearer, the seas around us were breaking and large slicks formed. They looked harmless but once in one, I found it pulled the boat around out of control. About this time three yachts literally shot out of the pass like cannon balls. This personal observation and another from the *Pilot* —"The tidal currents are so strong that eddies and rips can be found on the inside when the flood is in force" cinched it for us. With all the coral reefs and shallows within the pass itself, an entry under those conditions was just too hazardous. We then read about Tiputa pass and thought we would check it out. With the wind behind us, we roared toward the second pass, but just as we came closer, a nasty black squall swept through blacking out the entire atoll. By now, with sunset only a couple of hours away and the sky indicating more squalls, we deemed the fates had somehow decided we should not visit Rangiroa. This was a big disappointment for me because it meant totally missing the Tuamotus.

We changed our course for Papeete. During the night, the squalls subsided but reinforced trades, blowing 25-30 knots, created large breaking seas. Not terribly comfortable on a beam reach, but under just a reefed main we were easily making 6 knots. Five days later, the seas were still crashing over our decks. Close to midnight we heard such a loud crack we thought we had collided with another vessel! Time for a storm jib.

It was about 2 A.M. and ten days after leaving Taiohai when we spotted the light off Papeete pass. Many people think nothing of going into a strange harbor at night. Joy and I are conservative, especially in coral waters. We elected to heave to and wait for dawn before entering. It was a glorious morning, too. Soft sunshine, the color of straw, washed the shoreside trees and grass. The scene was reminiscent of an impressionistic painting. The harbor was teaming with yachts tied to the quay. The lineup extended down to the rocky shore where boats anchored bow out and tied stern lines to shoreside bollards. The glass-like harbor waters reflected the brightly colored hulls and the clean white ones, forming a watery kind of quilt. Soon we spotted old friends: Milt and Marie on *Moonchild*; Paul and Heather on *Guinevere*; Leo and Gerda; Pam and John on *Windchild*.

Ashore in time for lunch we feasted at a sidewalk café on American hamburgers and French fries and ice cream topped with a big mound of whipped cream.

****

After arriving in French Polynesia, I suddenly realized how ignorant I was of the history of South Pacific islands. Such ignorance is, unfortunately, typical of Americans. Our attitudes are abysmally provincial. What our media calls "international" news is hardly that. We cover the troubled spots, hijackings, outbreaks of terror and violence, and some of the social scandals of European countries but that is about the extent of it. My curiosity whetted, I began searching for more historical background as well as information about current affairs in the South Pacific.

I learned that Tahiti was ruled by the Pomare dynasty until 1880 when the islands became a French colony. In 1957 French Polynesia became a French Overseas Territory headed by a High Commissioner who personally represents the French Republic. I suppose this change in status was intended to grant Polynesian citizens more independence and autonomy. In terms of governmental structure, the French Polynesians have a legislative body, the Territorial Assembly, made up of 30 popularly elected members. This Assembly chooses seven councillors who compose the Government Council. French Polynesia also elects representatives to the French Senate, Parliament and the Economic and Social Council.

The population of French Polynesia numbers more than 167,000, almost half of whom live in Tahiti with 24,000 in Papeete. The ethnic percentages break down into 75% Polynesian; 10% Asian; 15% European. Geographically, French Polynesia comprises some 130 islands in five archipelagoes—the Society Islands, Marquesas, Tuamotus, Gambiers and Australs.

Thor Heyerdahl's *Kon Tiki* voyage was meant to demonstrate that the South Pacific Islands could have been populated by voyagers sailing from the west coast of South America. Most recent research, however, has refuted his hypothesis by convincingly providing evidence that the Polynesian peoples migrated from west to east. The so-called Polynesian triangle represents the spread of these migrations to three points: Hawaii in the north, Easter Island in the east and New Zealand to the south.

This triangle covers almost twice the area of the continental U.S., but the ratio of sea to land is 70 to 1. Settlement of this region took place from about 1600 B.C. to A.D. 800. Prior to A.D. 1500, the Polynesians were the most widespread peoples on earth.

The initial Polynesian migration began about 3,000 years ago when peoples of the Lapita culture—so named for their pottery— left from the Bismarck chain and the Solomon Islands. Archaeologists have proposed that the Lapita people began their sea migrations eastward, moving to Santa Cruz Island in the Solomons, south to the Banks and Vanuatu, New Caledonia and Fiji. From there they sailed in subsequent migrations to Tonga and Samoa.

About 1,000 years later, having evolved a distinct Polynesian

55

culture and proto-Polynesian language, they began another still further eastward migration. This carried them to the Marquesas perhaps as early as 200 B.C. but not later than A.D. 300. From the Marquesas they voyaged by ocean-going canoe and settled in Hawaii around A.D. 300 and to Easter Island about a century later.

Their migration to the Society Islands appears to have occurred shortly after their arrival in the Marquesas. It wasn't until A.D. 800 that they landed on the shores of New Zealand, thus completing the great migration across the Pacific Ocean.

The early Polynesians brought all their major foods—plant and animal—with them. Among these are coconut, taro, banana, yam, breadfruit, pig, dog and chicken.

Our knowledge of early Polynesians, their migrations and culture are gleaned from several fields of study—from oral traditions recounting epic voyages and cosmogonic myths, from linguistics, ethnobotany and physical anthropology.

Archaeological evidence has revealed not only similarities in religious practices but also differences which developed locally. Some of the most fascinating information comes from the stone images and temple platforms scattered around the Pacific. The Tahitian word *marae* describes low rectangular stone platforms with a rectangular court or terrace that has upright stone slabs erected at certain points in the court.

These structures are common to the early settlement period in East Polynesia. Variations occurred in Hawaii and the southern Marquesas where terracing became very prominent. In the Australs and Cooks, emphasis was placed on the uprights. In New Zealand, the stone temples are virtually absent but the term *marae* survives as does an elaborate structure—out of wood.

The famous Easter Island stone images are considered to be analogous to the upright slabs found in Central and East Polynesian *marae*. One can ask, are the anthropomorphic images an earlier representation of the slabs?

One of the most puzzling questions concerns the tiki, an anthropomorphic stone image—a male with round face, wide mouth and protruding eyes and ears. These figures occur in Hawaii, Easter Island, the Marquesas and Pitcairn—the island to which the Bounty mutineers fled. In Tahiti only sorcery gods were personified in stone. These were small and were placed on an adjacent shrine

Joy and Jeannine—
Welcome aboard!

Virgin's Bay (Hana Vave) on
Fatu Hiva in the Marquesas.

Our young Marquesan guide stands above a tiki hidden in the jungle vines.

Plotting out a course.

Trading with young girls in Raiatea.

A traditional Tahitian boat has planks lashed with sennit made from material found inside the outer hull of the coconut. The boat's seams are caulked with sticky milky liquid from the breadfruit.

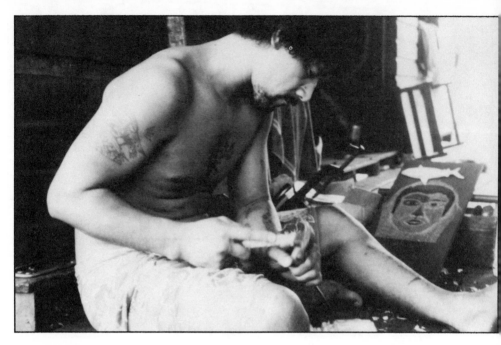

Mark carves in the shade of his family's *fale*, Western Samoa.

The shark that Mark carved for us has a place in front of the antique barograph in *Banshee's* cabin.

A Tongan woman paints a design on a huge *tapa*.

Tongan women pound bark for *tapa* cloth.

Pampas grass in New Zealand.

Looking up at four giant kauri trees in New Zealand. The trees were logged into extinction on Great Barrier Island.

without a platform. This is not the case in Hawaii, Easter Island or the Marquesas where the tiki is placed on the surrounding wall, suggesting they represented important deities in these areas.

After several months in the "bush," Papeete and its civilized amenities were most welcome. We were able to replace some gear. Yachting equipment, although terribly expensive—as is everything—was readily available. It was enjoyable to binge on French pastries, cheese, paté and eat out once in a while in a restaurant.

A lovely side trip was by *le truck* to the Paul Gauguin Museum 61 kilometers from Papeete. The museum is imaginatively laid out in five or six buildings connected by open air walkways. It is located between the botanical gardens and a serene lagoon.

For the first couple of weeks in the city, I enjoyed the hustle and the mixed European/Polynesian flavor. Then we tired of the noise and exhaust fumes. Anchored right on the main thoroughfare, we were bombarded with traffic noise that began at 5 A.M. and lasted until about 2 A.M. The Italian restaurant directly across the street blasted disco music nonstop nightly. What a contrast. Turn your back to the city and you faced a beautiful wide lagoon often dotted with native sailing and rowing canoes. This view recreated scenes right out of Polynesia's past. It was like having one foot in each world, except that one could never escape the ubiquitous clutter and clamor of contemporary capitalism at work. Little wonder then, that Joy and I opted to begin our exploration of other anchorages.

I remember talking to someone tied up in Papeete. At the time there were easily 200 yachts sitting there beside the city. This friend said to me that when all the boats are tied up here in Papeete, we remain cliquish, but when in an anchorage with just a few boats, we all get to know each other. I wonder if this same principle holds true on land? This in essence means the larger the community the less we get to know others and the less we venture out of our tight little circles.

Our first move out of the circle took us to the island of Moorea, about a half day sail from Papeete. Our first stop was to anchor inside the lagoon just off the reef in 30 feet of clear aquamarine water next to Tim and Heather's catamaran. In fact we said our farewells to them a day or so later when they left bound for New Zealand.

We leisurely moved on down to Papetoui Bay and anchored at

the famous Robinson's cove. On a walk we discovered an agricultural research center set in the midst of rolling green hills topped by stands of acacia. and, most unexpected of all, sleek coated horses and cows grazing on the velvety hillsides. Part of the experimental station consisted of fish ponds farming fish and shrimp. But the bucolic scene, so like the English countryside, was totally unexpected on a tropical isle.

Joy and I continued to explore various parts of Moorea, sometimes anchoring in areas where we were the only yacht. It seems to me that overcrowding such as we experienced in metropolitan areas takes a toll that we fail to realize until we leave it. Being the only person or two people walking on a small *motu* (little island) imparts a tremendous calmness and consequently one's whole being slows down. In urban areas we get out of step with nature to the point of forgetting that we are *part* of it, not some entity outside of and *controlling* it. Our sense of time is truly relative. An article in the November issue of *Science 85* throws the concept of time into and entirely new perspective. Sandra M. Farber wrote: "Because light travels at a constant rate, looking deeper into space means looking farther back in time. At the edge of this range, the telescope (the Hubble space telescope) will show us galaxies as they were billions of years ago. More than halfway back to the Big Bang when the universe was born." Similarly my experiences in the South Pacific have been like going through a time warp that transports me back to an earlier time in human existence. A side effect—a bonus really—has been a release of creative energy. I have found my mind seems more fluid and especially when sleeping or falling asleep thoughts and ideas come to the fore. I first noticed this activity in Moorea where I began having some very vivid and detailed dreams. It was not unusual to wake up in the morning with a complicated sentence echoing in my brain. Here's one I wrote down—"It's a shame to spend your money this year on bricabrac because frames bring the out-of-doors indoors." I'm not including this line here because I think it has great literary value. What I think it shows is the mind at work on another level. To be sure, the items juxtaposed don't even belong together on a rational level, but strictly on an image making level, the line is quite striking.

Emotionally many things were going on. I found I was missing my friends a great deal. And in a strange way I started missing having a job. I think I really missed the structure that work brings to one's life. I was used to interacting with many people socially, intellectually and professionally. My entire orientation to life had changed. I was meeting new people all the time, but I soon learned that most cruisers talk almost exclusively about yachts, parts, rigging, bad passages, etc. I have found myself really longing for good conversations and discussions on other topics and issues. The other problem for me was the need/desire to play a piano. Music has always been an important part of my life. Just before leaving the States I purchased an electronic keyboard. Unfortunately it stopped functioning in the Marquesas the first time I brought it out to play. Someone knowledgeable about electronic gadgets looked at it and told me what part I needed. I had friends send the IC (integrated circuit) but when I got to Papeete and found someone who could repair it, he said it still needed another IC. Months went by and in the end the keyboard never was repaired. So I attempted to satisfy my longing to make music by playing my recorders and guitar. It was not the same. One good musical moment happened when George Rudy brought his flute to *Moonchild* and I brought my recorder. The two of us sat on the deck playing flute duets while Moonbeam, a Siamese cat, lay nearby apparently enthralled with our dulcet tones.

In early December we went to Afareaitu, the Tahitian side of Moorea. Several days after arriving we decided to go in search of a waterfall that our friend, Margaret, had described to us. We dinghied into a small wharf at Afareaitu. The small village contains a little grocery store, the office of the gendarmes and a wonderful church built in 1912. Painted white with blue trim the European-style church standing out against towering mountain peaks—it could have been in an Alpine scene. The view from the sea was spectacular with the valley falling away from the sharp mountain as though scooped out by a giant hand.

We followed Margaret's map over a dirt road that narrowed to a footpath and led to a wooden bridge. Gradually the trail steepened. Much of the way was shaded by tall trees—mango and Tahitian chestnut trees predominating. The trail wound around the mountain basically following a river whose roar over boulders resounded in the otherwise quiet wilderness. About halfway up we encountered a flat area. From here the bay and the coral pass looked like a picture in relief. Suddenly a young man appeared and approached with a smile. He told us that this was his land, extending from the bridge to the waterfall. He welcomed us, told us to enjoy it then disappeared around the next bend.

Further up, as the sound of the falls grew louder, we suddenly came into view of the waterfall. At that moment the sun was in just the right place to cast a golden sparkle over the cascading sheet of water and the fine spray that misted the air. Finally we came into full view of the waterfall and the languid dark pool at its base. It's amazing that the pool is so still and quiet when there is such a tumultuous roar from the water as its liquid electricity leaps earthward.

We had spread ourselves out on some rocks beside the pool, trying to avoid a nest of ants, when the young Tahitian, looking much like a forest faun, reappeared. He busied himself as if he hadn't noticed us. When we yelled hello, he came over to greet us again and introduced himself as Richard Maui. The waterfall comes from a spring, he explained, the only one on Moorea that does. Richard pointed out a number of plants and described their use as food or medicine. He explained that his grandmother had taught him how to use plants medicinally and still it's the only kind of medicine he uses. Richard informed us that some years previously, part of the *Bounty* movie had been filmed here. He was in the film playing the part of a pirate!

We managed to get back to *Banshee* only seconds before a torrential downpour. With that deluge the monsoon began. The next day the rainfall became heavier. Heavy black clouds marched in a continuous procession across the mountains down to the lagoon where they turned the world and my mood into a sodden gray blob. Making things even worse, we had to keep hatches and ports closed so the boat felt like a Swedish steam bath. Sitting around inactive for several days at a time, sweaty and hot usually makes me depressed.

Perhaps without diversions I have too much time to think. I started feeling guilty, guilty for not having taken another direction in life, feeling that I've become useless and totally hedonistic! What is it that I need to do? Why must I *do* anything? Is it not enough to enjoy, to observe? No. I kept thinking everything must lead to some end, must amount to something. Life must have direction; activity must be purposeful. There I was again—back in the *Western* trap. For the past months I'd been seeing people just living each day, simply. No push, no rush to get ahead, to amass wealth or possessions. What for? The Polynesians take it easy. They have the sea, the sky, clouds, trees, flowers, fruit, plenty of food, family, friends, children, dogs and horses. Richard has his land, his waterfall. He doesn't want to sell his land, to see a hotel built on his lovely mountain. He never thinks about "progress." His land belonged to his father and will become his son's. The land goes on and on with the generations. Progress? Progress is a Western concept, foreign to Richard.

****

My mother flew to Tahiti from Florida for a visit over Christmas and New Years . I felt it was a courageous venture for a 74-year-old lady to fly alone to a foreign land. I was delighted to see her and had hoped that she would be as enchanted as I with Tahiti and Moorea.

Unfortunately, conditions were less than ideal with three of us closed up for much of the time on a steamy 34-foot yacht. The monsoon was upon us and this meant torrential rain for hours on end. Below in the cabin, it was hot, humid and most uncomfortable. Between bad weather we did manage a little sight seeing. One day we rented a car and drove all the way around Tahiti. On Moorea we had a prefect day when we toured the island by van.

On the day of my mother's arrival, there was a bit of excitement. We knew she was tired after the long flight, so Joy and I got her settled into the boat for a rest and we went off to town to do some shopping.

Unbeknownst to us, in our absence a vicious squall came through. The blow dislodged the anchor and *Banshee* was rapidly drifting down on a vessel anchored nearby. Fortunately our friend Ron Zaneveld on *Saga* and "English" Peter on *Eila* saw the impending disaster. Ron was the first to reach *Banshee*. Tall, strong Dutchman that he is, he leapt aboard in one great bound with a string of profanity issuing from his mouth.

Totally unaware of her precarious position, Mother was alarmed by the sudden appearance of a strange man charging across the deck. Who was he? What did he want? Then out of nowhere Peter appeared hoisting himself over the rail, his puckish fair face frozen in a grimace. The two men frantically ran back and forth from bow to stern, heaving up one anchor and throwing over another. All of this activity amidst a host of loud yells left Mother speechless. She stood on the companionway steps watching the commotion. Finally Peter and Ron, who thought no one was aboard, saw her standing there. She told them who she was and both men felt somewhat embarrassed and blond Peter blushed remembering their salty language.

With *Banshee* secured, the guys introduced themselves and Mother invited them in for tea and cookies. Having just arrived, she had no idea how to light the stove to heat water. Ron showed her how. To this day he remarks how calm she was throughout the ordeal.

I felt sad when Mother left to fly home. Joy and I had a long involved argument brought on by the pent-up emotions that had accumulated. I hoped Mother had enjoyed herself but I suspected the reality of traveling did not accord with the romance of it. So it must be with many people. They dream about exotic places but never consider at the outset such things as bad weather, traveler's trots, having things lost or stolen, missing trains and planes, etc. How much more people romanticize sailing by private yacht! Seldom do they grasp what it's like to have to carry in every drop of water, diesel fuel, kerosene, propane and heaps of provisions.

As Joy and I have discovered, we spend more time maintaining the boat, keeping equipment repaired and functioning than we do in lounging around living the good life.

****

"Having watched the passage of my Oriental babies from the trees, I now stand with the Statue of Liberty." This was another wild sentence coursing through my brain when I woke up—showing that the same kind of mental activity was continuing into the new year, 1986.

Chapter 8

Clouds over Paradise

While sitting on *Banshee* in Cook's Bay on the island of Moorea, my eyes trace the jagged peaks of Mt. Mauroa. From there I look toward Mt. Tohivea—a thick, gray cloud hovers over its face obscuring the steep peak. It is late January, summer in the Southern hemisphere. For at least the hundredth time I think how fortunate I am to be in French Polynesia now. In another decade—if current trends continue—these islands will be very different, possibly their majestic beauty destroyed.

Like other Westerners I have quickly succumbed to the ubiquitous tropical softness, gentle lagoons, warm clear waters, fragrant whiffs of frangipani, tiare, ginger and vanilla. It is intoxicating—all of it—the vibrant foliage and exotic flowers whose extravagant forms are often unreal. As I watch cumulus clouds charging across the verdant mountains, some primal response registers in my skin. In a few hours I will witness another blazing sunset invading the sky, overrunning the clouds, a wild artist's palette merging and changing with a riotous will. The last shades of rose turn orange, gradually fading into burnt tangerine. Silently the mountains darken, guarding ancient secrets of a mysterious past.

I had expected to be overwhelmed by this kind beauty. What I didn't anticipate were problems in paradise. If I had come to these islands as most tourists do with only two weeks to sample the setting, I would surely leave thinking I had found paradise. But I've lingered much longer, already six months. It's been long enough to become acquainted with both Polynesians and the expatriated from Europe and America. My eyes have been opened. These islands suffer from some of the same threats as the work-a-day world I left behind. They also have some special problems of their own. The most puzzling questions started cropping up in the Marquesas, especially in Atuona. An expression of apathy etched in the faces of the adults caused me to question, but at the time I knew too little about the history, past and present, to have much insight. Better informed now, I see many parallels with the American Indians.

Like the Indians, the Marquesans had no resistance to infectious diseases brought in by Europeans. Many died from fighting against the invaders and perhaps even more from in-fighting that developed as a direct result of European intrusion. There can be no mistake that the Marquesans were a vigorous people. Ruins of their villages—solid rock walls, religious sanctuaries and stone carved tikis—lie everywhere throughout the islands. Most tragic is the way the Polynesians, like the American Indians, have been divested of their culture and, in many instances, their land.

Perhaps the most vulnerable parts of pre-industrialized societies are their religious structures and their concepts of land distribution and ownership. Once their religious beliefs are invalidated or superseded by a foreign religion, the society virtually dies, much like a plant whose root has been chopped off. Even during the one to two centuries since Europeans first came to the Pacific, the Polynesians have not become fully enculturated. And why should they? It is pure arrogance on our part to assume in the first place that our society is inherently superior to theirs. For too long we have regarded our advanced technology as the ultimate proof of our superiority. Unfortunately this dogmatic view has blinded us to the human aspects of the question. By now it should be quite evident that Polynesians have nothing in their history to prepare them to embrace European culture fully. European society had evolved historically over centuries in a totally different physical environment.

Basically the Marquesans are a forgotten people living on very remote islands. Access to these islands is limited to small prop planes from Tahiti or to a cargo boat. In the main, the only visitors to these islands are aboard the hundred or so private yachts who stop each year while transiting the Pacific. The Marquesans have no industry—the once thriving copra market has bottomed out—and they long ago lost most of their culture when they were missionized. Of the four islands we visited in the Marquesas, the inhabitants of the little village of Atuona seemed to be suffering the most severely from colonial malaise.

Almost every Marquesan family living in Atuona owns an expensive four-wheel drive vehicle. There is one paved road that runs for two or three miles through the dusty little settlement. There is no place to drive, yet vehicles constantly move up and down the road that goes nowhere. Everywhere the people sit around, idle. The adults seemed dull and listless. How do they afford such expensive vehicles and who buys the grossly overpriced frozen foods and canned items found in all three of the tiny hole-in-the-wall stores in Atuona? Canned vegetables and fruits cost between two and six U.S. dollars a can! Most people coming through on yachts can't afford such prices. Only a limited number and quantity of fresh vegetables were sometimes available on some of the islands. This fact seemed strange to me until I realized that the traditional Marquesan diet does not include garden vegetables. Today they still grow and consume breadfruit, bananas, coconuts, taro, mangoes and a kind of grapefruit known as pomplemousse. Unfortunately, a very poor quality of tinned corned beef and white French bread have become major items in their diet. Everywhere chickens run about, yet no fresh chicken is available in the markets. The Marquesans buy frozen chicken imported from Arkansas! Pigs on the hoof are plentiful enough, but to find butchered pork or beef is quite rare.

Slowly I began to realize I was seeing a people who had been missionized and colonized. What had been a viable culture had been reduced to a kind of cultural "zombiism." Disease, alcohol, Western culture and religion had stripped them of their past and had really given little or nothing in return. In place of weaving, canoe building, fishing, carving and living in a society that worked in harmony with the natural environment, these people now spend their days and their government subsidies on motor vehicles, TV sets, VCRs, ghetto blasters, cigarettes and alcohol.

Subsidies. No one has to earn money. The French government provides families with money for each child. This form of financial support persuades some Marquesans to remain in these islands and certainly encourages them to increase their population. Why do the French wish to keep these islands inhabited? For one thing, if all the Marquesans descended upon Tahiti, the French would be faced with a severe problem. Already they are in a quandary about an increasing number of youths who come to the city, penniless and without skills. A second reason, quite likely, is that the French would like to hang on to the natural harbor at Taiohai which could easily accommodate a large naval fleet should the French ever lose Papeete.

After thinking about it, I concluded that the subsidy for children would not be sufficient for the purchase of the expensive items many of the Polynesians possessed. The answer, as I learned, is that many islanders borrow money, using their land as security. Jobless and unable to repay the loan, most of them lose their land. This then, was the ultimate step in dehumanization because the land passes from generation to generation and has always been thought of as forming an essential link between living Polynesians and their ancestors.

Government subsidy also serves another purpose. It keeps people dependent and thus functions as a prevention against political movement for independence. But the carefully wrought bulwark is beginning to crumble. Independence fever has struck some French Polynesians, especially those growing up in Papeete. Certainly the independence of other Polynesian nations in the South Pacific has influenced some French Polynesians.

As one would expect, colonialism works more efficiently in the remote island groups—the Marquesas, Tuamotus, Gambiers and Australs. But the plan is less successful in the city. Papeete, the capital, is more Europeanized, the people more sophisticated. In this urbanized hub, Polynesians are quick to spot discrepancies between how they are treated versus how the French are treated. Favoritism is, according to French Polynesians, rampant. Characteristically it's not Polynesians who hold high paying positions: it's the French or *"demis"*—half French, half Polynesian.

Many Polynesians know that the extreme high cost of living, the highest in the South Pacific, is directly related to the French pocketbook. When French citizens come to work in French Polynesia, they receive high wages and, on top of that a fifty percent bonus for hardship! (Imagine living in Tahiti being a hardship.) Furthermore, French workers don't have to buy their cars here where they would have to pay very large import duty. They have their cars sent in from France.

Typically the most telling discriminations come in employment and education. Louis, a Tahitian advocating Polynesian independence, pinpointed some of the most blatant problems. Until recently Tahitian was not spoken in the schools, only French. Today it is used in elementary school but is not taught in high school. Another area of discrimination occurs with respect to higher education. Since there are no universities in French Polynesia, students must go abroad—usually to France. Study abroad without government assistance is more expensive than most Polynesian families can afford. Very few Polynesian students receive this kind of aid which, Louis says, readily goes to French students. Of course, without the education Polynesians cannot compete for better paying jobs. Thus the classic Catch-22 situation continues.

By far the most serious issue is that of nuclear testing. On July 10, 1985, the world witnessed the sinking of the Greenpeace vessel *Rainbow Warrior* in Auckland Harbor. Months later the French government belatedly admitted complicity. Unfortunate as the incident was, at least it focused world attention on a major concern in the South Pacific. If some citizens of the world didn't know or had forgotten, they quickly learned that the French are still conducting underground nuclear tests on the atoll Mururoa. How many Americans know that French Polynesians want nuclear testing in their country to cease? In January and February, 1985, (and probably since) there were big demonstrations in Papeete against nuclear testing. As usual, the press failed to report the protests. Because of the remoteness of South Pacific islands and their lack of economic import, the world at large remains ignorant of what happens here, especially when the sentiments are anti-French.

Probably most Europeans and Americans think that Polynesians living in the Tuamotus, Gambiers and Australs are unconcerned, oblivious to the nuclear issue. To be sure, they are not. A friend returning from a two-month stay in Mangareva (Gambiers) doing fieldwork, reports that the inhabitants are quite concerned. For one thing, they are distressed that fish—a staple of their diet—are contaminated.

At issue is not simply that islanders have lost a culinary delight. Nor is the real issue that these remote islanders live where land is scarce, forcing them to be dependent on supplies brought in by cargo ships that sometimes are delayed. No, the real issue is a moral one: what right do the French have to take over land belonging to another people and to make it unfit for human habitation? And why do we Western nations remain silent when French nuclear testing poses a severe threat of nuclear pollution which could well be injurious to the entire world?

For two decades the French government has been acting as

though it is a law unto itself. Beginning in 1964, when other nations agreed to cease above ground nuclear testing, the French continued to blast away at Mururoa from the air. In 1971, David McTaggart, representing Greenpeace, sailed his own vessel, a 38-foot sailboat, into the area to protest not only the bombing but the French government's violation of international maritime law. They had restricted 100,000 square miles of ocean when by international agreement they only had rights to control up to 12 miles offshore. McTaggart's book, *Sailing into the Bomb*, a report on his 41-day protest at Murora, is quite informative. His vigil and that of his two crew ended only when a French naval vessel rammed his little boat, causing so much damage that the French Navy had to tow McTaggart's boat into Mururoa for repairs.

More than four years ago, the Protestant church in Papeete wrote to the French government requesting that French Polynesians be allowed to vote on whether to allow nuclear testing in their country. The French government has never even acknowledged receipt of the letter.

Logically it can only be a matter of time before the French must relinquish their colonial holdings. Pressure to do so is exerted not only from within but from other South Pacific nations. Historically, ethnically and geographically the Polynesians belong to the South Pacific island community. It makes sense for these nations to form an alliance to deal with issues of common concern. This is precisely what has happened. For the past 18 years, the South Pacific Forum has served as a body airing problems and proposing solutions. On August 6, 1985, eight nations—Australia, the Cook Islands, Fiji, Kiribati, Niue, New Zealand, Tuvalu and Western Samoa—signed the Treaty of Rarotonga which designates a nuclear-free zone in the South Pacific. Specifically the treaty prohibits the manufacture, testing, storing, dumping and use of nuclear weapons and materials in the region. Of course, France is openly in defiance of the treaty. Because of their continued nuclear testing and the government's failure to set a date of independence for French Polynesia, the latter country has been barred from becoming a member of the South Pacific Forum.

Certainly the tourism issue pales when compared with nuclear testing, yet it looms as a major concern in the Society Islands. In the last half year, a dramatic increase in the number of tourists has been alarming. Recently I read a newspaper story that said the community leaders were pushing to develop the tourist industry. Their goal was to increase the number of tourists from the current 100,000 a year to 200,000 within five years. This information was a bit shocking because Moorea's scattered hotels are usually no more than fifty percent occupied at any given time. What's impressive about Moorea is that it retains a serene atmosphere with its scattered villages tucked neatly back into its valleys. The only form of public transportation are the "trucks" which drive people to and from two ferry docks. The ferries serve as a lifeline between Papeete and Moorea. There are no cities on Moorea, no hustle, no bustle. Tourism has been basically low keyed with nothing ostentatious. But this is changing. Now the *Liberté*, an American-Hawaiian cruise liner, has taken up "residence" in the Society Islands. With 750 passengers, the ship cruises weekly from Rangiroa in the Tuamotus to all six of the Society Islands. The first 22 weeks on the cruise ship were sold out. Imagine 750 tourists invading Cook's Bay where there is one small hotel, two small restaurants and three small grocery stores! Who stands to gain from developing the tourist industry? Certainly not the Tahitians. The investors are large American, European and Saudi Arabian companies. No one has bothered to ask the indigenous population if they want their islands turned into an adult Fantasy Island or a Disney-styled Polynesian isle.

Will the Society Islands end up like the Caribbean where mass invasion of tourists has brought out strong resentment of the indigenous people? Surrounded by wealthy tourists, the native inhabitants struggle along in menial jobs earning subsistence wages. Meanwhile their fragile island ecology quickly deteriorates.

I fear such a future for Moorea with its majestic beauty and its friendly people. The ecological balance of the barrier reef and the fringing reef is so delicate. Fresh water and sewage kill coral. If the coral goes, so does all the marine life connected to it.

So, early in my voyaging I have seen that paradise is endangered. Nuclear pollution, over-development and injudicious use of islands are causing damage that may well be irreparable. At present no one knows the extent of damage nuclear testing in Mururoa does to the natural environment or to human health. The French government suppresses health statistics and information on environmental changes in its South Pacific Territory. Instead they insist that nuclear testing has not caused any detrimental effects. Still, it is no secret to the people inhabiting these islands that fish in many areas are now toxic. Our Hawaiian friend doing fieldwork in the Gambiers reported that some fish actually glow in the dark. Any intelligent person will reflect that repeated underwater blasting of an atoll presents a possibility of triggering tectonic plate movement. What ultimate damage may occur is really beyond our ability to project. We know how important the oceans are to life on our planet. If we pollute to the extent of disrupting the life chain at this level, we are surely playing against odds with consequences that could affect the entire globe.

Perhaps the most staggering thought of all is that disruption from one cause might be reversible, if found in time. Unfortunately, our assaults on the environment come from several directions at once. We have chemical pollution coupled with pollution resulting from the congregation of too many humans in fragile environments. Humans bring wastes, their own and those of our civilization. Discarded plastics litter the ground. If burned, they pollute the air and if dumped into the ocean, they cause enormous problems because they never biodegrade. Still another stress on the environment is the fisheries who overfish to the point of depleting or even exhausting some species of sea life.

Before it's too late, I hope Americans and Europeans will join the South Pacific nations in pressuring the French to return French Polynesia to its rightful owners. When this day comes, I hope we will be generous and assist the Polynesians to find ways of establishing an economy that benefits them while still preserving the natural beauty of their islands. Part of my desire is personal. I would like to return to paradise in ten years time and find it is still paradise.

Chapter 9

La Dame de Mer

Like many other explorers, travelers and adventurers who have come to the South Seas, I came with preconceived ideas about the remote islands representing paradise. No doubt many of my impressions were formed from literature on the South Seas. James Michener, Jack London, Eugene Burdick and Somerset Maugham—to name some of the more prominent authors—described a male world, a world often filled with manipulation, lust, greed, alcoholism, a world where human emotions, gone amok, reached their ultimate in desolation and destruction. Another part of its allure comes from our conceptions of the South Pacific isles as the realm of the exotic and the ultimate in terms of romance. This paradise is a place of extremes and excesses. Skillfully, writers have portrayed the lives of their misguided characters set against the dazzling beauty of the tropics where palm fronds sway hypnotically and wavelets gently sweep across long stretches of pristine beaches. Hoving into view around the curved reach of the turquoise lagoon, the full sails of a brigantine glint bone white against a deep azure sky.

But paradise is threatened. Our imaginations crave antithesis, motion and resolution. Most of the South Pacific vignettes, short stories or novels vividly describe a smoldering human decadence that mirrors the natural world where rotting vegetation permeates the air with foulness. Yet a paradox persists: the jungle also emits the heavenly fragrance of vanilla and frangipani. The same paradox exists between human and natural forces. Nature is divine—the setting being paradise—but man corrupts and thus diminishes or tarnishes the perfection of creation. This portrayal, I finally realized, accords with primitive Christian religion. It is a modern Garden of Eden and man's falling from grace. It is also a world devoid of women except for Polynesian women who function as a kind of exotic fruit to be devoured by white men.

Times have changed and I hope literature of the South Seas will begin to include women, portraying them as real people. Coming to these shores in increasing numbers are European and American women. Some travel alone, in search of adventure, and some, like men of earlier times, to escape the demons of their pasts. So, here is raw material, waiting to be put down in print. Because I believe the time has come to accord women a central role in this genre, I offer the following true story. It is about a shipwrecked woman who calls herself *La Dame de Mer*.

****

It was my first day anchored in Cook's Bay on the lovely island called Moorea. The deep bay is bounded on three sides by steep mountain peaks. The small village of Pao Pao quietly lies at the head of the bay. On the north shore, the individual thatched roof *fares* of the Bali Hai Hotel look like a traditional Polynesian village poised at the water's edge. Off to one side of the hotel grounds is a dinghy landing where visiting cruisers tie up to go ashore.

The dark tropical night was soft, almost caressing. We were on our way to dinner at a nearby restaurant. In the dusk as Joy and I landed our dinghy at the little dock, I could just barely see the silhouettes of a young French couple arriving just ahead of us. We exchanged greetings and introductions. Then, from out of the shadows, came a rather high-pitched voice speaking in a cultured British accent. "I'm here because I was shipwrecked." A childlike giggle followed and then, a woman with long blondish hair bobbing about her shoulders, looking every bit the part of a siren, emerged from the shadows and continued in a rapid voice, "I'm a singlehander, a sailor without a boat." All four of us were a bit startled by the intruder and her strange tidings. She certainly knew how to get our rapt attention. Say the word "shipwrecked" to sailors and their ears will stand at attention. She introduced herself as Margaret Hicks. We spoke with her momentarily and invited her to visit us aboard our vessel the following day.

Over the next few months I came to know more about Margaret's disaster and her life as a whole. Some of our meetings were casual, meeting accidentally in Papeete and chatting over lunch at a sidewalk café. Other encounters were by invitation to the houseboat where she was living or on our yacht for dinner. Once she sailed with us to Papeete, steering most of the way. When I met her, Margaret was looking after a houseboat moored in Cook's Bay. In exchange for her time and effort, she had live-aboard privileges.

In 1982, Margaret was sailing alone around the world, and her 24-foot sailboat was run down by a local fishing boat in broad daylight on a clear day at about 2:30 in the afternoon. She was sailing just outside the barrier reef, about one mile from the pass into Cook's Bay. Margaret watched in startled amazement as the fishing boat operator changed course, putting his boat on a collision course with hers! His boat was not far away and he was moving at a much faster speed than her three or four knots. It was impossible for her to avoid the accident. As she said, "One minute I was in the cockpit of my boat and the next I was sitting in the water!"

Split in half, her boat sank immediately. Margaret literally had nothing but the clothes on her back because she had no time to take anything from the yacht. She quickly took bearings by eye on landmarks to note the location of the sinking. The fishing boat, without having incurred any serious damage, eased up beside Margaret and took her aboard.

Margaret had hoped to get divers to retrieve some of her possessions—mostly equipment—from the wreck, but before she was able to arrange it, scavengers had stripped it bare.

Next ensued lengthy litigation in court. She hired a French attorney to represent her. After trial and retrial, in the end the court ruled in Margaret's favor, awarding her full compensation for her loss. The offender's insurance company paid the maximum benefit which fell considerably short of the court award; the amount Margaret needed to buy a comparable sailboat. The court had ruled that whatever the insurance did not pay would be the personal responsibility of the owner. The difficulty came in trying to collect. The owner had no intention of paying and looked for a loophole. The owner's attorney came back with the argument that since his client was not aboard at the time of the accident, he was not financially responsible. Such a notion is totally at odds with international maritime law which holds that the owner is always responsible. A good part of the frustration of this experience was this kind of contrived ignorance. Local politics slowed down the legal machinery and even, eventually, intervened to protect the owner of the fishing boat. Belonging to one of the most influential families in Moorea, he was untouchable, above the law.

From the beginning the French Polynesians reacted with exceeding kindness and generosity. They realized Margaret had limited funds and they understood litigation could drag on indefinitely. One family offered her food and a place to live. For two and a half years, Margaret lived with them in their village, learning first hand about contemporary Tahitian culture. At the same time Margaret became a living legend in Moorea. One day a young Tahitian woman gave me a lift. As we were driving down the road in her Jeep, we passed Margaret peddling along on her bicycle, her floppy straw hat waving in the breeze. Margaret returned our waves with her own arm stretched out like the wing of a frigate bird. The Tahitian woman smiled at me and said, "We call her the Survive Woman."

Initially, of course, Margaret had no idea that she would spend three years in Moorea. She had anticipated a few months; long enough to settle legal matters and time enough to find and outfit a seaworthy craft in which to continue her singlehanded circumnavigation.

Since girlhood Margaret had been sailing in English waters. At 21 she bought her first boat. It was an antiquated gaff rigger that she restored to a reasonable facsimile of the vessel's maiden beauty. Well educated, Margaret had taught English literature in her own country and in Norway. Having a natural proclivity for languages, she picked up Norwegian easily and spoke French fluently.

What a memory! I often asked Margaret difficult questions about Polynesian culture and history and even about English history. She could recite the order of British kings and queens from beginning to present, and not just names. She could entertainingly chatter on for hours with anecdotal material about any royal person you might choose. As for Polynesian history, she knew myths, legends and customs and could speak authoritatively about anthropological and archaeological studies.

While furthering her teaching career, Margaret continued to sail. Singlehanding was her thing. She entered several singlehanded long distance races prior to her attempted solo circumnavigation. When I met her, and even after knowing her for a while, there were times when Margaret looked like a woman in her thirties rather than one in her late fifties! Her lean body and playful exuberance gave her a radiance associated with youth. Sometimes there was an innocence about her, fresh as a field of spring flowers.

I will always remember one day I spent with Margaret. It was special. For the first time she showed herself as a vulnerable human being whose inner reserves had been tremendously depleted. She talked freely about her family, her life, her decision not to marry so she could devote time to sailing, to adventuring. On that particular day she was even feeling as though her own sister, an established physician, had rejected her because of deep-seated sibling rivalry and jealousy. Margaret was very dejected. She cried. I held her and tried to offer words of encouragement. The crying and talking resulted in a catharsis. Finally she stopped crying and confided that it was the third anniversary of her sinking.

As the months passed, I tired of hearing cruisers being critical of Margaret's concern. Where was their empathy? Somehow three years of her life had sifted away, day after day of waiting, hoping and waiting. Caught up in the special magic that pervades Moorea, one becomes unaware of the passage of time. The beautiful days blend together, a collage of bright colors and soft breezes. Time moves as lazily as the brilliantly colored fish in the turquoise lagoons. Yet in one split second, Margaret's dream of a lifetime had sunk to the bottom of the ocean. In another flash, three years had gone and she was no closer to resuming her circumnavigation than on the unfortunate day the fishing boat ran her down.

When I left Moorea, she was already two months beyond her visa. She was daring the French to throw her out. Margaret was prepared to have a Mexican standoff with the French. She would have delighted in being party to setting off a war between the French and the English. She loves drama. More and more frequently in those last days, she was voicing delight about the time when finally she could launch her revenge against the "Froggies." I understand it was not inflated ego; it was inflated humor. How else to relieve three years of accumulated anger and frustration? After having exhausted every legal avenue to compensation as well as her own limited financial resources, what was left except physical violence or voicing a desire to have revenge?

She had outlined her plan to me months before, and when we left, it still was to go to New Zealand and earn enough money to buy another little boat that would enable her to complete what had begun as the greatest challenge of her life, sailing around the world alone.

****

February 6, 1986, was a scorching day in Moorea. The weather report soon clarified the reason for the muggy air. Tropical cyclone Ima was 900 miles away, headed directly on a course for us! The news spread like wildfire on the 8 A.M. ham set and by "coconut telegraph," word of mouth.

We took a long dinghy ride across Cook's Bay going to the village to do some shopping. On the way we saw Milt and Marie bringing *Moonchild* through the pass and exchanged greetings with them. Around 4 in the afternoon we returned to *Banshee* to learn that the hurricane was veering south. It appeared that the high situated above us would protect us by deflecting the cyclone. Nonetheless, we already knew if it should head for us, we would nip into Pig's Bay (which we renamed Hog Haven) for shelter. We were anchored out behind the reef in the lagoon with about 11 other yachts. There would probably be a mass exodus if Ima came.

For obvious reasons we wanted the hurricane to miss us. But another pressing reason was that we had planned to meet our friends Margie Anderson and Mary Thompson in Huahine. They had left Alaska on an extended South Pacific tour and they were joining us in Huahine for several weeks of cruising. A hurricane would delay our passage to Huahine, only an overnight sail, but we had no way to contact Margie and Mary.

The next day it seemed quite certain the hurricane would miss us. Yet Brian and Janet on *Foxy Lady II* powered over to Pig's Bay. Being from Hawaii and hurricane conscious, they were taking no chances. Joy took the ferry to Tahiti so she could get our clearance papers and visas. I stayed on board and made potato salad for a barbecue on the beach that night.

It was a lovely barbecue, but just after dark the wind picked up and Joy and I hurriedly dinghied back to *Banshee*. We decided to remove the outboard from the dinghy. We didn't know it then, but that was a very good thing. We went to bed thinking the hurricane watch was over.

Wrong. We awoke the next morning to a very dark sky, 25 to 30 knot winds and heavy seas breaking over the coral reef. Everyone, keyed up and knowing what these signs indicated, began preparing to move to Pig's Bay. The weather forecast confirmed our dreads:

Ima had altered her course once more and was expected to be a direct hit on Tahiti and Moorea.

We took up anchor, intending to tow *Nessie* behind since the distance to Pig's Bay was only about two miles. We hadn't moved far down the lagoon under power when Bob on *Tanamara* called us on the VHF channel which all of us were monitoring to say our dinghy had overturned! We didn't even know it. He volunteered to right it for us if we brought *Banshee* close to his boat. Bob swam over and pushed down on the stern to drain as much water out as possible. We were glad we had removed the outboard the previous night.

Apparently there was enough remaining water in *Nessie* to reduce her stability. As soon as we powered forward again, *Nessie* turned turtle. Our choices were to cut her loose and probably lose her or try to tow her bottom side up. We chose the latter, but it was like towing a sea anchor. In no time the dinghy was totally submerged. Even though the wind and seas were behind us, we could barely move.

Slowly, ever so slowly, we crept across the large bay to the far edge. *Foxy Lady II, Merriman, Fiddler's Green* and *Mariah* were already there anchoring or anchored.

Brian had already been apprised by radio of our predicament. As we approached Pig's Bay, he and ten-year-old Brian Junior sped alongside in their inflatable and took *Nessie's* painter. They towed her ashore, thus leaving us free to anchor. After dropping *Nessie* off, they returned and took two of our stern lines ashore which we later secured around trees with chains. In addition to the stern lines, we set a 35-pound CQR, a 22-pound Danforth and a 50-pound fisherman's anchor off our bow. We lay only about 30 feet offshore, well protected from what would be the prevailing wind direction when Ima struck. Even if blown ashore, it would pose no real hazard as we would go up on soft mud.

Now the hurricane watch began for real. Joy and I decided to strip everything off the deck, a monumental task. As more and more gear went below, every bit of space inside the cabin was filling up. As we were below stuffing things into whatever space we could, I heard a voice ring out, "Ahoy, *Banshee!*" My heart did a double beat. It had to be Margie and Mary! But how? I dashed on deck and sure enough there they stood on shore, laughing and waving excitedly to us.

What a reunion! I pulled the dinghy ashore by one stern line and after a quick leap onto land, we were all hugging and squeezing each other with such joy and glee. We loaded their bags into the dinghy and went back to *Banshee* where they met Joy for the first time.

It was nothing short of miraculous that they had found us. Margie and Mary had taken the ferry from Tahiti to Moorea, then jumped on the ferry truck which would drop them at a campground on the opposite side of the island. To their utter amazement, as they were whisked down the road, they spied *Banshee*. Margie said to Mary, "We *have* to get off and see them!" It's not every day that you have guests arriving on the eve of a hurricane.

It's not everyone you would invite to stay with you under such crowded and confused circumstances. But Margie and Mary are two very exceptional and hardy individuals. Sailors themselves and great outdoors women, they don't expect luxury. To prepare for their own eventual blue water cruising, they bought and almost totally rebuilt *Felicity Ann*. This boat was made famous by English-woman Ann Davison, the first woman to singlehand across the Atlantic in 1953.

Immediately the two of them pitched in, helping us ready *Banshee* for the blow. They stayed on board with us from Sunday through Thursday, the duration of the wait and the arrival of Ima.

How four of us managed to live, cook, eat, sleep and play inside the crowded interior for five days and maintain a joyous and cheerful camaraderie speaks well for all of us.

All our preparations turned out to be anti-climatic. The hurricane kept coming one way, then changing course, sometimes aiming at us only to charge off in another direction. From Saturday until Wednesday afternoon, it had us all hanging from weather report to weather report. In the end, Ima missed us by 200 miles. The worst winds we got were 45 to 50 knots, mostly gusts. There was no scarcity of rain, though, which kept us inside for long stretches.

Once the weather settled down, the four of us set sail one lovely evening for Fare, Huahine. We wanted to leave just at dark so as to arrive at our destination the next day in daylight. Unfortunately, we had to power the entire way due to lack of wind. Once there, we spent time moving from one anchorage to another. Some nights Margie and Mary opted to camp ashore in their two-person tent.

One morning Joy filled the outboard with gasoline. She overfilled it just a bit. As soon as she cranked it, the outboard started smoking. She was staring dumbfounded at it, holding a half-filled gas can in her hands. I was on *Banshee* and yelled at her excitedly, "Get off the dinghy now! Bring the gas can with you!" Meanwhile I grabbed the boat hook and pushed *Nessie* away as soon as Joy was on board. *Nessie* drifted about 50 feet away and the outboard burst into flames. Blobs of plastic from the outboard body were dropping into the sea with great hisses. Any moment we expected it to explode. Just about the time Margie and Mary had seen it from shore and started swimming out, Joy had her fins on and dived into the water. When we saw fire on the water we knew the danger had passed. The gas tank had melted, releasing the fuel. Margie and Mary reached the dinghy ahead of Joy and began splashing water over *Nessie's* stern. Once the fire was out, we could see the stern was badly checked and blackened but otherwise okay. The outboard was totaled. Because of the high prices in French Polynesia, we would not be able to replace the outboard until some months later when we went to Pago Pago. At a nice little marina in Ralatea, we spent a week fairing, sanding and painting *Nessie*, restoring her to her former beauty.

Throughout Margie and Mary's visit, the rain came in almost steady torrents, leaving little time for activities. One fine morning Margie put her expertise to use reinforcing the dinghy rudder in preparation for a sail. The rudder's original construction was so flimsy that it had caused two rudder blades to crack through. Margie cut and shaped a piece of aluminum for each side of the upper part of the rudder where it takes the greatest stress when sailing. With the repair completed, the two Alaskans went exploring in *Nessie*, sailing in light puffs of wind that rippled the bay.

One of our last dinners together resulted in each of us having vivid dreams, we attributed the dreams to the food. We ate Cuban black beans and yellow rice. I dreamed I had gone to visit Joy's mother for a few days. She had several other guests with her. After fixing a large dinner for everyone, she came over to me and said I must put a tattoo on her! I put blue stars on her arms which went nicely with the various colored designs already covering her. Neither Joy nor I could could figure out the symbolism of this crazy dream. Evidently I was more impressed than I realized with the body tattooing we saw in French Polynesia.

Chapter 10

Mopelia, a Special Atoll

"Where is the pass?" I asked Joy. Anticipation had raised my voice a few decibels beyond normal.

"You heard Cliff." Cliff, along with other friends of ours, stood on a sandspit overlooking the hazardous pass into Mopelia. It's unmarked and only thirty feet wide. Cliff was talking to us on his hand-held VHF radio. Our egos were on the line. About 16 yachts had already entered the atoll that lies approximately 100 miles west of Bora Bora. Their skippers and crews had proved themselves in this ordeal by water. Furthermore, Paul and Heather, only 45 minutes ahead of us on *Guinevere*, had maneuvered their little yacht through the pass.

"Yes, I heard him say look for the area of greatest turbulence," I said steering away from what looked like white water I had seen when river rafting. "But, I don't see any pass! Do you?"

"No. Circle by again," Joy said authoritatively.

"No way. If I circle again, I'll never have the nerve to go in. It's now or never. If *Guinevere* can do it, so can we!"

My heart was pounding. My mouth dry. The wind opposed the current and all that water inside the atoll was racing out, being squeezed between the narrow coral pass.

"Joy, we're going this time." I brought the wheel hard over. *Banshee* responded, cutting through the seas whipped steep by 10 knots of wind.

On the radio a good hour before, John, on *Different Concept,* had assured us the pass was a piece of cake. He said if for some reason the forces were too great, the current would spit us out the pass, backwards. Talk is cheap. My eyes told me there was danger ahead. But, with my own eyes I had seen—from a distance—Paul take *Guinevere* through.

I steered for the turbulence. Standing waves frothed and hissed against our bow. Joy was shouting alternately "More to starboard. More to port." I stood with one foot up on each side of the cockpit so I could see better. I bent at the waist, using all my strength to hold onto the wheel. I envisioned us going broadside into the pass. I could see the dark color of the water to each side of us where massive coral heads lurked. On we went. It seemed the seas were rushing past us at tremendous speed. In actuality, as my darting glances shoreward told me, we were slowly inching forward through chaotic waters.

"Steer hard to the right," Joy shouted. "It's a dogleg."

Finally, after what seemed an eternity, we were inside the atoll. Now all we had to do was sight carefully so as to avoid huge coral heads strewn about the clear turquoise water. Joy was in tears— whether from relieved fear or elation I didn't know. Ahead of us, other yachts belonging to friends with whom we'd been cruising off and on for several months, rested, their masts standing tall and poised as their hulls rocked gently.

At last anchored and exhausted by all the emotional suspense and adrenaline rushes, we made a stiff drink of orange juice and Rhum Dou Dou, the dark rum we'd grown fond of in French Polynesia. Barely collapsed in the cockpit, sipping our celebratory cocktails, we were periodically interrupted by various friends who'd motor up in their dinghies for a personal greeting and congratulations on our entry. I felt as if we had passed through some rigorous hazing ritual for joining a collegiate sorority.

Fortunately the weather had cooperated. With our drinks just drained, a nasty squall hit and continued even after sunset. In no time without any land mass to protect us, the fetch had become quite steep and we were bouncing up and down with a vengeance. Suddenly there was a loud report followed by a series of terrifying cracking sounds. I thought another boat had smashed down on us. We both dashed on deck in the thundering rain and discovered the spring line on the anchor chain had gone. Joy quickly fashioned another one and put on chaffing gear.

Our experience on Mopelia can be likened to a leisurely summer at the seashore that will forever stand out as one of life's high points. We ended up becoming a regular community with exercise classes on the beach, snorkeling and fishing expeditions, lobstering at midnight on the reef at low tide, and banquet barbecues and potlucks on the beach. The four Polynesians temporarily living on the atoll, working copra, became our friends and shared in our extravaganzas.

There are several small motus within the atoll. One of these we named "bird island" as it was the breeding and nesting spot for frigates, boobies and terns. Walking around the perimeters of that island, we were able to observe the nesting habits of these species. At one end of the atoll, a lovely white sandspit surrounded by a shallow lagoon was the perfect place to sail a dinghy. Here you could slip noiselessly over the light green water, sometimes racing along with a ray. The snorkeling was magnificent. The water was so transparent it was easy to forget you were underwater. The fact that the area was uninhabited and thus unexploited was most evident underwater. The sea was full of many large fish and exquisite coral gardens where these gigantic aquatic creatures elegantly moved as if engaged in an intricately choreographed ballet. It was here that I learned that the very large snapper, grouper and parrot fish I was seeing were 50 or 75 years old! I found myself wanting to spend all my time underwater just looking. There were sharks, too, but I had long ago become accustomed to seeing three- to four-foot black tips who zipped rapidly off in the opposite direction when they spotted me.

From people who had visited the atoll before us, we had heard that one could go to the seaside of the atoll at low tide and just pick up crayfish off the reef in ankle deep water. One night about ten of us went on the expedition. We had bright diving lights and lanterns so we could see the creatures. No one really wanted to waste batteries or fuel on the tramp across land, so we felt our way through a mass of vines, underbrush and fallen coconut trees, stumbling and blundering as we went, swatting pesky mosquitos. Whoever had checked on the tide had miscalculated because instead of low ankle-deep water on the reef, it was mid-calf to mid-thigh. The biggest problem though was that the wind was quite stiff, making up a tremendous surf and strong surge. Bright lights or no, the turbulent waters made it impossible to see where you were stepping, which, as often as not was in a deep hole or crevice in the coral. With each step I was afraid of sticking my foot into the living room of a moray eel. Neither I nor anyone else saw one single crayfish. The only thing I caught, and under these conditions it was amazing, was a live cowrie.

Life at Mopelia was so pleasant it made moving on very difficult. But we couldn't delay forever. There was no way to replenish provisions on Mopelia and we planned to go to another atoll,

Suvarrow, enroute to Pago Pago, a passage of about two weeks. Our friends Jack and Lura on *Tamarac II* left Mopelia on April 30 bound for Suvarrow. We planned to meet them there.

By May 6 we were still waiting for wind. We decided to move across the lagoon to be closer to the pass for our departure and to see our bird island again. With light winds we sailed *Nessie*, around the motus. I was struck by our location. Here we were in the middle of the ocean where a bit of coral reef rises above the breaking seas. How easily we are deceived, thinking of land as a kind of fortress, something safe. In fact this atoll is a hazard to passing ships. Here we sit in the South Pacific several thousand miles from any continent and hundreds of miles from any sizeable island. Here we sit happy as boobies.

We talked by ham radio with friends who had left. They were experiencing light winds, so light they had to power. We would wait for wind.

By May 8, we finally had some wind. It started up the previous night and held. By 10 A.M. we were sailing out the infamous pass. Such a contrast to when we entered. Now it was tranquil. We could plainly see the coral wall lining the pass. The bright colors glinted and sparkled in the clear water.

A day or so after leaving we heard about the Soviet nuclear catastrophe at Chernobl and the evacuation of 49,000 people, possibly more.

We had not made more than a two-day passage for about eight months and Joy and I were a bit rusty. So was some of our equipment. Mildred, the windvane, didn't want to steer; then I discovered we had forgotten to release the wind wand. Once we did, the vane worked perfectly. The tow generator was not making electricity. Joy troubleshot and found corroded wires, which she replaced.

The third day out we covered only 50 miles. Not from lack of wind. We had plenty of that. A low system was giving us heavy northwesterlies, just the direction we needed to sail to make Suvarrow. In addition to heavy winds, we had heavy, confused seas and shifty winds. Joy had to change her bunk three times as wind changes forced us to tack. By the end of my second watch at 4 A.M., the winds had lightened to the point we could not sail. We dropped the genny and powered until daylight. At sunrise the wind returned so we hoisted sail again. For the remainder of the day, light, variable winds plagued us. One positive thing: in these light wind conditions we can operate all the alternative energy systems—the tow generator, the wind generator and two solar panels. With everything going full blast, we have plenty of electricity to run the refrigerator, the SatNav and the tape deck. I love it: Bach's Brandenberg Concertos powered by the sun, wind and water. He would have liked that.

It was the calm before the storm. By 10:30 P.M. we encountered the first high winds of a gale that would later be upgraded to a 55-knot storm. We changed to the smaller staysail, then reefed the main, following the principle that as the wind rises, sail area is decreased. Close to midnight, we were hit by intense black squalls that increased with intensity. As conditions deteriorated, Joy and I disagreed about what we should do. She wanted to heave to; I wanted to continue sailing. During my watch we continued to sail. At this time I had what I thought of as a personal encounter with a massive squall. I watched in fearful fascination as it approached— a low, dark, menacing, ominous black cloud. It was almost touching the surface of the sea and every now and then a light blinked from its interior, like the evil eye of a giant. I wondered, with trepidation, if it was a whirlwind or a cyclone. I sat in the cockpit unable to take my eyes off the awesome black mass that steadily moved closer and closer. Then the wind started, a low moan that rapidly crescendoed into a roar. Suddenly the inky sea was heaped up into a frenzied froth of foam and waves. The winds hit *Banshee's* shortened sails like a ton of concrete and she smashed over onto her side with seas rushing over her decks. The giant black squall sat on us for ten or fifteen minutes, its awesome power palpable. Then it was gone. Overhead a clear trail of stars appeared as the blackness passed. It looked as though nothing had happened. I was staring at the friendly glitter of stars.

But the bad weather had not passed, it was just the beginning. When Joy came on watch, we hove to until the squalls played out. For the next day and a half we alternated between periods of sailing in 15-20 knots and powering in calms. Then by 3 A.M. of the second day we found ourselves in the thick of it—a 55-knot storm with a low of 996 millibars, extending out to 300 miles. When our steering vane hopped out of its gears, we were forced to hand steer. The 30 to 40 foot seas were too much for the autopilot to handle. Too much for human beings, too. We decided to heave to and stayed hove to for the next thirty hours.

Heaving to can be done several different ways—with foresail and main raised, with main only, or with no sails. The purpose of heaving to is to stop the boat's movement (or at least slow it down). Steering is not necessary because the wheel or tiller is tied over to one side. The effect is to keep the bow about 50 degrees off the seas. The vessel tends to turn her beam alternately to the seas, then pull her bow back toward the wind and seas. The turning motion and the sidewise movement of the boat creates a slick, thus considerably calming or flattening the sea action around the hull. Nonetheless, the vessel crabs sideways, making leeway sometimes up to as much as two knots. Below decks in the cabin, where you stay when conditions are this bad, the motion is horrendous. To me it feels as if the boat is corkscrewing! It is a motion that I most detest.

After heaving to, I was awakened around 6 A.M. when *Banshee* suddenly went over on her side. Joy raced to close the hatch. The water was up to the middle of our ports. We lay there in that position for ten or fifteen minutes, each second expecting that we would be rolled over if the wind increased. It didn't and we leveled off when the 55 or 60 knot gust abated.

Joy and I discussed what we should do. I thought we should drop the staysail to reduce windage. She agreed that would be good but felt it was too risky to go on deck. Another gust like the one we just had or a knockdown would not be the time to be on deck dropping a sail. We left the sail up and fortunately had no recurrences of this kind of wind. For the next 24 hours it continued to howl 35-45 knots. During this time the seas built into monstrous wedges that frequently broke right on top of us.

In this situation—constantly thrown up and down, twist, up and down, twist—we had little or no desire to eat. Cooking was not a good idea because with the hatches closed most of the time we had little ventilation. We cooked things that took very little time and effort and always found eating improved our morale.

By the time the low passed, we had changed our minds about going to Suvarrow. We talked with Lura on the radio and learned they had been anchored there through the storm. It was not a secure place to be in heavy winds. One boat with them had dragged onto the reef and sustained some damage. The weather report indicated there was more bad weather coming.

We had about a two-day reprieve; then the second gale was upon us. We had not been able to repair the windvane. In calm conditions with both of us handling the vane, we could get it lowered into the water and the gears would stay meshed. In heavier winds and seas, however, the gear jumped out, leaving the steering to us. When this happened, we hove to for the night, agreeing to start sailing again at first light. By daylight the winds had subsided to 30-35 knots, but the seas were a mountainous 20 to 30 feet high. It was almost humorous, our little boat with a handkerchief of sail—a triple reefed main—speeding down the seas at five or six knots into the steel gray valleys. Throughout the day, conditions moderated. By the following day, conditions were so light we flew the spinnaker for five or six hours. Being low on fuel, we were hesitant to power any great distance.

It took a couple of days to recover from the fatigue induced by this passage attributable, mainly, to motion and noise. Pago Pago was the most welcome port, only because of the two storms preceding our arrival. Otherwise, the harbor is a filthy hole, an embarrassment to any American! Our government may subsidize American Samoa with an annual budget of 93 million U.S. dollars, but not one penny of that money is spent to clean up one of the largest natural harbors in the South Pacific. The harbor reeks from fish offal dumped and pumped into the water by the Starkist Tuna packing plant. The odor permeates the air night and day. Because of the filth and garbage clogging the harbor area, anchoring is very poor. Boats slip and slide every time it blows—which is almost continuously. After failing three times to stay in place, we set two anchors. They held.

Pago Pago has another very serous problem: power failures. Every other day, if not every other hour, the electricity generating plant suffered massive failures. While we were there, many clinics at the LBJ Hospital, including the dental clinic, had to close down semi-permanently because of blackouts. Kidney dialysis patients were flown to Hawaii because they could not be cared for under those circumstances. Ninety-three million dollars and Pago Pago can't have a steady supply of electricity? Something is drastically wrong. Misappropriation of funds?

On the positive side, American Samoans were friendly to us. We enjoyed taking the bus to different parts of the island where we found quite a wide variety of foods for provisioning, many brands that we hadn't seen since leaving the States. Again we were able to indulge our taste for Mexican foods—canned chiles and salsa and, once, fresh corn tortillas flown in from California!

In Pago Pago, we met and began a friendship with Tania Aebi, an 18 year old American woman who was solo sailing around the world on her 26-foot sailboat, *Varuna*. In fact it was Tania who helped us find our stolen dinghy late one night. The three of us came back to the dinghy dock after a late dinner with several other women. The only dinghy at the dock was Tania's. Ours was gone. We had heard that dinghy theft was a problem. As a precaution, we had locked our new outboard and oars, but the dinghy was simply tied up. A Samoan fishing at the pier, when questioned, said he had seen someone leave in a dinghy like ours ten or fifteen minutes earlier. He thought the man had taken it to a tuna boat anchored in the middle of the harbor. We looked but could see nothing. Tania offered to drive us around the harbor in her dinghy, figuring that it had to be somewhere along the shore. When getting in her dink, she noticed that her oars were missing! We powered around the harbor and sure enough we found *Nessie* up on the rocks half full of water, one oar missing. In our recovered dinghy, Joy and I persisted in the search for the missing oar. Suddenly a big squall struck and we sought shelter in the cabin of an empty fishing boat tied up alongside a small dock. It was about 1 A.M. when the torrential rain abated and we continued our search. To our surprise, the flashlight beam picked up the white oar caught up in some rocks at the head of the bay. Unfortunately Tania was not so lucky. Her oars were never seen again.

After only three weeks in Pago Pago Harbor, the bottom of our dinghy was a solid mass of barnacles. As we discovered while driving *Banshee* around the harbor in high winds to bring her to the wharf for checkout with customs, barnacles were restricting the propeller. Once tied up at the wharf, Frank Caper offered to clean our prop while he was down cleaning his. Chivalry is still alive! Thanks, Frank.

By 1530, on a brisk wind, *Banshee* and four other U.S. yachts sailed out of Pago Pago harbor. We would be arriving sometime the next day at Apia, Western Samoa. By sunset the taller peaks of Pago

Pago were no more than a gray lump on the horizon. I said my final farewell and felt a heavy sadness—the melancholy that fills me when I leave a place I never expect to see again.

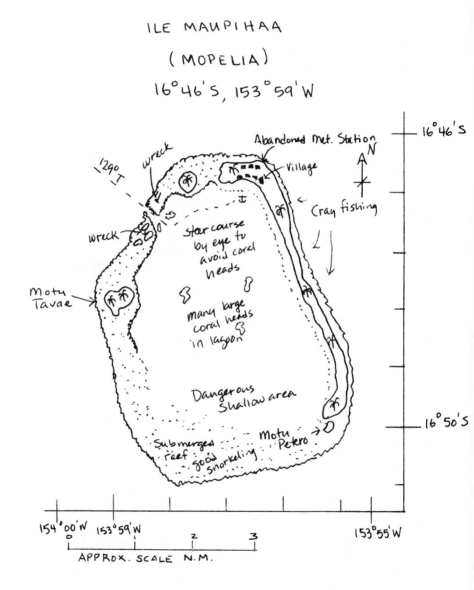

ILE MAUPIHAA

(MOPELIA)

16°46'S, 153°59'W

Abandoned Met. Station
Village
Cray fishing
wreck
1290 T
wreck
Star course by eye to avoid coral heads
Motu Tavae
many large coral heads in lagoon
Dangerous Shallow area
Submerged reef good snorkeling
Motu Petero
16°46'S
16°50'S
154°00'W 153°59'W 153°55'W
APPROX. SCALE N.M.

Chapter 11

Apia, Western Samoa, a City of Contrasts

It is Sunday morning. Overhead peach-tinged clouds announce dawn. The barely perceptible rocking of *Banshee* is comforting. After living aboard for one year and four months, I wonder if I could sleep ashore again. It's the end of June. We are in Western Samoa, considered by many to be the place from which Polynesians spread across the Pacific. The northernmost outreach of the Polynesians lies in the Hawaiian Islands. The other two parts of the so-called Polynesian triangle are Easter Island in the east and New Zealand in the south. Polynesian legends tell of the journeys made by canoe to these far-flung places. To this day Western Samoans claim that ninety percent of the people on their islands are full Polynesian.

Certainly the way of life here shows adherence to many of the old traditions. Even now, just after sunrise, the acrid smoke emitted from multiple *umus* stings my nostrils. Nowadays these earth ovens are fired up only for Sunday or for special occasions. The buildings lining Apia's waterfront are shadowy phantoms lurking in the heavy mist. Layers of gray smoke snake around the mountains, momentarily obscuring most of the lush green hillside. To seaward a thick smoky haze engulfs a large cargo vessel tied to the wharf. Suddenly the low metallic ring of the bell from the twin-towered cathedral cuts through the grayness. Soon it is joined by the ringing of another bell. The two pitches, not quite in harmony, seem perfectly suited to the eerie smoke-draped world.

Apia, the capital of Western Samoa on the island of Upolu, is a city that combines modern amenities and traditional ways. The city's shoreline boasts a large share of churches and highrises, but the pedestrians scurrying along the busy streets mostly wear the traditional lava lava. Formal business attire for men consists of a western coat atop a somber colored lava lava. In the center of town the clock tower, reminiscent of Samoa's early German settlers, strikes the hour. Nearby the local market buzzes with shoppers bargaining with sellers seated on mats, their fruits and vegetables spread around them. The marketplace is dominated by stalks of green bananas, baskets of husked coconuts, piles of taro roots and freshly caught seafood. Such foods form the staples of traditional Samoan diet. Other foods found here include oranges, pineapples, papayas, eggplant, green beans, squash, tomatoes and even several kinds of herbs. One section contains locally grown tobacco, some shredded and stacked in small piles, some compressed and rendered into decorative twists that resemble miniature canes. Most venders in the market have several piles of pinkish or whitish beans that look somewhat like lima beans. These are cocoa beans, grown locally in the mountains. Many sellers of cocoa beans line the sidewalks, their beans in piles drying on pieces of newspaper. In Samoa, cocoa is drunk the way Americans drink coffee. The beans are ground up and boiled in water. Sugar or honey is added to sweeten the drink. It is common to see young boys running about the streets carrying a large aluminum teakettle in one hand and a plastic bag full of cups in the other hand. Usually they are on their way to a group of workmen, bringing them their morning or afternoon cocoa on the job.

Several good grocery stores in town offer a wide selection of foods, including many items found in an American supermarket. For a cruiser who has come by way of French Polynesia, the prices seem extremely reasonable.

The main street is a façade or a veneer of the western world, but half a block up a side street leads you into the midst of a Samoan village. Here families still live much as they have for centuries, many in the nicely contoured thatched *fales*. In all, there are 362 villages on Upolu. Most of these are located along the palm-fringed shore.

Not many cruising yachts visit Western Samoa and American yachts are easily outnumbered by European, Australian and New Zealand boats. One reason for so few yachts may be because there are few places to anchor on the two big islands, Upolu and Savaii.

Although Western Samoa has been an independent country since 1962 and has an established parliamentary system of government, at heart it continues to be a Polynesian society. Many of the people speak good English, some excellent, so talking with Samoans is relatively easy. However, the ability to communicate easily may tend to confuse our perception of Samoan people and their culture. Without thinking, we can easily assume they think and act the same as Americans or Europeans. In fact, their culture and values differ considerably from ours. One of the biggest differences is reflected in Samoan houses. The *fale* is usually kept open on all sides, although they have attached mats which can be rolled down. Additionally, the interior is without partitions. This construction makes it one of the least private dwellings to be found anywhere. Samoan social structure accords well with the public or communal nature of the *fale*. The social unit, the *aiga* (pronounced eye-ing-a) consists of an extended family composed of parents, grandparents, children, uncles, aunts, cousins and adopted children. Each of these extended families is directed by a *matai* who oversees the social, economic and political affairs of the *aiga*. His word is law.

There are definite customs one should observe when visiting a Samoan *fale*. Everyone sits crosslegged on the floor. It is considered bad manners to eat or talk while standing up in a *fale*. One should not wear bathing suits or abbreviated clothing, except at poolside, at the beach or on board. Knee-length shorts are acceptable in Apia, but are hardly ever worn by Samoan women. On the whole we've found that Samoans appreciate it when we wear our lava lavas. Covering the body is one of the more unpleasant legacies of the missionaries. Most of the time the temperature is very hot and the humidity high.

The easiest way to see the country is to sign up for various bus tours. Aggie Grey's Hotel and several tour agencies have tours that cover different parts of the island. By taking about three tours one can see the whole of Upolu. We went on an all-day tour that followed the coastline to the easternmost point, looped around the other side of the island and about midway took a road across the interior that eventually brought us back to Apia, our point of departure. During the day we had three swimming stops. The first was at a fresh water pool located three steps from the ocean! The second stop was at a lovely beach on a lagoon where they served us a delicious picnic lunch. The third stop was at a tiered waterfall with a deep, cool pool at its base. As the bus climbed upward to one of the highest points inland, we observed lush tropical plants of all kinds: tree ferns, cocoa trees, coral trees (planted in the plantations to impart nitrogen to the soil) and giant banyan trees. In the midst of the clouds that encircle the peaks, we paused to view an awesome waterfall cascading down a sheer mountain face.

For me the high point in Western Somoa was our contact and acquaintance with several Samoan families. One Sunday afternoon we unfolded our bicycles from their box on our deck and set out for a nearby area where we intended to snorkel. Desiring to do a little sightseeing first, Joy and I rode by the beach and continued on down the road. We had not gone far when an attractive young girl waved us over. She asked if we would like to go swimming on her family's beach. Naturally we said yes. We were quickly escorted down a narrow dirt path past several *fales*, one belonging to her grandparents, another to her parents, and then others owned by additional family members. As we went along, other young people joined us. By the time we reached the beach at a little islet with very clear water, ten or more children had joined us. With our permission they took turns riding our bikes on the beach. Once we'd had a swim, we were inundated with requests to use our masks and fins. Three of the young people wanted to come out to the boat that afternoon for a visit. We asked their father if they might come with us. He gave permission. Before leaving their village, they insisted we take along some coconuts and mangoes. Instantly Califa, a 15-year-old boy, scrambled up a very tall coconut tree. He tied a twisted bandana around his ankles. It supported him on the front side of the tree while his hands held him up from the back side. In less than a minute he had reached the top and was pulling down green coconuts which hit the ground with a loud thud.

We became friends with another Samoan family who generously opened their door and their hearts to us. Afa, the father, a 62-year-old man of great intelligence and wit, loved telling us Samoan history, customs, songs. A natural born entertainer, he could keep us laughing for an evening. His gentle wife, Sina, took particular delight in instructing us in the preparation of traditional dishes. Victoria, one of their daughters, had recently returned after spending several years in the States where she had gone with a Samoan dance troupe. Her brother, Mark, is a talented wood carver. Victoria's three young children and one of Mark's also occupy Afa and Sina's *fale*. More than once we sat with them while Mark or Afa played the guitar and all of us sang along. Sometimes in the afternoon we'd all sit at the back of the house. While Mark carved, we chated. Piglets rooted around, three dogs snoozed under the *fale*, and two kittens batted each other across the face. It was cool in the shade with trade winds fanning us. Life is unhurried in this village and, I suspect, not much changed from the way it has been for centuries among the Polynesian peoples.

For better or for worse, Western Somoa is in transition. Even as government forges ahead attempting to bring the country and its people into the twentieth century, many younger Samoans must look abroad for employment. Lesser people, embittered by the stresses of a society in transition, turn against foreigners. Not the Samoans. They greet visitors on the street with cheerful smiles and are eager to introduce you to their country. I especially enjoyed talking to Victoria, whom we came to call Vita, as do her family and friends. Since Vita had been a Samoan dancer, I asked her if she thought the missionaries had caused their dances to change in any way? She said no. But I'm almost certain that Samoan and Tongan dances altered drastically with the coming of the missions. Both of these countries have dances which are sedate, entirely different from the suggestive dances we watched in French Polynesia. Another big difference in the two areas is also seen in the clothing. Tahitians and Marquesans expose much of their bodies. Samoans (and Tongans, as we soon discovered) cover their bodies completely, usually in drab, dark clothing.

One day Vita told me the following legend about how Samoans ceased being cannibals.

Every night the Samoan king had to have two young men for his dinner. His son strongly disapproved of this practice and because of his great love for the Samoan people he determined that he would make his father stop.

Each night two young men were delivered alive to the king in a large basket. One night the son released one of the captives and crawled into the basket himself.

When the king opened the container, he was most amazed to find his son inside.

"What are you doing there, my son?"

"I am your dinner, Father."

"Oh, no. How silly! I cannot eat you, my son! Why do you do this?"

"I do it, Father, because I love the Samoan people. You have to eat me tonight if you are going to continue eating other humans."

"Oh, my son, I can't do that. I won't eat you and I will cease eating humans for your sake!"

After telling me the story, Vita assured me it was exactly how cannibalism had ended in Samoa. The story is especially fascinating in that it implies none of the commoners still engaged in cannibalism. It may well be true that the practice lingered the longest among nobility who practiced cannibalism as a sacred rite.

When Joy had sailed to Samoa 13 years earlier, she came to know the harbor master at Apia, a man named Joe Evans. She mentioned him in a conversation with Afa. Several days later Afa said he found out where Evans lived. We decided to go find Joe. Joy and I hopped on the bus and asked the driver if he knew Joe's house. He did and told us where to get off.

Joe, or "Frog" as he prefers to be called, was then a young 78-year-old retired sea captain; his wife, a 38-year-old Samoan woman. Together they have three beautiful children and Frog has adopted her two children from a previous marriage.

Frog seemed genuinely elated to see Joy and we were immediately seated in the living room of their two-story home—a caravan—he called it. Most of the building, except the living room, was open, conforming to Samoan style houses. Seated in a dark room with walls cluttered with a lifetime of mementos from his worldwide travels, we drank a cup of dark rich Samoan coffee. Later, Fava, his wife, a deep-voiced and well-poised woman, joined us. Her black eyes portrayed a person of heightened vitality and abundant sexual energy.

The longer we stayed in Apia the more people we met. One of the most interesting friends we made was Judy Royer, a young Minnesotan who was finishing her second year in Samoa with the Peace Corps. From her we learned much about Samoan life and customs.

On July 10, the *Canterbury*, a New Zealand frigate, left Apia. The first day she was in port, we had gone aboard for the open house. The next day we came back from town to find an engraved invitation to a cocktail party aboard the *Canterbury*. It was the biggest social event of the season. In our most respectable clothes, dug out from moth balls, we joined a stream of dignitaries. At least half of Apia was there decked out in their finest lava lavas. The Maori crew members entertained the crowd with traditional Maori song and dance. The navy officers stood by in full dress, looking smart and dignified.

Until Western Samoa, we'd had no untoward behavior from any men in any place. Here, unfortunately, we had several instances. One night just as I had put out the light, intending to go to bed, I heard a noise at the stern of the boat. Looking outside, I saw a shadowy figure standing behind the stern, apparently standing in a dinghy or canoe and holding onto our stern pulpit. Softly I spoke to Joy who was already in bed. In a flash she was up and had bounded up the companionway. She asked the young Samoan man, "What do you want?" He feigned ignorance, as if he couldn't understand her. Rephrasing the question, Joy asked him several times.

In the meantime, I noticed that he had moved from the stern around to the port side, coming up to the gate in the lifelines. By now I had located a large bottle and decided if he tried to board, I would leap outside and bring it down on his head. I was grasping it by the neck, in position.

Joy had a sudden inspiration and grabbed the VHF radio mike and held it so the man could see it. With a low, threatening voice she said to him, "If you don't leave now, I will call the police on the radio." It was a complete bluff because the police don't monitor the VHF. Suddenly the man got the meaning very quickly. He understood "police" and "radio." Instantly he took off, paddling rapidly across the bay.

Both of us had an unpleasant experience with an enormous Samoan who worked as a guard at the ferry wharf where we landed our dinghy each time we went ashore and where we went to fill our water jugs. Once as I tied the dinghy up there, he lumbered over to me, leering and said, "I love you. I want to take you dancing."

Experience has taught me that sometimes silence or ignoring someone works. So, I ignored him and very rapidly walked away.

Some days later Joy went up to the wharf alone to fill the water jugs. The same grossly overweight guard came over to her and pulled the hose—our water hose—out of her hand and shouted, "I told you, you go to ship's wharf. Ships have to pay for water at ship's wharf."

Trembling inside, Joy walked over to him and snatched the hose out of his beefy hands, "Give me my hose!" She then took our water jugs, placed them in the dinghy and locked them up with a wire painter. Meanwhile he was still shouting at her in his faulty

English, being vulgar and rude.

With all the dignity she could muster, Joy strode away from the wharf, carrying her hose, and went to the office to report the incident to the officials. They were mortified and most apologetic. One man reconfirmed that yachtspeople could indeed get water there. He walked back to the wharf with her, saying the guard was an "ignorant, stupid man." He then had it out with the guard.

Several days later we came back together and the fat old guard was there again. This time he meekly walked up to me and said he wanted to speak with my friend. I told Joy, she came over and he apologized for his behavior and put out his hand to shake Joy's and then mine. Both of us shook hands with him and from then on he was polite and friendly.

Perhaps another incident will help shed light on the cultural background that contributed to the guard's initial attitude and behavior toward us.

For some time Vita and Mark had been expressing a desire to go for a day sail. Finally George said he would take them on *Io* and he invited me to go along. The big day came and when George came back from shore he had only Mark with him. I asked where Vita was and Mark said she was afraid and she was sick.

It sounded a bit strange to me since Vita had never expressed any fear. The next day when I saw Vita, I asked her about it. She replied that Mark wouldn't let her come! *Let!* When I pressed her for more information she said that Mark said as her brother it would diminish his stature if she came. In Mark's eyes sailing was for men, not women, and sisters must do as their brothers instruct them. Of course Mark accepted Joy and me as sailors. He would have gladly gone out on our boat. He accepts it from us because we are Americans.

The crux of the situation between us and the old guard was that he was treating us like Samoan women. That is what the official meant when he said the guard was "ignorant and stupid."

Chapter 12

Tonga, the Last Polynesian Kingdom

The day we said our farewell to Afa's family was a sad time. We took them gifts of food—taro, corned beef, tangerines, cocoa beans, candies. Vita finished the last few yarns on a mat she had decorated for us with our names and *Banshee's*. Sina had woven the mat for us. Afa gave us a fishing lure and extra feathers so we could make our own lures. Mark presented us his lovely carvings—a shark and a relief head of a *matai*. Afa and Mark played and sang farewell songs and together we all sang "Now Is the Hour."

I was struck by how little his family has by way of possessions but how rich they are in their giving and how their friendship has enriched us. They give of themselves, sharing their home and experiences with us. So many hours of singing and talking, eating and laughing. In our society it seems people have little or no time for giving of themselves.

It was a short sail—three and a half days—to Neiafu in the Vava'u group of Tonga. Nasty weather and darkness arrived when we did, preventing us from picking our way through the almost landlocked passage into Neiafu Harbor. We hove to for the night. By daylight we had been pushed about 25 miles away and it took most of the day to tack back and make the harbor. We had talked to Milt and Marie on the radio the previous evening. They had expressed their delight that we had arrived. We anchored close to them and they came to pick us up for an evening at the Paradise Hotel where other friends were waiting to have a drink with us at the happy hour.

It was surprisingly cold with the wind out of the south, straight from the Antarctic, I thought. We pulled out wool shirts and long pants. Bone weary from hard sailing, we still went in to spend a few hours with old friends and enjoy a nice lobster dinner. There's always a special feeling going ashore after completing a passage. A kind of sereneness settles over me. The land smells are especially pungent and the colors of plants look quite vibrant.

Sailing in the Vava'u group presents some of the most inviting scenes and easiest sailing. Some 30 to 40 islands cluster together within protected, almost fjordlike passageways. Most cruisers treat Neiafu as a home base where they can provision at the little town, collect mail and then go explore the nearby islands for a week or two.

Our first anchorage in the group was at Port Maurelle on the island of Kapa. We put the hook down in 74 feet and could see the bottom! As I looked shoreward the banded colors—marine blue, shading into emerald and light green—beckoned. I got out my snorkeling gear and dived in. Burr . . . it was icy, but I managed about 20 minutes totally absorbed in the coral reefs filled with schools of brightly painted fish.

A walk on the powder-soft sand beach proved warmer. Here I found a number of shells in good condition. Only two other boats were anchored in the cove with us. The only sounds were the lapping of the water against our hull, the soughing wind and a symphony of calls from land birds. What a welcome sound—one I missed all the months at sea.

Another famous pastime in Tonga are the feasts. We chose Matoto's feast because of his low-keyed, genial manner. Matoto arranged to pick us up at the hotel and drove us to his beach where the feast was being prepared. Smells wafted from the *umus* where traditional foods slowly cooked. Musicians sat on mats under a thatched roof, singing and playing. In their midst was a large *kava* bowl from which they dipped the mild narcotic liquid in a half coconut shell. They downed the muddy colored drink in a single gulp and continued singing and playing. We were offered kava, but we declined, being put off by the idea that *kava* would numb my lips. Too reminiscent of the dentist! Joy had tried it on her previous visit and said she couldn't recommend it.

About 30 people had come to the feast. For at least an hour before the food was served, we enjoyed traditional singing and dancing by various groups. Then we were instructed to sit on the mats in two lines, facing each other. Six very large Tongan men brought in the food carried on banana leaves. Before they had finished, they had laid five or six "boards" between the two rows of people sitting crosslegged. What a colorful array of foods: several kinds of baked roots, baked green papaya with coconut cream, fish—cooked many different ways—raw fish salad with chopped vegetables and coconut cream, fish wrapped in taro leaves and soaked in coconut cream, baked octopus and clams, a delicious fresh fruit salad. We attacked the attractive and succulent delights Tongan style—with our fingers. A primitive spoon, fashioned from the stem of a palm frond, was provided for scooping up the fruit salad.

This meal, fit for the Tongan royal family, was sufficient for at least two days, but on the morrow—being true gluttons—we went to Gunther the German's feast. It was a Sunday afternoon barbecue with chicken, lamb chops, sausage, steak, fish and liver with potato and macaroni salads, green salad, fresh green beans and carrots, fresh pineapple and for dessert a choice of chocolate cake, apple streussel, or cheese cake and ice cream. Feasting and feeding has become a cottage industry throughout these islands. On other islands in the Vava'u group, we went to feasts prepared just for us and a small gathering of our friends, but the choice and amount of food provided was always five or six times more than we could possibly handle!

One of the first things we heard in Tonga was how cheaply one could hire Tongans to do boat work. We decided to employ William, a nice looking 28-year-old, to sand before we varnished. This turned out to be a controversial step which caused a bit of a ruckus. William had barely started sanding when another yachtie we knew stormed up in his dinghy and yelled at William, "I thought you had a stomach ache and quit work on my boat for that reason." Fire shot from his eyes. Poor William looked not only dumbfounded but frightened. I too was dumbfounded, but Joy quickly found her voice and politely said to the American, "Please don't bring your problems here. If you need to talk to William, do so somewhere else." The yachtie left in a huff but soon returned to apologize. Later I saw him ashore. He apologized again and offered an explanation. We had agreed to pay William $1.00 U.S. an hour, about 30 cents more than he and others had been paying William. Talk about a tempest in a teapot! We felt guilty paying someone as little as a dollar an hour.

It takes a while to become accustomed to the much lower economic level in South Pacific countries. Most of the locals do not live on a cash economy. They grow their own food. Cash money buys extras—an outboard motor, a radio, cigarettes, beer.

A friend invited me to come along on a bus tour of the countryside. It was an enjoyable and informative day. Since vanilla beans are a major export item from Tonga, we visited a vanilla plantation and learned why the bean (or its extract) is so expensive. While vanilla is an orchid, still it is a trailing plant needing something on which to climb. A special plant is grown and kept trimmed waist high just for this purpose. But the most labor intensive part of cultivation is hand pollination. Strangely enough only one insect is capable of pollinating the vanilla flower, therefore, without human intervention, vanilla beans are rare. Once harvested the beans are first put into 65° water for four minutes. Then they are dried in the sun for at least three weeks. Each night the drying trays are moved inside. Once the outside drying period has ended, the beans are dried inside for another week or so. Finally the beans are sorted, graded, weighed and tied up in stacks of one kilo. One of the pleasures of going about the Tongan countryside is coming upon places where beans are drying. Long before you see the drying beans, you will smell them.

On the same outing we came upon a group of women making *tapa* cloth. We could hear the pounding and followed our ears. Probably because the making of *tapa* is so involved, it is often done by several women rather than alone. The very first step is removing and drying the bark from the paper mulberry tree. A 3/4 inch strip is pounded to a width of about ten inches! Ten-inch strips are joined together by a kind of glue derived from the manioc plant. The seams don't show. Finally, once the piece of cloth is prepared—many times 50 feet long and half as wide—the women paint designs in rich brown and black colors. One 50-foot long *tapa* I saw took 28 women three months to complete. They were willing to sell the *tapa* for $500 Tongan. Most of the crafts are as labor intensive and sell for very little. Obviously there are no unions in Tonga. On the other hand, what else is there to do? You spend a little time tending the garden. While you gossip with neighbors and relatives, you can busy yourself with carving, weaving, *tapa* making. Not a bad life, really.

On this tour I noticed that almost all the land we passed was under cultivation. Many plots contained rows identified by an owner's name and number. As I later learned, Tongans must work their land or they lose it. Incidentally, individuals—commoners— do not own land, rather it is owned by the king and 33 nobles. Many horses, cows, pigs and even a fair number of goats showed that Tongans are seriously engaged in raising their own food—more so than other peoples we had visited. In the villages people still depend heavily on horses for transportation, far more so than on fuel-guzzling vehicles which are expensive to purchase, run and maintain. Often horses carried not only their rider, or riders in the case of children, but heavy loads of coconuts, yams, papayas, or bananas.

Once a year King Taufa'ahau Tupou IV comes around to inspect his subjects and see how they are getting on with the business of living. It's the equivalent of a country fair with prizes awarded for winners of each category. People exhibit their crops, seafood catch, fishing gear and all sorts of crafts from quilts to mats. On September 2, we put on our good dress and followed the the hordes of people on their way to the exhibition grounds. Here were beautiful displays of fruits and vegetables, crafts and domestic animals. Before the king spoke in the pavilion, a 200-voice choir sang two selections in gorgeous harmony. The band, too, gaily played to the enthusiastic crowd. Everyone had to be seated when the royal family took the stage because no one is allowed to have his head higher than the king's.

In the old days Tongans equated size with prestige. Persons of rank were expected to be enormous. Perhaps something of this attitude still lingers. The king probably weighs close to 400 pounds. We heard that his doctor had advised him to lose some weight and he had complied. His health did not appear to be very robust. He spoke in gasps—a characteristic that has earned him the nickname Darth Vader—and he supported himself with a cane. He wore support boots that came just under his knees. Otherwise he was attired in a gray one-piece suit with a formal lava lava. He wore sunglasses even indoors. When he exited the hall and sat in an open vehicle to be driven around the grounds to view the exhibits, he donned a large Mexican sombrero!

As I spent more time with various Polynesian peoples, I started to understand how we are alike and how we differ. One of the biggest differences is that they do not function as individuals. Things are done communally. It's not that individualism is discouraged, it's simply not thought about. Polynesians do not spend time alone and have trouble understanding someone's desire to be alone. Repeatedly we were asked in Tonga and elsewhere: Where is your family? Why are they not with you—your mother, father, sisters, brothers? Many have expressed that they don't know why anyone would sail alone. Not only do they not function as individuals, they are not prone to introspection. Introspection and abstract thinking go hand in hand with literacy, that is, they develop within the framework of a written language. Polynesians are still basically living in an oral society.

A friend recounted an instance to me that is absolutely fascinating. He went to a film with a Samoan friend. The film was "Third World War" but was not about a nuclear war. The war was fought with guns and even clubs. The Samoan kept asking my friend, "Where did this war happen and when?" My friend answered, "Never. It is imaginary. It is fiction." The Samoan could not understand: the image on the screen is too real; it is taking place. This reaction is akin to the misconception that many Westerners suffered from—especially several decades ago—that if it's in print, it must be true. More to the point, Polynesians simply do not have a concept of fiction. Stories for them, based on their legends or myths, tell about their history, are reality not fiction.

I believe that literacy causes us to view the world in an entirely new perspective. "Compare and contrast" are critical skills that develop another part of the brain just as learning things by rote develops another skill, involving a different part of the brain. In oral societies people learn by rote. This difference may well be one of the reasons why most Polynesian children, when educated in school to read and write, have difficulty grasping these skills. They are still living in a society which for the most part operates as an oral society.

In Apia I made the mistake of going to the movies one day with Mark. We saw two horrible films. One was called *Jungle Warriors*. Both films were cut from the same mold and contain nothing of value. Their subjects—drugs, violence and brutal sex—made me extremely angry. What a thing to show people, most of whom believe that what they see on the screen has actually occurred. Is it not dangerous (surely irresponsible) to export the most porno-graphic and violent films and videos to places where the people have no knowledge or background to enable them to see these portrayals in perspective? More than one Polynesian has asked me if I wasn't afraid to live in America. They think that everyone carries a gun and at any minor disagreement pulls it out and shoots down the other person! It is a rather startling concept: first the missionaries damned sex, made the Polynesians feel ashamed of their bodies so that they dress in layers of clothing; now they can rent a video that shows it all in glorious color. Surely these contrasts must cause a form of social schizophrenia.

Just walking through the small town of Neiafu early in the morning gave no hint of such vagaries. All appeared serene on the surface.

I read from my journal:

I saw a white pig lying on a porch like a dog with its legs tucked up under it; it was contentedly snoozing. I thought poor pig, it has no idea what's in store for it. The rest of the scene was homey . . . The porch belonged to an old frame house. Everything had the appearance of being old and well used. Chickens were pecking and scratching around the bushes. Down the hill a fire was smouldering and some of the smoke hovered at the back of a bleak house. Down the street at the wharf a supply ship named Sima was in. A cool breeze swept in off the bay and rain clouds sat low. Off and on it rained lightly. I walked slowly back through town, listening and looking. Here and there an excited voice would call out and uninhibited laughter rang out. Some people were sitting on the benches in front of Burns Philp, talking with others who stood in front of them . . . Mothers with infants in their arms strolled by. A line of people stood at the bank. An occasional truck or car idled by on the dusty road.

Momentarily the rain came, lightly wetting my hair and face. Past town I walked uphill toward the big Catholic church. I looked out at the yachts—about 40—riding peacefully at anchor in the deep bay that stretched out below me. What a wonderful sight, the blues and greens streaked like marble. Pangaimotu sat across the bay, rising up to the clouds. Its shaggy coconut palms thick on the hillside. Magnificent. Breathtakingly beautiful.

I've seen this view almost every day for a month. Always it is different according to the time of day, whether it's windy or still, sunny or cloudy, warm or cold.

One event shows how remote from the world the Vava'u group is. Our electric windlass, made in New Zealand, developed some

103

problems. We needed to order replacement parts from New Zealand, but there was no way to phone from Neiafu. We sent a telegram. One friend made a phone call for us from Pago Pago and another helpful person, sailing to Auckland, offered to call the Maxwell-Nilsson company. Further, we had a ham radio contact in New Zealand who went to bat for us. The repair parts, we learned, could not be sent directly to Neiafu. First they had to go to Nuku'alofa several hundred miles away in the Tongatapu group! We had to find an agent in Nuku'alofa and send a letter employing him to get the package on to us, bonded by customs. By this cumbersome process it took a month. In the meantime we had to stay anchored in Neiafu, waiting.

A rather spidery looking trimaran was anchored near us. It was named *Bullfrog*. We learned the forty foot wide, forty foot long tri had just won the Singlehanded Transpacific Race. One day a vivacious young woman came over to ask if she could borrow our clothes pegs. She was Cathy Hawkins, half owner of the boat with Ian Johnston. Soon thereafter we were invited to go for an afternoon sail with them—and what an exciting sail that was. We couldn't have had more than four to five knots of wind, but this racing machine was doing nine knots, almost double our normal cruising speed! Cathy was everywhere at once, bouncing around trimming this sheet or that and steering. She was apologizing that the boat speed was so slow! Normally, Cathy said, they try to hold *Bullfrog's* speed down to 25 knots when racing.

Cathy and Ian, who built the boat together, often race it in doublehanded races, but each of them also races it solo. The boat's name came from their sponsor, Bullfrog Sunscreen. That meant Cathy was a professional racer who lived by the sponsorship and money won racing. Not too many women have this kind of occupation or this kind of success in the competitive sailing world.

We certainly admired Cathy. Handling a lightweight multihull racing machine like that requires special skills and knowledge and to my mind really requires guts.

In Neiafu I went through another period of nostalgic longing for the structure and human interaction I enjoyed when landbased. I was definitely feeling aimless and useless. I did not like the feeling. I examined what my expectations about this voyage had been. I came up with two basic answers: terrific experiences and plenty of time to write. On the first count I was satisfied; I was learning about other people and their way of life. As far as writing—I was doing less. Why? A big part of it was that I needed time alone and space—a place of my own to spread things out. Hard in the confines of a small boat when you're sharing that space with someone else. But all was not lost. I was reading more fiction than ever before and developing quite an analytical eye for technique, characterization and plot development.

Still, the unsatisfied sensation persisted. I thought I should be doing something fulfilling. I was not a good hedonist and felt compelled to do something productive, beneficial. Shouldn't life have a purpose? But a tiny voice in the back of my mind said, "You must sing the song that is inside. We don't do what we must do for the 'good' of someone else. We must live what is inside, following those yearnings and urges to the end. Perhaps something of that will touch another, but most likely in a fashion you could never anticipate."

At the little island of Nuku we joined with the crews from *Saga* —Ron, Jackie, Jessie—and *Io*—George and Jan. Together we went on *Io* and anchored off Mariners Cave to dive into this well-known underwater cave. To find it, one must go down about six feet and swim underwater about 20 feet to enter the cave. Ron volunteered to help anyone who needed it. It is a free dive with snorkel and fins. I asked Ron to assist. He grabbed my arm and pulled me rapidly, then very forcefully pushed me up to the surface inside the cave. Wham! My head cracked into a hard mass with dizzying pain. I had hit an overhang! Then, as I looked into the cave's interior, it began to grow foggy! I thought the whack on the head had really done me in. Maybe I was going to faint. But no, just then the fog disappeared. Just as I was feeling relieved, the fog came back. Later we concluded that the fog resulted from the change in pressure. As the surge came and receded, so did the fog.

What a spectacular sight. The only light into the cave was reflected up through the water, giving everything an iridescent glow. Pretty and eerie. Swimming around, I gazed through my mask at the bottom some 50 or 60 feet below. Overhead the ceiling arched about 70 feet. The cave's massive stalactites and stalagmites looked as if great globs of wet cement had cascaded downward, suddenly hardening into graceful swirls and cylindrical forms resembling organ pipes. But, I realized, these took thousands of years to form. Awesome. I could also smell a strange acrid odor in the air. Water sounds plopped with a hollow echo that bounced around the vaulted expanse.

We had been in Tonga for about six weeks when Tongan immigration threatened to throw me in jail and fine me $10,000! What happened was this. Upon entering Tonga we informed the immigration officer how long we wished to stay—about four months. He stamped the passports and wrote a date on them. The date was not legible but stretching our imaginations, it looked like the date we had specified. I only became concerned when everyone we knew was constantly renewing their visas, saying they could only get them for one month at a time.

I went to Immigration and explained to a very large young man what had happened. He became quite agitated and in poor and halting English threatened me with jail and a $10,000 fine. I was quite apologetic and contrite and talked slowly and simply, but not in the pigeon English I've heard some Americans use. I also immediately told him that I did not have $10,000. My concern was based on a number of horror stories we've heard about the liberties Tongan customs and immigration officers take with yachts. Of course, yachts owners are as much at fault as the officials if the owners allow officials to drink huge quantities of liquor on their boat or give them several bottles as "gifts." Our standing rule is that we never offer a drink to an official.

At any rate, the immigration officer, like so many petty officials, was terribly impressed with his authority and I suspect, too, a good portion of his bravado came from his being a man dealing with a woman.

Our encounter was stretching on close to half an hour and we had not made any progress toward a resolution. If the truth be known, I think he was enjoying his position because it gave him an opportunity to reprimand me repeatedly. About this time he said something that almost made me burst into boisterous laughter. He said, "What language you speak? You no speak English." I was hesitant to respond but finally said as neutrally as I could, "Yes, I'm an American. I speak English." Suddenly I had an inspiration. "Sir, give me two visa forms so Joy and I can fill them out. I'll just take it to the boat so she can do hers and sign it. Then, I'll be right back."

Confronted with something positive—and a way out—he complied.

In early November we had to move on south as the Southern hemisphere hurricane season was approaching. On the way to Nuku'alofa we wanted to cruise through the islands of the Ha'api group. Going with us were George and Jan on *Io* and Loren and Georgia on *American Flyer*. Georgia and I had gotten to know each other in Neiafu when we got together with George Rudy and formed a trio and played tons of music. George had his flute, I had my two recorders and Georgia had her five recorders and guitar. It was good fun in an evening as the sun set, sitting in the cockpit of one of our boats playing chamber music.

It was only 57 miles to our first anchorage on Ha'ano, but the wind shifted, making it a beat and thus increasing our mileage. Once night set in, *American Flyer*, a faster racing boat, left us in her wake. We left *Io* in ours as their roller furling gear was malfunctioning and prevented them from pointing well. Through most of the night, when on watch, I could see running lights from both boats on opposite sides of the horizon. We stayed in radio contact with each other but lost contact with *Io* even though we could still see them. By sunrise *American Flyer* was out of sight but still in radio range.

When running the engine to charge our batteries, we discovered the engine was overheating. The sea was rough; a situation not conducive to trouble shooting and repairing an engine. We found if we ran the engine in neutral at only 1500 RPMs we could charge for a while. Under load, though, the engine overheated immediately. The next day, when approaching Ha'ano, the wind died and we could not use our engine to come in to anchor. We spoke to Loren on *American Flyer* about our plight. Immediately he took up his anchor and powered out and towed us in. We were very grateful for his assistance. We knew we were in good hands—he's a towboat captain!

While anchored at Ha'ano, Joy began searching for the source of the overheating. After taking apart and checking the water pump—which was fine—and pursuing other likely avenues, she found nothing. This was another case of check the simple things first! It turned out that the thermostat was faulty. Fortunately we had a spare.

The Ha'api group proved to be one of the nicest cruising areas: lovely wide beaches, beautiful reefs and few inhabitants. Its only drawback is the lack of protected anchorages. As long as the weather remains settled, it's a nice place to be. When it changes, leave. We did. We left from Nomuka, where we had anchored with *Io* behind the reef, but so close that we were almost on top of it. When the tide came in, the breakers were almost crashing over our beam! Neither of us felt safe here. We awoke at 6 A.M. to a wind shift to NE. Not what we needed. It meant we had to leave immediately. In the middle of a heavy rain squall, we managed to make our way out through the winding narrow pass with George and Jan on *Io* just behind us.

Shortly after arriving in Nuku'alofa, we had a hurricane watch. In all about 15 cruising boats were anchored at Pangimotu, just across the bay from the city wharf at Nuku'alofa. Everyone was provisioning and waiting for the right weather to begin the passage to New Zealand. With no known hurricane holes in the area, we were feeling rather nervous.

George, Jan, Joy and I had gone to town to renew our visas and do some shopping. In the market George and I met another yachtie who informed us that hurricane Osea was predicted to hit Tonga in about 36 hours! As soon as we could, we all got back on *Banshee* and headed back to Pangimotu. On the radio, we learned the rest of the cruising fleet had left Pangimotu. They managed to find a narrow channel, which they marked, that wound through the reefs and back to a lagoon, a perfect hurricane hole. Captain Cook had also sailed into this lagoon. Unfortunately we couldn't get through because the tide was falling and our draft too deep. We went only part way and anchored behind Pangimotu. Lady Luck was with us. Osea never came our way. Hitting some cold water, she lost some of her fury and was downgraded from 70 knots to a 45-knot storm.

Before leaving Tonga I had another unsettling encounter with Third World bureaucracy. Upon entering Nuku'alofa, customs wanted to see my receipt for port fees paid in Neiafu. That receipt was not with my other papers. I knew I had kept it. They were reasonable and said I could show it to them when I checked out. I went back and tore the boat apart but could not find it. I found old receipts for other port fees paid in Neiafu—one paid by the month, in advance. The one I paid just before leaving Neiafu was good for an entire month.

It was nowhere to be found.

On the day I went back to customs to check out, I was in line with about ten other captains who were also trying to check out. I showed all my receipts to the official and told him I had lost the most recent one, but obviously Neiafu would not have given me clearance if I owed them money. I had been in conversation for about ten minutes. Of course, the entire matter could have been straightened out right away if one could phone Neiafu—but that was not possible since there was no phone service to that outpost. Several others standing in line had heard the entire exchange between me and the official. They spoke up too and said I was right—without paying the fees Neiafu would not have given me clearance. With that the official to whom I had been speaking simply walked off and left me standing at the window. About ten minutes later he came back and asked me to step inside the office. That was one way to separate me from my supporters!

He had me sit down in a chair across from his desk and said he needed information for the clearance form from Tonga. Instead of simply giving me the form to fill out, he filled it out—a laborious process since I had to spell each word out several times and he still made mistakes. It was a two-page form and took quite a bit of time. Finally the question of port fees arose again. We finally struck a compromise. It was then, on the day of checking out of the country, one day into a new month and customs was systematically waving this for other cruisers. Rather than make me pay two months, he would accept the fees for one month. I knew I could have refused and left paying nothing. But I had already spent at least an hour haggling. It just didn't seem worth it for $12.00 or for the principle of the thing. I paid it, having won half the battle. Later I figured out what happened to the receipt. The customs official in Lifuka, in the Ha'apai group, failed to return it to me on my departure. As I learned, the same thing happened to others. Intentional? Perhaps.

On Thanksgiving Day some dozen yachts left Nuku'alofa bound for Opua, the Bay of Islands, New Zealand. We left with good weather, not knowing that most of us were going to get hit by a very fierce low before making New Zealand.

Chapter 13

To the Land of Lamb, Milk and Honey

December 1, 0500. Looking overhead I saw what I first thought was a plane. However, it moved too fast and the light was different. A satellite? I raced below and looked at the SatNav. It was locked into a satellite. I pressed the button to see which one: number 50, rising at 20° from the SW. That was it! The first time I had knowingly seen a satellite.

Three days later, on December 4, the dreaded happened. We sailed into a low. Joy awakened me at 0545, saying we needed to reduce sail. We did and watched while a massive pile of ugly black squall clouds marched down upon our port beam. Winds crept up in the next half hour from 20 to 30 knots and eventually, as the stormy blackness enveloped us, heavy rainfall sliced at us horizontally, stinging our faces like sharp needles.

Throughout the morning we continued to think that within an hour or so we would escape the squall zone. Then the sky all around became a sodden lead ceiling that lowered oppressively. No squall, we suspected, but the weather report mentioned no lows.

By noon the wind was howling a steady 35 with gusts up to 45. We kept reducing sail, but every ten minutes it seemed the wind rose another five knots. The seas had mounted, becoming a furious mass of crests toppling over themselves. With more frequency they broke over our decks. We were sailing under only a triple reefed main and as the wind increased even more, I realized the boat could not handle this much sail! We were overpowered. By now the groaning winds thrashed us at 50 plus knots. The deck was heaving back and forth in a motion threatening to roll us over. We dropped the reefed main and hove to under bare poles and went below to wait it out.

The fury continued. The screaming and howling penetrated and reverberated through my head. Building seas pounded us more frequently. The knot of dread tightened in my stomach. After hours of horrendous motion, I lost my appetite and felt a kind of quasi-

motion sickness, coupled with an aching head but no outright
nausea.

At 6 P.M. we spoke to other boats underway to New Zealand. Ron
on *Saga*, also in transit, mentioned that the latest weather report
had noted a low with gale force winds. This low, which we were in
the midst of, was joining with a trough extending down from Fiji.
Moreover, there was the further threat of a tropical depression that
could shoot down the trough directly at us. Ron's advice: GET OUT
NOW! He suggested sailing out under our storm jib on a beam reach
so we could continue sailing south on our course. This was a tactic
we'd never tried.

Joy and I hurried on deck, working as fast as we could in the
rapidly failing light. Before it was completely dark, we had hanked
on the storm jib and run the sheets—no easy feat on a heaving deck.
At times we sustained heavy seas that washed right over our decks
and the two of us. Once again we were sailing, albeit through walls
of water and sheets of spray.

That night we experienced the worst weather I have ever
endured. Both of us were so involved in sailing the boat that it was
8:30 before we finally managed to have some much needed hot food.
Joy heated up some baked beans with ham which we washed down
with a cup of hot coffee. Then we began the long and arduous night,
each of us taking a watch of one hour on and one off. On the off watch,
one of us could lie below in a bunk, fully clothed in foul weather gear,
harness and seaboots so as to be ready to go on deck at a moment's
notice. Our main concerns were that the windvane would stop
steering, in which case the boat would be instantly out of control
and, secondly, that the wind generator blades would break loose
and start turning! One time we caught them just in time. While Joy
frantically reached up, grabbed the blade that was just beginning
to rotate, and began to tie it down, I was hanging on to her so she
would not fall overboard when the boat lurched or a sudden sea
broke over us.

What stands out most about that night is the coldness, the
fatigue, the wetness and the feel of it. The sky and sea were an inky
black. Breaking seas sent a sheath of phosphorescence across the
blackness like a jolt of electricity. The frothing, blazing sea resembled some form of giant algae, spreading over itself in heaped
up confusion. The high whine and howling sound of the wind was

almost deafening. One minute we were rising on a steep dark mountain and the next, sliding down the back side into a deep, deep valley that fell away 30 or 40 feet. Breaking seas racked the boat, sometimes half filling the cockpit. Within no time, each of us was soaking wet; our foul weather gear failed to keep out the water.

I don't recall any sense of fear—only dread, knowing the kind of bone weary exhaustion one suffers after hours of this kind of exposure and violent motion. It was my first experience with *mal de mer*. By 0400 I was so overtired and cold that I was ready to heave to and fall into a sound sleep. Joy offered to take my watch, but this time she stayed below rather than going into the cockpit as we had been doing. She suggested I remove my wet clothes and wrap up in a sleeping bag so as to sleep in comfort. As usual our worst enemy was exposure. It robs one's body of vitality and stamina.

Through the next day we took turns sleeping for three or four hour stretches to recover our strength. Though the gale moderated somewhat, the conditions continued to be heavy. We left the storm jib up and added no more sail. Toward nightfall I developed a headache and nausea, no doubt because I had been staying below for so long with only occasional time of pulling back the hatch to look out. By the second day of the storm, December 6, when conditions moderated, we pulled down the storm sail and hoisted a staysail and double reefed main. By nightfall the wind had diminished even more, to 10 to 12 knots. Leftover seas and light southwesterlies made it impossible to sail our course. The same wind pattern persisted for the next three days and we alternated between sailing and powering. Finally, on the fourteenth day after leaving Nuku' alofa, we sailed into the Bay of Islands. Under a nice stiff breeze and fair skies on a day drenched with warm sun, *Banshee* sailed down the 12-mile channel. With pleasure we stared at the hilly islands, evergreens ridging the hillsides, brilliant green valleys, snug little coves with rocky outcroppings. The islands looked as if they were floating on the translucent greenish sea. The air smelled of hay and earth. New Zealand was more beautiful than I had dreamed.

At 2:30 P.M. we dropped our sails in front of the wooden wharf at Opua and powered in alongside *Io*. George took our docklines and we joyously tied up to await the New Zealand officials to arrive and clear us in.

Opua, a quaint little seaside settlement, is comprised of a ferry dock, a little convenience store, a tiny post office and three boatyards. We came to know Elliott's boatyard, the one tucked into the woods with an A-frame shed, quite well since we hauled out there for a month and had an unexpected return visit there five months later.

After clearing customs, we eagerly went ashore to purchase fresh fruit, vegetables and milk with cream on top in a bottle! A stack of mail awaited us at the post office where we were warmly welcomed by Margaret, the Post Mistress, and her assistant, Colleen. It was so homey. We could have been residents returning after a long absence! One little note brought a feeling of great warmth. It was from Joyce and Jim Irving, welcoming us to New Zealand and confirming that our beds were ready and waiting. We had no way of knowing then that Joyce and Jim—complete strangers—were to become some of our most treasured friends, and even more, like family.

In this small, island nation, I began to realize just how varied and rich the English language is. Added to the list of different British accents we'd been hearing across the Pacific was Kiwiese. Where "e" becomes "i" and vise versa, and vowels are often dipthongized. Suddenly a whole new vocabulary assaulted my ears. The word "mate" (with "a" pronounced as "ai") replaces "friend." "Crook" means something's wrong—"my back's crook" means my back hurts. One of the most colorful expressions is "a box of birds" which means the opposite of "a can of worms." When I read in the *New Zealand Herald* about the "beer-swilling hoons," I thought it was a misprint for "goons." But, as I soon learned, "hoon" is a common word in New Zealand. Is it a shortening for hooligan? To be sure Australians and New Zealanders like to shorten words. But the Aussies (from Oz) engage in abbreviation far more readily than the Kiwis who look down on "Strain," Australian speech. "They talk with their teeth clenched," I was told by someone in the know. By far the most humorous and completely foreign phrase I heard in New Zealand was spoken by an Australian woman who said, "I went to hossy to get a hissy." Translated into English, I comprehend, "I went to the hospital to get a hysterectomy."

Some expressions leave me thinking the worst: for example, "He shot through his wife for a bird" means simply that he stepped out on his wife. A "bird" means a girl. The first time a friend said to me he'd "jacked up some of his friends for me," I felt a twinge of embarrassment. I soon learned he was just saying he'd arranged for his friends to come and help me. Men are "blokes" or "chaps." If someone invites you to "tucker," you might feel inclined to say never mind, in which case you would miss out on a good dinner. Dinner is also called "tea." At the end of a meal you have "pud" which is any kind of dessert. One of the most peculiar terms is "cobber." Males often refer to a comrade as a "cobber." The term is Australian for comrade, its origin unknown according to the New College Edition of *The American Heritage Dictionary of the English Language.* I suspect that "cobber" comes from the mining milieu. "Cob" means small lump or mass, as of coal, and in British regional dialect "cob" means a great leader. Perhaps my favorite phrase is "to take the mickey out of you." This means pulling someone's leg.

After a couple of weeks resting up from our passage, we sailed out to see some places in the Bay of Islands. With Lou and Liz on *Silver Cloud* and with *Io,* we anchored in Otahei Bay on the lovely island of Puka Puka. Joy and I spent the better part of one day tramping across the island. This trek took us up and down steep green paddocks filled with grazing sheep. But the most magnificent sight was of the hillside ablaze with masses of red—the flowers from the *pohutukawa* tree (*Metrosideros tomentosa*). Of the same family as the bottle brush, the flower closely resembles that one in color and shape, but the trees are gigantic.

In a couple of days we all moved over to Waipiro Bay to celebrate Lou's birthday. At low tide we waded around in the deepest mud to dig pipis, a small, ubiquitous clam. Fortunately, the pipis live closer inshore, past the soggiest mud. In no time we had two buckets half full of clams. After soaking and rinsing them in fresh water for three hours, we cooked them for dinner. We put them on a trivet in a large pot with a bit of water along with a bit of fresh rosemary, fresh tarragon and bay leaf. We cooked them until they opened, then dipped the clams in garlic lemon butter. Eaten with rice pilaff, we had a very tasty meal.

On January 2, we came out on the railway at Elliott's Boatyard in Opua for some prearranged work. *Banshee* had not been out of the water since Papeete. We were hauled out for only a month, but the work that we did and had done during that month was staggering. Three major jobs had become very evident in the heavy weather sustained off the New Zealand coast. The bulkheads in the main

Banshee's wind generator, "Frieda," refitted with a two-bladed propeller, and one of the two solar panels on *Banshee's* stern.

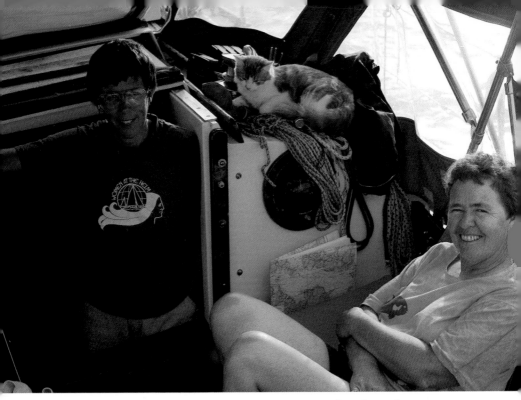

Joy, Jason, the cat we adopted in New Zealand, and me.

The lagoon at Moorea, looking out to the barrier reef.

Early morning at Cook's Bay, Moorea.

Banshee blocked up in the boatyard in Papeete, Tahiti.

Cape Brett light. I felt excited and warm, like I was coming home!

The Bay of Islands, New Zealand, where we were settled in at Opua to relax, pick up mail and put the boat straight.

saloon had bowed in so much we could no longer close the head door. Our floor, or rather cabin sole, moved around like a trampoline! And the deck under our staysail had started lifting up and down when we were flying the storm jib in the worst of a storm. Important things that Brian Elliott found and repaired were a faulty skeg shoe, a near failure of the rudder post, and the steering cable that had almost parted.

To solve the problem of our moving cabin sole, Brian Harris removed the old cabin sole and cut away some of the fiberglass liner that had slipped. He rebuilt new floors, bracing up the lines and putting in running cleats along port and starboard sides. Upon this new foundation, I built a cabin sole from rebated teak board which I glued and "secret" nailed to marine plywood. Then I filled the rebated area with West Systems microballoons. Once hardened, I belt sanded the sole. Harris screwed the sole to the floors and I finished off the sole with five coats of satin varnish.

To move the bulkheads back into place, Elliott sprang them apart with a car jack. He then fashioned a deck beam from laminated kauri. Once it was in place, the bulkheads were staunchly back in place.

We sent out all the chain and anchors to be regalvinized and bought new chain for our main anchor. The propane tanks went out for sand blasting and zinc spraying and we painted them upon their return. The dodger was repaired and its plexiglass windows replaced. Inside the boat, we began varnishing and painting.

We also had some pleasant activities during our stay at the boatyard. We made the acquaintance of Purrbox, a small, very gregarious black cat who chose to live in the boatyard. We had barely come out of the water in our cradle when she appeared, her green eyes alert. Being cat lovers, Joy and I were delighted to see a friendly cat. We were both in great need of a cat fix. Elliott, who had grasped the situation astutely, said, "Purrbox, it's Christmas!"

Purrbox allowed one of us to carry her up the ladder and bring her inside the boat. She quickly made herself comfortable and especially settled in after we gave her a can of tuna for dinner. As she was curled up sleeping, Joy and I discussed whether we dared let her stay in for the night, afraid she could not get down the ladder if she needed to. What a silly discussion! As if she understood us, Purrbox bounded out on the deck and facilely scooted down the ladder. Later, she returned, coming up the ladder with no assistance, thank you.

Purrbox settled in, arriving every morning for her milk, except on cold rainy nights when she slept in and woke us for milk in the morning. She regularly arrived in the evenings for her dinner. But Purrbox was no moocher. She showed her appreciation by bringing us rats or birds around two or three A.M. and characteristically dropping them on the cabin sole for our inspection and praise. She would wake us by making a strange insistent kind of meowing. Once, when I responded too slowly, she deposited the dead bird at my feet—on my bunk. That was too much for me. Somehow she must have gotten the message because from then on, the early morning gifts were deposited at the foot of our ladder, on the ground. Smart cat!

Another pleasant break in the drudgery was a visit by our friend Judy Royer. After completing her time with the Peace Corps in Apia, Judy came to visit friends in New Zealand. She arrived on the very day Joy had painted the forward cabin. This meant we had only two sleeping bunks available. We solved the problem. I brought some of our cushions out of the boatshed and made my bed on the floor between the two bunks. Like a good sailor, Judy pitched in, helping with cleaning and painting. It's always a pleasure to have guests like her.

Opua, as tiny as it is, was the place where we met two world-renowned yachtswomen—Ann Gash and Susan Hiscock—and also Lynn Service, a Kiwi, interested in becoming a singlehander. One morning in the boatyard while I was standing in *Banshee's* cockpit, a booming voice yelled up at me, "Good morning! I hear you're on your own." I looked down to see a rather good-sized woman with an enormous braid hanging down her back.

Several days previously, I had watched—from a distance—as Ann Gash had sailed her 23-foot Folkboat up to the Opua wharf. I suspected this was she. "No. I'm sailing with another woman. Not alone. Are you by chance Ann Gash?"

"Yes, I am." It was only a short introductory exchange that ended with Ann inviting us to dinner on her little boat, *Stella Ilimo.*

We arrived on Ann's boat and we were greeted by a big welcome. She had cooked up a pot of potatoes, carrots, onions and green beans in a small pressure cooker. She asked if we'd like orange juice, then proceeded to cut and squeeze fresh orange juice into a glass by hand. About halfway through dinner, we heard a knock on the hull. It was Lynn Service, the Kiwi woman who wanted to become a long distance singlehander. She had just come over to make her acquaintance with Ann.

Here we were—a collection of women at the helm. Although we didn't meet Susan Hiscock until our second visit to Opua, we will remember the port as a woman sailor's place.

****

Once back in the water we set about getting *Banshee* shipshape so we could leisurely cruise around the Bay of Islands and then move south to Auckland. Shortly after our arrival in New Zealand we had gone to Auckland for a couple of days to meet Jim and Joyce. Before we came back to Opua, they asked if we'd be interested in staying in their home for three weeks in March while they traveled in the South Island. It was perfect for us, a chance to live ashore while completing *Banshee's* painting. We could look after their vegetable garden and their two cats. And I could play Jim's piano! What an offer.

Bad weather delayed our departure from the Bay of Islands. We roughed it out in Matauwhi Bay, catching and eating our fill of snapper. While eating popcorn one day, I felt a strange, sharp crunch. Part of a molar had broken off. Getting to a dentist from here would be an all day project: go ashore at Matauwhi, walk to Russell, take a ferry across to Pahia and hope that a dentist would take me in on the spot. Unlikely. I wasn't in pain so I could wait until Auckland. But the sharp edge was annoying my tongue. I tore off a small piece of 220 sandpaper and in less than a minute had smoothed the tooth.

Finally the weather broke enough to sail from Matauwhi to Pipi Bay, a well protected cove where we sat out a nasty gale for two days. In this little millpond, we watched the wind whipping the tree tops and felt absolutely no effects. We went ashore to cut each others' hair and Joy gathered pipis at the water's edge. She found enough to add to the three small fish I'd caught that morning. Altogether they made a fine Pacific chowder.

February 19. Early morning. A crisp day. Sky cleared from

yesterday's strong winds. A morning chill clung to the hills in layers of wispy fog, giving the hills a bewhiskered look. By 0845 we were silently gliding out of the bay, our mainsail all the way out, a single white wing. Noiselessly we ghosted past the headland heading for the open sea—our first glimpse of the ocean in over two months. None too soon, either. I was beginning to feel I could never go to sea again. The trip to Auckland somehow seemed overwhelming. I voiced these thoughts and reservations to Joy. She said she felt the same way. We were getting back on the horse.

Soon the wind picked up. Whitecaps dotted the green water. *Banshee* raced along at 6 knots as if she were glad to be sailing again. As we neared Cape Brett, we sailed into a massive flock of shearwaters. They bobbed all around us. When we came too close, they flew away. Their method of takeoff is distinctive. At first they almost walk on the water. As their wings flap, their feet paddle the surface and then suddenly, with a lurch, they lift off, rapidly gaining height. Occasionally some of the birds didn't leave the water; instead they skied a few feet with the wing-and-foot routine only to slide back into a serene floating position.

Off Piercey's Rock—we sailed between it and the end of Cape Brett—hundreds of seagulls swarmed just inches off the water, moving as if all were controlled by a single invisible string, swooping, turning, rising, falling in perfect unison.

For several days we anchored at different places along the North Island mainland. On February 22, we sailed to Boulder Bay on Matapuka, one of the islands of a group called the Hen and Chickens. All of these offlying islands are wildlife sanctuaries. No one can go ashore without special permission. We loved the view from the boat and found the land bird calls exquisite. But the anchorage proved very rolly.

The next morning we left under power, cutting a sharp wake over the glassy surface. Before we were out of the bay, a pod of dolphins joined us and escorted us to the end of the Chickens. They took turns rubbing their backs on our bow. We took turns going up forward to watch them. One continued to roll over on its side and look up at me. Periodically a pair would jump out of the water or do other tricks. I talked to them and sometimes I could hear a high-pitched squeak. Perhaps they were responding to me.

For three hours it was almost impossible to detect where the sky ended and the sea began. It was a study in gray, silver and pewter. The sea had no ripples, no swell—a flat surface upon which an occasional bird floated, took off from or landed on. No jumping fish, no wind waves, nothing. For the first time the sea looked like a desert to me, desolate, empty.

Around 12:30, a light northeasterly breeze rippled the metallic surface. We hoisted sail and turned the engine off. The rush of water against the hull punctuated the stillness. Then gradually, like a ghostly phantom, Great Barrier Island began to emerge, a darker lump just showing on the horizon. Slowly, as the sun burned a hole in the cloud cover, texture and color filled in, flooding the island with life and distinct features. Forested hillsides, rocky coastline stood still and clear like a calendar photo. Two sailboats still a couple of miles ahead of us turned into a deeply chiseled bay, their white sails dwarfed against the mountainous background.

We too entered the wide-mouthed bay. The steeply rising mountains on each side reminded me of the Swiss Alps. This bay could have been an Alpine lake, smooth, reflecting the greens and browns of the landscape. We wound around the fjordlike fingers until we found the leg into the village of Port Fitzroy. It lay nestled amongst trees and grass green paddocks. On an adjoining, almost barren hill, scattered cows grazed.

Just as we were anchoring, I heard a sudden ear-splitting sound. Looking over my shoulder, I saw a seaplane splashing to a landing. It roared across the water at tremendous speed, slowing only as it closed on the shore. It rolled ashore and passengers leaped out onto the beach. Just as quickly, the plane plunged back into the bay. Buzzing like an angry bumblebee, it wove between anchored boats, leaving a large wake that violently rolled every vessel in the bay. After this rude intrusion, it became airborne and disappeared around the bend.

Other equally combative "attacks" of the seaplane through the evening and early the next morning persuaded us it was time to explore the island. We loaded on fresh water and a few supplies from the little store, then went in search of a quieter, less active cove. We found Kiwiriki Bay, a secure flat anchorage where we were the only boat.

Ashore we found a cave and inspected the fault lines running along a cliff. The striations showed a massive geological upheaval had occurred in the distant past.

Today Great Barrier Island supports some scattered stands of recently planted trees—mostly pine. Otherwise there are scrubby bush commonly seen all over New Zealand's North Island. The area also contains a fair number of pohutukawa trees that line the shore, ruggedly growing right out of rock.

For centuries before the Europeans came, Great Barrier was covered with the native kauri trees. Unfortunately these regal giants that were several thousand years old were logged. In 1909 the Kauri Timber Company opened a sawmill at Whangaparapara Harbor. It closed down in 1928 after cutting some 20 million feet of kauri. In a mere two decades these venerable old trees were gone, the island denuded of its kauri.

Bay of Islands
New Zealand

Chapter 14

Impressions Down Under

We joke that in New Zealand you can have three seasons in one day. Without the moderating influence of a continental landmass, weather and temperature fluctuate rapidly. One minute a cold breeze and clouds covering the sun send one scurrying for a sweater. Ten minutes later, the sun is burning and off comes the sweater. Such changes may be even more exaggerated in Auckland because of its location. Situated roughly two-thirds of the way down the length of the North Island, Auckland has the Hauraki Gulf on the east side and Manukau Harbor on the Tasman coast on the west. Except for a bit of land approximately one-fourth mile wide, the Pacific and the Tasman would meet. Hence, when weather systems roar across the Tasman—which they do with great regularity—Auckland has no buffer zone.

Settling in at Joyce and Jim's home on Kipling Avenue in early March, Joy and I began to develop our land legs. I soon discovered that Auckland resembles Los Angeles and San Francisco in many respects. Auckland is hilly and its waterfront in downtown Auckland shares the salty flavor of the beautiful northern California City. Many of the plants growing here are also at home in California. Many of the older villas here are identical in style to the Victorian homes recently renovated in San Francisco. But there are differences, too.

One of my most outstanding impressions of New Zealand goes back to our early days on Kipling Avenue, sitting in the living room, which faces the front garden. A line of several kinds of trees and a high hedge across the front lawn totally block the view of the street. In the center of the lawn is a ring of rose bushes. One sunny day I simply sat there letting the scene wash over me. Sun drenched the garden and the breeze rustled the transparent curtains and gently nudged the trees. A Bach choral, soft and soaring, added to the ambience. I slowly became aware of something else. What had been part of an indeterminate background suddenly became the feature. It dominated everything. The buzzing seemed to grow in volume until everything else receded. It was the sound of many cicadas. For me this buzzing became synonymous with summer in New Zealand. Every sunny day they droned a continuous, sonorous symphony. Where do they go when it rains?

The rain. I remember nights under the corrugated iron roof of the house. When it rained, it made a thunderous clamor. I pulled the blanket just a bit snugger around my ears, happy not be standing watch in the downpour. For some inexplicable reason it made me think of New Zealand's early days of isolated pioneers living on their paddocks miles from any settlement. Tough, rugged, self-reliant people, friendly and warm to strangers.

In this house, our social life increased tremendously. Just having the space, I guess, we felt more inclined to have dinner parties. George Rudy came to stay a couple of weeks while looking for a medical post. He also brought his flute and a pile of music for piano and flute or two flutes. We read through much of it, sometimes beginning at 7 A.M., sometimes playing late into the night. Here Joy and I renewed our acquaintance with cruising friends we hadn't seen since French Polynesia. Tim and Heather had bought a house here and had their first child.

We also got to know new friends. Foremost among these were Hilton and Melva Ward. We met them at an anchorage on Kawau Island when Hilton rowed up, started talking and invited us to join them for a cookout ashore. We went. They were cooking kawahai. Three or four cheeky wekas kept circling around. One grabbed a piece of fish right off the grill and another helped itself to a piece from Melva's plate! Wekas look a lot like the kiwi, with its vestigial wings and long, slender bill, except they have a much shorter beak. Like the kiwi, the weka is a large, flightless bird. They have a very distinctive, deliberate walk and can run very fast. Around 1940 the birds were becoming scarcer in the North Island. It is thought that a disease caused their disappearance. Concerned, conservationists captured some wekas from the Gisborne area where the birds were thriving and released them in regions that seemed favorable for their survival. In some places the weka has reestablished itself.

When Joyce and Jim returned from the South Island, they offered the room to us for as long as we wanted or needed it. We stayed on for about a week, wanting to have some time with them. Both of them were so helpful driving us all over Auckland to purchase items necessary to our ocean existence.

Finally, with ourselves and *Banshee* back together, we left Auckland temporarily to do a bit of local cruising. The Hauraki Gulf is strewn with many lovely islands and safe coves for anchoring. Our first stop was Islington Bay, affectionately called by Kiwis "Izzy" Bay, on Rangitoto. This 800-year-old volcanic island dominates the view from most of Auckland. Its 5708 acres are part of the Hauraki Gulf Maritime Park.

On a very bright day we hiked to the summit of Rangitoto where we had a commanding view of Auckland, the entire gulf and even Little Barrier and Great Barrier Islands. Just as we arrived at the summit path, two buses disgorged a hundred or so tourists! Joy and I could not believe it. The wilderness quiet was suddenly disrupted by the chatter of a mass of *homo sapiens*. I was somehow reminded of seagulls swarming and screeching behind a fishing boat. We were saved, though. Most of the tourists were unable or unwilling to tackle the very steep path to the top. We had the lovely vista to ourselves and enjoyed our picnic brought along in our pack.

The next day I woke and saw a little bird perched on our lifelines. As it preened and cleaned itself, its tiny body vibrated vigorously. It had a long, V-shaped tail and very long wingtips. A rust orange band extended from the throat to the upper breast. The remainder of the underside was a silvery white while the back feathers were dark brown. From my North American bird book I determined that the little creature closely resembled a barn swallow of which here are 80 species worldwide. North American and European swallows migrate to Central and South America. Where do the New Zealand birds go? A New Zealand bird book only confused my efforts to identify the bird.

Around 11 A.M., we sailed from Rangitoto to Waiheke Island and anchored in a very pretty cove off the town of Oneroa. Ashore we soon found the important things—a vegetable market and the ice cream parlor.

The north side of Waiheke is mostly grassy with patches of pine and grazing sheep and cattle—a pastoral scene evoking the British Isles.

We had a quiet night there with a half moon in a clear sky. Outside on deck we could hear the pounding surf. The barometer remained high—indicating good weather, but the forecast was for wind moving from south to northwest. That meant a front was on the way.

I woke suddenly in the morning. Something had bumped *Banshee* and we actually rocked a little. I went topside to investigate only to have the episode repeated. Something was hitting us from the underside. As I watched, I saw one very good-sized three-and-a-half-foot king fish. It was followed by two small fish of the same species. Periodically the large one charged into the side of the boat and vigorously thrashed the water. We had witnessed the same behavior of this fish at Great Barrier. Why? I don't know the answer.

With no wind, we left Oneroa under power, rounded the north side of Waiheke and anchored in a nice place called Hooks Bay. We both thought the name referred to the shape of the land surrounding the bay. Later we learned differently, when we went ashore.

We landed the dinghy on a sandy beach. A short walk brought us to a deserted frame house at the head of the bay. The floor, some of the interior and exterior walls had fallen away. Every shred of paint had long since weathered off. Huge ironwood trees standing behind the dwelling dwarfed it but also protected it from prevailing winds. The rocky beach abruptly rose into soft rolling hills etched with sheep trails that stood out like rust colored fingers against the green velvet slopes. Behind the house, a narrow valley extended a few hundred feet onto a small rock-studded bay. It was here where we walked along slowly, with sheep scattering in front of us with an occasional mournful deep "bah," that we found a fenced-in grave. The wooden fence, protectively marking the final resting place, was eroded to bare wood that shone a weathered silvery gray. Little of its former glory was present, but I could imagine how crisp it looked painted white—the new, spiked white fence rails and the turned dome corners. There in the middle, a large engraved stone slab told it all: "In memory of my husband Stephen Hooks, died 1921, aged 64, sleeping, peacefully sleeping." A story told with a minimum of words. So some 60 odd years ago, Hooks Bay was home to at least two people. What a view they had and such a variety of landscape. If they tired of looking at a rocky wooded shore, it was easy to shift their eyes to the shoreline of sandy beaches with a backdrop of barren yellow-brown hills. What were their lives like? Whatever happened to Mrs. Hooks? What was her first name? Were there any little Hooks? Does this family prosper today?

"Red sky in the morning, sailors take warning" confirmed the weather report of wind and rain. The low we had been expecting was upon us. We were rolling from side to side. The further north the wind went, the more unprotected this bay became. At 8:30 A.M., we had the anchor up and sailed out of Hooks Bay. As we cleared the point, a nasty squall of 30-35 knots overtook us. The seas were heaped up and unpleasant. Heavy rain not only drenched us but blotted out the island towards which we were sailing. Once the rain abated we headed for Man O'War Bay, and coming into a protected lee, we escaped most of the horrendous blow. We sailed into the flat waters of Rotoroa Island and anchored. Here was another fantastic view of a hillside with cattle, a small settlement (an alcoholic cure center) with a church steeple reaching up toward the clouds.

Once the bad weather passed, we determined to move on to the Coromandel Peninsula. We couldn't have selected a nicer day: sunshine, fair winds and brilliant, colorful clouds. New Zealand has some of the world's most beautiful clouds. I didn't know it then, but we were going to end up in Squadron Bay, my favorite of all the places we went for the month. It was calm as a lake and was tucked in on three sides where the hills roll right down to the sea. Cows and pine trees perched picturesquely as if waiting for my camera. Looking out the entrance, we could see peaks of other islands cloaked in a purplish haze. Magical, especially in the light of a full moon.

A few days later we moved on to Coromandel Bay to see new sights and also to go to town and purchase a few fresh provisions. It is a huge bay, but, shallow. Very shallow. We knew we couldn't go up to the Coromandel Wharf except at high water, so we anchored safely across the bay and dinghied into the pier at mid tide. Les on *Mithra* told us to tie *Nessie* at the seaward end of the pier and all would be well.

We had a nice walk into town. We visited the baker, two food markets, butcher, fruit and vegetable stall and a dairy. We lunched at a tea shop and then left to go back to the pier and fill our water jugs. We had been gone two and a half hours. Walking along the shore, we could see how far the tide had gone out. I began to have intimations that we were in for a big surprise at the pier. We were. All the commercial fishing boats alongside were sitting high and dry in the ooze! The water was a good half mile beyond the end of the pier! There was no one, absolutely no one on the pier. Just us. Well, a good time to watch the wading birds. It was rewarding. We saw two gray herons, some sandpipers and a number of noisy gulls foraging on the mud flats for tasty morsels. But the real sighting was a spoonbill. As I learned, the Royal Spoonbill, a large white heronlike bird with a black spatulate bill has only become established in New Zealand over the last 40 years. Even so, they are still rather rare. This is the only one we've seen. Watching the birds feed proved entertaining, especially noting the variety of behaviors. The gulls waded into a puddle and then scratched like mad. Apparently this activity stirs edible creatures to the surface. The strangest looking feeder, though, was the spoonbill. Its bill swept back and forth through the puddles much like a vacuum cleaner. Periodically its head came up, neck stretched to swallow some succulent bit.

Joy's impatience to get back to *Banshee* got the better of her good judgment. She wanted to drag the dinghy across the mud to the water. I countered with, "The mud's probably knee deep. It should create a wonderful suction on the dinghy. But, if you really want to, we can fill the two water jugs, I'll jump in and you pull it across the mud flats Alaskan husky style!" She didn't think much of my humor, but at least it made her come to her senses.

Our dinghy sat askance in the mud, her prop down two or three inches into the mud but half of her stern tipped up in the air. She was pinioned up under the pier pilings next to rocks that were covered with several inches of slippery green slime. Nothing to do but wait; let nature take its course. It did. It took two and a half hours of waiting. Looking out in the distance, I located several marks to use for judging the state of the tide. Around 3 P.M. I determined that the tide had turned and was coming in. It was. It came so fast I could see it encroaching on the mud. First one stake and then another were surrounded by water, and finally an old tire tipped up on end disappeared as the sea rose above it. Little by little the wading birds were retreating towards land.

We had a cold ride back in *Nessie* across the bay, arriving just before dark. The wind howled all night, creating a terrible fetch that caused us to leave the next day. We went to Deep Cove, a protected anchorage on the west side of the island, almost exactly opposite where we had been on Home Bay. Deep Cove turned out to be a pleasant place with not too many boats when we arrived. That soon changed because it was Easter weekend. With half of New Zealand out in their yachts and launches and not too many protected anchorages on the Coromandel in easterlies, the bay filled up rapidly. The weekenders began arriving that evening and, much to our surprise and delight, Hilton and Melva came in *Marduk* and anchored nearby.

The following day they invited us over for lunch. Later Melva cut Joy's and my hair on shore and then the four of us went pipi hunting. We invited them to *Banshee* for dinner and a game of Nautical Nonsense. They brought freshly caught fish in a beer batter and we made pipi chowder to go with the fried fish, fresh steamed carrots, wine and coffee.

With *Marduk* we moved to Deadman's Bay and went fishing in the dinghy. After catching a good mess of snapper, we had another communal feast. Early the next morning, Melva and Hilton left, trying to make it back to Auckland before another low hit.

We returned to Squadron Bay knowing it was a secure holding place to weather out the adverse weather. That afternoon and night it blew fierce. Winds were 35-40 with gusts higher. There was no fetch but *Banshee* thrashed around and some of the williwaws threw us over on our side.

Two days later when the low had passed, we went ashore to look for mushrooms. We found two kinds but, not being able to identify them, left them. The variety of trees was nice: pohutukawa, oak, Ponderosa pine, poplar and cedar, as well as some we didn't know. We picked rose hips and made tea with them and lemon balsam. Quite good, actually. We also found the drying-out place for the shags. They were perched on branches at the shore's edge in characteristic pose with their wings held out to dry.

The weather turned cold. We lit a coal fire in our little fireplace and carried on: reading, writing, doing various repair jobs as we waited for the wind to abate. We were sitting in the middle of a 200-mile band of gale force winds that was not passing quickly. By now it was almost the end of April. Despite the heavy winds, we had to leave and return to Auckland where we were meeting a friend flying in from the States to make the passage with us to Fiji.

We met Jackie at the airport on May 2. The three of us spent the next nine days preparing for our passage to Suva. On the Thursday before we left, a reporter and a photographer from the *New Zealand Herald* came to interview us. Joyce had tipped them off. On Saturday morning, Joyce and Jim surprised us by coming to Admiralty Steps to see us off when we checked out with customs.

There was not a breath of wind. We left under power and continued powering all the way to Kawau Island where we anchored for the night in Bon Accord Bay. Early morning we hoisted sail in a good steady wind and set a course for the Moko Hinau Islands. Around midday the wind died and we changed to a course for Great Barrier, under power, knowing we could not make the Moko Hinaus before nightfall.

Light winds continued to plague us even after leaving Great Barrier. We sailed when we could but had to run the engine for long stretches. Then the unexpected happened. On Jackie's watch in the middle of night on May 13, but not a Friday, she noticed that suddenly the engine sounded different. Suspecting something was amiss, she aroused Joy who soon discovered that the propeller shaft had sheered. She woke me and we determined there was absolutely nothing we could do before morning.

On the morning net we talked with various boats and reported that we would be returning to Opua, 130 miles distant, to make repairs. Harrison on *Aquavit* suggested we tie off the prop before trying to sail—to prevent it from jamming into the rudder. We talked with Russ on *Paul Bunyon* in Opua and he said he would speak with Elliott to see if he could haul us out for repairs. Now it was up to us. Someone had to dive into the water and tie off the prop.

Chapter 15

Sailing to Fiji on the Heels of a Coup

Joy and I looked at each other, communicating without speaking. Each of us knew she was going over the side to tie off the prop. She had the only wet suit; a shorty she had bought just before leaving Auckland. It was a light weight suit, but better than nothing. Although she is an experienced diver and took her scuba training many years ago with Mel Fisher himself, she opted not to wear a scuba tank. The swell was rocking *Banshee*. The tank would be an encumbrance. Even before she mentioned it, I knew her concerns: sharks and cold water. We decided the quickest thing would be to send her down with lines. We first tied slip knots in the lines. All she had to do underwater was slip each line over one blade of the prop, pull tight and the line would be secure. Topside, Jackie and I had to keep tension on the lines and then tie one line to each side of the boat once Joy had completed her job. We also had another line around Joy for safety. When both lines were secure, she dove back under and pushed hard on the prop. It slid back into place with a clang.

The entire operation probably took about ten minutes, but to us it dragged on for an eternity. Joy came back aboard, shaking—as much from cold as from apprehension. She was the heroine of the day. As soon as she had dressed in dry clothes, we pressed a glass of brandy in her hand. It was well earned—even if it was only 10 A.M.

Later in the day we had a scheduled talk with Russ in Opua. He confirmed that Elliott could haul us out—the tide was even cooperating! We could also be towed back to Opua, if we wished. We declined. We were perfectly capable of sailing back. John Cullen on Kerikeri radio had also offered us a tow if we needed it once we reached the Bay of Islands. Other hams were standing by in case we should have an emergency. We gave Russ the measurements of the shaft so it could be machined in advance. It was a morale booster to know so many people were willing to help. We carefully monitored our water intake. It was surprisingly negligible.

Once warmed up, Joy clamped a pair of vice grips on the shaft from the inside to prevent it from slipping in case something happened to one of the lines.

Over the next two days, the wind continued to be light and variable. Our course fluctuated accordingly from 177° to 240°! On the morning of the second day at 0230, Jackie and I spotted Cape Brett light. With the light winds, it still took the entire day, tacking to get inside the Bay of Islands. It became apparent that the wind was lightening even more as the day was ending. We radioed John Cullen and advised him we would need a tow into Opua. The last ten miles, in fading light, John towed us to Elliott's mooring. Brian and Russ both came out to greet us at the mooring.

In addition to our excitement, we heard on the news that there had been a coup in Fiji! Naturally we were concerned. We talked by ham radio to cruisers who were sitting in Suva Harbor. Of course they were not free to discuss the political situation over the radio. Back in Opua, we read the *New Zealand Herald* daily and listened to radio New Zealand and Australia. Both countries were proclaiming the situation as grave. The New Zealand Navy sent a ship to stand by to remove any New Zealand nationals should they need to be evacuated. Still, we thought the New Zealand and Australian reports were suspect. If the situation had been life-threatening or dangerous, surely our cruising friends would not be hanging around; they would leave and somehow they would warn others not to come to Fiji. It was strange to feel that I trusted people I knew personally over and above two governments.

Later when we got to Fiji and talked with friends who were there through the coup, our suspicions were confirmed. The media had been creating headlines, deliberately misrepresenting the facts. No one can dispute the legitimate concern that a military takeover violates the principles of democratic rule. In this instance the military was not physically violent. The news media stated that within hours the stores were depleted of staples. Friends who were there said there was no shortage of food and the rioting—reported by the media—was non-existent!

The return to Opua also gave us an opportunity to meet Susan Hiscock. She and her late husband Eric were one of the earliest husband and wife teams to take up cruising in small boats as a way of life. Their varied experiences, prodigiously set down in books and articles, have benefitted countless others who've decided to go to sea in small crafts. It was an honor and pleasure to have tea with Susan aboard *Wanderer V*.

A week after returning for repairs, we were once again heading out for Suva, having satisfied ourselves that it was safe to go there despite grim news reports. We had said our farewell to Purrbox who had been happy to have us back. We also said good-bye to Jackie who returned to California after deciding not to continue. Jackie's decision was based on several factors. She felt she was running short of time. She also expressed a lot of concern about the political situation in Fiji. But the deciding factor may well have been that the three of us were not getting on too well. We had had several disagreements, mostly to do with conserving fresh food and using water sparingly. Joy and I spoke with Jackie about this concern once we were back in Opua. Jackie's decision to leave was made shortly after our discussion.

Initially we had light wind behind us. After two days the conditions changed—for the worse—as the wind came forward and stayed there in the northern quarter for the entire passage. Intermittent gale conditions made it and uncomfortable passage. These strong winds resulted from the amalgamation of five highs!

Not all was bad. My journal recounts some scenes of spectacular beauty.

> *Yesterday a spectacular dawn—a drama lasting well over an hour. In the east the clouds parted as if to make a path for the royal sun. The attendants stood at the ready—a crescent moon gleaming against a delicate translucent blue and close by the planet Jupiter. Halfway between the moon and the horizon Venus, a penetrating yellow, is backed by a faint lavender overlaid with lace of pewter. Low on the horizon deep orange and deep gray clouds. If color had sound, this would be the sonorous bass notes of a solitary cello.*

While the weather remained calm, we discovered that one end-fitting on the spinnaker pole was held by just one rivet. What a disaster that could have been! Joy drilled out the old rivets and put in new ones. Amazing to me how cruising is a series of one near accident after another. We work hard to stay on top of it all—

keeping everything fit and working and still we come close to having serious problems.

For the first time we participated on the roll call of the Pacific Maritime Net. Run by volunteer land based hams, daily they contact and track yachts making ocean passages. They tabulate each yacht's speed, course sailed and weather conditions so they can put the yachts on a computerized grid to see their whereabouts. The net also frequently helps by getting special weather forecasts for those who need it and has got doctors on the radio to provide necessary medical advice in emergencies. These men and women perform a wonderful service to those of us at sea. Through them we are also able to make phone patches to friends and family back home.

Sometimes the nasty weather does not bring out the best in me. On May 29 I wrote:

> *Just lost two days. I was seasick. Gale force winds. My first experience with long term seasickness. All I could do was function minimally, doing what absolutely had to be done to keep the boat sailing. We reefed down to triple reefed main and even reefed the staysail. I was able to do night watches by lengthening the periods between checks to half an hour instead of twenty minutes. Otherwise I spent my time sleeping, day and night. Only ate a few crackers and drank an occasional cup of tea with sugar. . . A gray day when I finally woke up this morning feeling depressed, wishing I was anywhere but here in the middle of this gray lumpy ocean! My spirits improved with sail handling and steering, but I'd feel better if we had nice weather and a fair wind. The temperature has warmed considerably. I can sit outside without a sweater or wool shirt.*

Our best day of sailing was the final day of the 14-day passage. Heeled over, charging along at six knots for Suva harbor, I took a much longed for fresh water shower while bracing myself against the boat's gyrations. I eased sails a bit for Joy's shower. We anchored next to *White Cloud* in Suva Harbor and waited for the launch with the doctor to clear quarantine. As scheduled in advance with the harbor authorities on the radio, the doctor arrived at three P.M. He was a young East Indian man who talked quite freely about the coup and its effect on life in Fiji. Indians are forbidden to gather in numbers greater than two. This law does not apply to Fijians, he assured us.

We then tied up at the wharf to await the arrival of customs and immigration. Both of these officers were also Indian. They stated their sentiments: sadness that their home was no longer their home and fear that physical and economic damage may result from the military takeover. Many Indians have fled; others are desperately trying to go to Australia, New Zealand, Canada or the States.

Fiji proved to be the most interesting and most colorful place we have visited. The main reason for this is because of the two extremely diverse cultures currently inhabiting these islands. East Indians, brought in as indentured laborers in 1879, have increased to the point that they presently outnumber the indigenous Fijians, a Melanesian race that came to these islands around 500 B.C. Not only have the Indians increased their numbers, many of them have prospered financially. It is Indian effort and ingenuity for the most part that have made Fiji the most stable economy in the South Pacific. The Indians are hard working, studious, ambitious and sometimes overbearing. In contrast, the Fijians are easy going, friendly, warm and exuberant. Many Indians cluster in urban areas such as Suva and Lautoka where they maintain the culture and tradition as if they were still in India. They are a multireligious group of Hindus, Sikhs, Muslims and even Christians. The Fijians are basically either Methodist or Catholic. To be sure the seeds for discord between the two races have obviously had sufficient time to take root. Unfortunately the overthrow of a democratic government will and has left the Indians fearful, angry and perhaps foremost, anxious to leave the country. When we arrived, the coup had only happened two weeks before, so life was still fairly well in equilibrium. As our five months there progressed, we were to see subtle and overt changes—all adverse.

Suva, the capital, sits on a lovely blue, deep-water harbor tucked inside a wide barrier reef on Viti Levu, the main island. Cruise ships from many world ports testify to Fiji's viable economy. Upon our arrival, though, its commerce with Australia and New Zealand had ceased. Wanting to show their disapproval of the military intrusion, the labor unions in Australia and New Zealand

initially placed an embargo on shipments to Fiji. Both the Australian and New Zealand governments realized this was not a viable
option. Within a month, trade was reestablished, fortunately,
because otherwise Fiji would have come to a standstill and shortage
of certain food stuffs would have severely disadvantaged Fijian and
Indian alike.

The tourist trade, however, suffered a serious setback and
nowhere was it more manifest than at the Handicraft Center. Here
stall after stall of Fijian carvings, weavings and *tapa* being sold by
Indians and Fijians were totally empty of customers. They descended upon us like bees upon honey. The reaction of the races was
astounding. The Fijian people, usually women, would talk to us
soulfully about the coup. They said for us to write to our friends and
tell them to come to Fiji as no harm would come to them. "You see,
it is peaceful," they would say. And it was. On the streets, life went
on as usual. Indian women garbed in gorgeous saris flowed down
the streets and chocolate-colored big Fijians clad in brightly colored
sulus passed by saying *"bula bula,"* the Fijian greeting. In contrast,
the Indian shopkeepers were practically nabbing us by the collar.
They would step out in front of us and begin their salesmanship
spiel. Always it was that they had the best bargain in town for us.
Several even approached me to buy U.S. dollars. They were not at
all pleased when we refused their offers. Naturally their attitude
was annoying and left me with a bad impression. Fortunately, other
favorable exchanges with Indians who became friends erased my
negative feelings.

The heartbeat of Fijian life lies not in the cities but in the
scattered villages found on both large islands, Viti Levu and Vanua
Levu, and on numbers of small islands, some forming chains like
the Yasawas and the eastern group known as the Lau group. The
latter, populated primarily by Polynesian peoples, many of them
from Tonga, is the most remote area of the country. Over 100 of Fiji's
300 plus islands are permanently inhabited and most of the others
are used for planting.

Historically, Fijians have had the reputation for being among
the most ferocious of South Pacific islanders, reflected in the early
name, the "Cannibal Islands." Not only cannibalism but extreme
warlike behavior and a plethora of cruel, callous and tyrannical
customs earned them this reputation. Compared with the Polyne-

sian groups, Fijians were Christianized much later. It wasn't until the early 1830s that Tongan missionaries came and they made little headway until thirty years later. Many of them ended up on the spit. As late as 1867, a white missionary was killed and eaten. Even though the Fijians make and sell cannibal forks, many of them are very sensitive about the subject. I learned through personal conversation with some of the educated Fijians that they deal with the subject by "distancing" themselves. For example, I asked one Methodist preacher when the Bible was translated into Fijian. He answered, "Hundreds of years ago!"

The colonial period began in 1874 when one of Fiji's principal chiefs, Thakombau, ceded the island to Queen Victoria. English planters came, determined to grow cotton. The Fijians refused to work on plantations for wages: Needing a cheap labor force, the planters initially brought in Solomon Islanders, even kidnapping them when they refused to come willingly. The British put a stop to these abuses by imposing the Polynesian Islanders Protection Act in 1872. Sugar cane finally replaced cotton as the Indian laborer replaced other islanders. Gradually the indenture system fell out of favor and the Indians became tenant farmers in 1916. This system continues today. On October 10, 1970, Fiji became a fully independent nation with a parliamentary form of government that actually included some power vested in the Fijian chiefs. In village life, the chief still rules and the structure here retains essentially the form it has had for centuries. A large part of the discussion following the coup has been to grant even more power and control to the chiefs and at the same time curtail Indian power and influence.

One of the major problems has been over land rights. The 1970 Constitution for Independence asserted that all persons born in Fiji would have equal rights. But the land laws have always favored the Fijians, forbidding Indians from owning the land they farm. This hurts the majority of the Indian population who grow cane. About 83 percent of the land is administered by the Native Lands Trust Board as inalienable Fijian land.

Despite these basic problems, pre-coup racial antagonism was minimal with Indians and Fijians often working and playing together.

Ironically English is the language that unites all of these peoples. Fijians speak several different dialects and Indians likewise speak several languages—Urdu and Hindi being the most prevalent. In order to communicate, everyone must know English and they do. To be sure the Indians have mastered English far better than the average Fijian, but even in the remotest village, most Fijians can get by with rudimentary English, and some, especially those who have worked for a time in Australia or New Zealand, speak quite well.

The current political situation in Fiji challenges whatever preconceived notions one may hold about democracy as the best form of government for everyone. No question about it, from the Indian point of view, democracy appears to be the only approach that could offer them any hope of equality. But democracy is absolutely the antithesis of Fijian communal life. Fijian life, as presently practiced in the villages, adheres to a hierarchal social structure. This ranking system pertains to chiefs, readily seen in various terms for chief—such as *ratu* and *tui*. Furthermore, chiefdom is inherited, not elected. The hierarchy runs right through families and exists within the family as well. For example, the oldest son will always be the most important of all the sons. He becomes head of the family when the father dies or decides he no longer wants to function in this capacity. The eldest son is privileged; he does not have to work. His brothers will supply him with food and so will his wife. Respect for the eldest son manifests in ways that may seem very strange to Westerners. In some villages, the eldest son's wife, even though she sees her brothers-in-law on a daily basis, may not speak to them or they to her! She speaks to them through her husband or through each of his brother's wifes.

In the order of rank, women are lesser than men. When women marry, they move to their husband's village. Naturally this is not a favored position, as it places her below the women in her husband's family. Even with education that has promoted literacy at an elementary level, it has still not altered the basic practice of using women as beasts of burden. They raise the children, tend the plantations, feed and care for domestic animals, wash, cook and go fishing almost daily to supply necessary protein. What do the men do? They may fish a little, engage for a few hours a week in a communal project, but the majority of their time is spent talking with each other, smoking and drinking *kava*, in general sitting around at ease.

To comprehend how difficult it is to come up with a kind of government that would serve Indians and Fijians equally well, one must understand the gulf existing between the two peoples. Most Fijians live in villages. They live a traditional way of life growing bananas, papayas, several root crops (tapioca being the main one) and fishing on the reef. Most villages have no electricity. Most Fijians have no strong feelings about the type of government they have, but they do have strong feelings about their lives in the village. What they don't want is all of Fiji being turned into a tourist resort. One of their biggest concerns is that if the Indians gain more political clout, Fiji will change as the Indians continue to expand industry and tremendously enlarge their tourist trade.

Indians, on the other hand, strive to educate themselves well and to increase their incomes. Those who own businesses that sell duty free goods of all kinds benefit considerably from the tourist industry. Indians are running other tourist related businesses—car rentals, hotels, resorts and restaurants. It is to their benefit to increase tourism. Above all, Indians want to propel themselves into a twentieth century urban lifestyle. Fijians wish to preserve the lifestyle they have, their simple village life.

It is difficult to fault either group with what they desire. Theirs is an intrinsic dilemma: what kind of government can serve the interests of both groups without infringing on the other's rights? The real irony, though, is that neither the Fijians nor the Indians are responsible for their present plight. Their disparity was engineered by the British who personally will lose nothing regardless of the final outcome.

One further irony prevails. Like so many underdeveloped countries today, Fiji is easily made a pawn to be bandied about, pushed and pulled between Western and Soviet power blocks. I wonder if this concept can be comprehended by more than a handful of Fijians. I'm convinced that Fijians, be they Melanesian or Indian, are politically naive. It is tragic.

I laughed the first time I heard the theory that the CIA engineered the Fiji coup. Months later, after coming upon bits and pieces of information from disparate sources, I found myself looking at the idea from a very different perspective. The motive: Fiji along with New Zealand is one of the South Pacific countries to take a positive stand against nuclear power and nuclear weapons. If the

US supported a rebel coup, in exchange the radical Fijians would gain military support from a major power and the US would gain another stronghold in the South Pacific, getting one up on the Soviets.

Plausible.

Chapter 16

Life Fijian Style

In order to cruise to some of the outlying islands, we had to visit the Fijian Affairs Office, place an itinerary before them and request permission to go. While this procedure may conjure up ideas of tyrannical red tape, I believe the idea is sound. Primarily it assures the Fijians that visitors have been instructed in the proper way to approach a village. One doesn't just barge into a village or start fishing or swimming in a lagoon. Lagoons, like the land, belong to people. Before doing anything, the visitor must go to the village and speak with the chief or the head man and ask permission to visit. The Fijian Affairs Officer explains the procedure to prevent misunderstanding. It would be wrong to disregard this protocol. Surprisingly many of the same customs also pertain to intervillage exchanges. For example, people from one village do not fish in another village's area without the chief's permission.

We decided to begin our cruising with the Astrolabe Reef. In preparation, we went to the large public market to provision with fresh vegetables and fruit. Crowds milled around stalls crammed full of picture perfect produce and piles of grains and spices—cinnamon, cloves, curry powders, garam masala, fenugreek, coriander. The wonderful scent permeated the air. Loaded down with two large tote bags, we got on the bus to return to the Royal Suva Yacht Club where we were anchored. Several Fijian ladies seated close by on the bus looked at me, smiled while saying *"bula bula"* and then giggled uproariously. I concluded it was because I was carrying a two-kilo bundle of *kava* root. Maybe they thought I was planning a big party. The *kava* root, though, was intended as gifts for various chiefs when visiting their villages.

At 0645 we, along with *Io*, powered across the flat, windless bay on our way to Ndravuni Island in the Astrolabe. By mid afternoon we had anchored in clear aquamarine water in front of the small village. Upon landing on the sandy beach we were met by a young man. We asked him to take us to the chief. Off we went, soon reaching the center of the village where all the village men were laying a large cement floor for the new community hall. We were escorted to an ugly old man with one tooth who was sitting on the sidelines. He was the chief. We each gave our names, extending our hands for a welcome shake. The chief spoke no English but instructed a young man to speak with us. He invited us to a nearby *bure* and took us around to a back door while the chief entered through the front door. We left our thongs outside and were gestured by the chief to sit next to him crosslegged on clean woven mats. In addition to the four of us and the chief were two young men who were our interpreters. The translators positioned themselves facing us seated in a semi-circle.

In the midst of us was a very big wooden *kava* bowl. I noticed it was quite full. George and I each presented our papers from the Fijian Affairs to the chief and then each of us placed a neatly tied bundle of *kava* in front of him. It would be impolite to hand the *kava* to a chief. *Kava* acts as a symbolic thing. If the chief picks it up, you have been accepted into the village. If, however, the chief doesn't touch it, you are not welcome. The older of the two interpreters began to read aloud in Fijian the permission papers which the chief had passed to him. Once the paper had been read, we asked the chief if we could visit several of his islands in the vicinity. *"Io,"* (Yes) he smiled. Could we return tomorrow to visit his village and take some photos? *"Io."*

Then he invited us to drink *kava* with him. Although I had not drunk *kava* in Tonga, somehow I sensed that in the present circumstances it would be rude of me to abstain. *Kava* is presented to people in their order of rank. Naturally the chief had the first cup. George was second because he is a male captain. I was third because I was also a captain, but being female, of lesser rank than a male! Jan and Joy were next and the two translators last. We asked instructions for drinking *kava*. Clap once before accepting the *kava* cup—half coconut shell. Drink the entire portion down in one gulp and clap three times. While this was happening, the chief and two young men were chanting and clapping. This is the *sevu sevu* ceremony. It is a binding ceremony in which the chief pledged to take us under his protection for the duration of our stay. Before leaving we would need to take formal leave of the chief.

Rather soon after downing the slug of *kava*, my tongue began to tingle. We continued to talk back and forth. Billy, the 17-year-old interpreter, expressed his surprise several times that Joy and I had sailed to Fiji from Los Angeles. The young man wondered if we listened to the news and what did we think of the coalition? For once language differences acted in our favor. None of us wanted to get in a political discussion. Very adamantly Billy stated that Fijians don't like Indians. His sentiments, fortunately, are not typical. I felt his was the voice of youth. After a bit more conversation and a second round of *kava*, the four of us thanked the chief for his hospitality and we left.

On the second day after a tour of the village, accompanied by the chief's three-year-old grandson—who chattered non-stop to us in Fijian—and an entourage of older children, we left for the nearby smaller island Yaukuve. Only two Fijian families live here. There were five other yachts already anchored here. Most nights we had communal feasts on the shore—the day's catch of fish wrapped in banana leaves and cooked over a wood fire—and other dishes brought ashore from each yacht. Always we invited the two Fijian families to join us. They did and ate the tasty dishes with gusto.

On Yaukuve, we witnessed for the first time one of the Fijian's favorite pastimes—setting fires. We didn't know the import or the extent of this activity then, but we did think it unusual. We thought the fire strange because a very strong minor storm system came in towards evening. It blew very intensely for several hours and we watched with concern as the fire ashore blazed out of control very near the dwellings. When we spoke to the Fijians the next day, they seemed totally blasé about the fire. Why were they burning? To clear land for their plantation. This was the standard answer we always got, but we noticed that the area of land cleared always greatly exceeded the planted area. In fact, entire islands are denuded in this manner. Of course the repeated burning sets in motion a destructive cycle of land erosion and consequently, without vegetation, rain does not come. In a short time the land is turned into a desert. Much of the burning appears to be "recreational," that is, a big fire out of control provides excitement. But burning or setting fire is an age-old form of revenge in Fiji. In some areas of Fiji, New Zealand and Australia have provided money to reforest some land. Many of the reforestation projects are set afire just when the lumbering begins. The Fijians feel they get so little money for their trees while some middle man, usually an Indian, makes a killing on the timber. So, in anger, the Fijians burn the remaining trees.

Asete, 21, married to a man whose family has traditionally lived on Yaukuve, invited Joy, Jan and me to go walking on the island with her. She spoke English quite well. With us also was Lisa, the six-year-old daughter of Liku. Even at that young age Lisa knew the island, what things were dangerous or harmless and how to gather food from ocean, reef and shore. Much of the time she was in the lead, pointing out things of interest. Lisa knew no English, so Asete explained for her.

Asete told us several legends and myths involving Yaukuve. One was how the spring of Yaukuve was first discovered. Once many years ago when no one lived on this island, a grandmother and her grandson were left here alone. After a while the young child began to cry because he wanted some water. Just as the grandmother was explaining to the child that there was no water here as on Kandavu, the main island in the Astrolabe, the spring started flowing right out of the rock on which she was sitting. Since that day the water has continued to flow and that is why the Qovu family has been able to live on this island for years and years.

The Qovu family still lives here. The spring is used for bathing and laundry, but is not suitable for drinking because of salt intrusion.

Another bit of folklore Asete told us concerns the Devil and devils. According to her, before the missionaries came, the Devil ruled this island. Christianity drove the Devil out. Today, however, there are still little devils here—like children—and they do prankish things. In fact these devils frighten some people so much that they stay clear of the island. Only the day before yesterday Asete's husband went to the spring for a bath. He set the soap down and turned away momentarily. When he turned back to pick up his soap, it was gone! The little devils had hidden it.

Asete told us about the devils with a half embarrassed, half apologetic expression. I thought her feelings stemmed from concern about how we would accept what she was saying. Our response was to accept it just as we would anything she might tell us about Yaukuve.

After almost two weeks, we left Yaukuve and together with *Io* sailed to Mbengga, a rather large island about 15 miles southwest of Suva. A large barrier reef surrounds the island, making it, for the most part, a very comfortable place to anchor. We had a vigorous sail to Malumu Bay, one of the larger bays on the island. The bay is breath-taking in its splendor. The dark green water cuts through high, densely overgrown hills. At its head, various rivers and streams disappear into the emerald jungle. Immediately I felt myself drawn to this unknown mysterious beauty and decided that I was going on a river exploration the next day. Little did I know just how it would evolve.

About an hour after we had anchored, a long flat-bottomed boat came along side *Banshee*. Smiling up at us was a very handsome young man in his twenties and two young boys. He inquired if we would like some crabs. We agreed on a very reasonable price. Savenaca (the "c" is pronounced "th") asked if we would like to come to his village the next day for a visit and for some bananas. Yes, we would. He gave us directions, saying he would meet us at the bridge at eleven.

We left too late. The tide was almost at dead low. The water had dried out leaving thick mud and mangroves between us and the river, which was rapidly going down too. An older man on the reef kept waving. We went to him and learned he was Savenaca Senior. His wife, Liku Bula, was with him in a long boat. They knew about their son's invitation and offered to take us up the river and to their village. We got out and sank to our knees in the oozing mud, but with their help, we managed to pole, portage and wade up the river with our dinghies through huge mangroves and thick rain forest. Much of the time the area was bathed in misty rain. As the tide fell even more, it revealed a complex jumble of mangrove roots along the river bank. Bird calls resounded from the solid green canopy and wonderful luxuriant ferns clung to massive branches. Barefooted, we hobbled over the stony river bottom until we could momentarily jump in and paddle over a deep spot or pole our way up the winding tea-colored river.

At the bridge where we tied up our dinghies, the river had shrunk to a mere trickle. Then we followed the rangy Savenaca along a narrow path. It had been hand cut with a machete through thick jungle that towered overhead. Along the way we came to a ridge overlooking the bay where our two yachts quietly rested at anchor. Misty rains came and went, wetting us and draping the landscape with an ethereal gauze. Finally, after climbing for a long

143

time, the path led downhill and within a short distance we came upon a garden planted in *dalo* (*taro*) cassava, papayas and bananas. Then we reached a summit looking down on the village. A very steep, well-worn clay trail angled down to Dakuni which lies on the opposite side of the island, facing a wide lagoon on the southeastern side.

Village children sounded the alarm as we approached, laughing and calling out to us. Adults, noticing us, gave a friendly wave or cheerfully called out *"bula"* or "good morning."

Savenaca was a superb organizer. His abilities earned him the nickname "Used car salesman." Before we had arrived at Dakuni he had convinced George and me to give him a bundle of *kava* even before we went to see the chief. And before the day was over, Savenaca managed to persuade us to go to the little store (he even got the owner to open up) so we could buy him several packs of cigarettes and a can or two of corned beef.

Savenaca took us to his *bure* where his son and several other men were sitting around the kava bowl. Their glazed eyes and languid behavior told us they had been imbibing steadily for some time. As we sat there drinking *kava* and talking with Savenaca Senior, one by one, other villagers dropped in to meet us. We kept moving back to enlarge the circle. Two of Savenaca's daughters came in. Until then, Joy, Jan and I were the only women present.

After several cups of *kava* and one of tea, Savenaca decided it was time for us to meet Ratu Whami, a high chief. A man near 80, and his white hair gleaming, Ratu Whami greeted us in flawless English, laughed jovially and proceeded to tell us about his days in the Solomon Islands during the Second World War. He pointed to photos of his comrades in arms prominently hung in his beautifully constructed thatched *bure*. We presented him with a *kava* bundle and some native tobacco which Savenaca had told us he was partial to. We politely declined Ratu Whami's *kava*, telling Savenaca had seen to our *kava* needs quite generously

Savenaca took us on a tour of his village. I was struck by the open friendliness of the people who came up and introduced themselves and shook our hands. Three or four children, the little ones especially, followed us everywhere in every village and delighted in coming up to touch us. White skin is still a source of wonder to them.

We were anchored between two villages and knew we had to

present ourselves to the head man at Lalati, too. In fact he had sent someone out to inquire about us when we'd been there about 24 hours. In we went with our obligatory papers and our gift of *kava*. Lalati is a sparkling village situated between two hillsides on a calm bay, much more prosperous looking than Dakuni and much tidier.

As we approached Lalati, an attractive young woman came to greet us and took us to Daniel, the head man. He was sitting with about ten other men and a couple of children in a half completed building with a floor and roof made of blocks and timber. We paused because the group was chanting and clapping, performing a *kava* ceremony. As usual we were graciously welcomed and had *sevu sevu* before a young woman proudly took us on a tour of the compact village.

Much to the credit of these islanders, Mbengga is the only island we visited in Fiji that was not being burned to the ground. One can only hope they will continue to let their green island flourish.

Chapter 17

The Yasawas

High volcanic islands with isolated beaches, steep cliffs and colorful reefs characterize the Yasawas. This chain of six islands lies northwest of Viti Levu. On our way to the Yasawas we stopped off at Navandra, locally known as the "Haunted Island." Actually there are two uninhabited islands here, the other is called Vanua Levu, not to be confused with the big island of the same name. Both are tricky to approach as they lie behind a submerged reef that is not visible in settled weather. *Banshee* and *Io* arrived in settled weather. About two hours later it became unsettled.

Southeasterlies came up so that the wind was blowing on shore. Still, we wanted to go ashore because the setting was wild and beautiful. Deserted islands have a special appeal. Strong winds sent the surf crashing on the steep sandy, rock strewn shore. Knowing it would be a difficult landing (we learned a lesson not to be soon forgotten in Omoa on Fatu Hiva when we were overturned), Joy and I removed the outboard from the dinghy and rowed ashore. The trick to landing in surf is to approach the shore with the bow out, pointing into the seas so the skiff rises to the swell. Joy sat in the stern rowing so she could watch the surf. I could see where we were going and thus guide her through the patches of reef and coral heads. We had to maneuver three surf lines before it was shallow enough to step out of the dinghy and walk over the "sheet" coral to the beach. At low tide the sand mound rose 20 to 30 feet and proved to be a treasure chest for shells. Particularly in abundance were turban shells, most of them inhabited by hermit crabs. From the crest of the exposed hill we could see the other side of the island, its shallows a lace work of variegated blue and green.

At one end of the beach a huge volcanic formation jutted up with a wide band running through the middle that looked like molten iron long ago trapped and sandwiched in the lava flows. Heavy foliage covered much of the small island as it is not subject to constant burning.

That night we discovered why Navandra is called the haunted

island. Heavy winds kicked up a nasty swell. In the moonlight, looking shoreward we could see the froth of wild seas and looking behind us—perhaps 50 yards—a deafening sound of blind rollers as they smashed violently into the reef we had so carefully passed on our way in. The wind rose and fell from moan to shriek, humanlike, unnerving, blasting from one direction and madly veering to another direction. The entire area was shimmering, as if caught up by an uncanny supernatural power. Later a Fijian told me that the moaning sounds were the voices of seven fishermen who had disappeared here and hence the name Haunted Island.

After two uncomfortable days of horrendous rocking and thrashing, we decided to leave and head for Waya, the southernmost island of the Yasawas. Before leaving we reefed both the main and the staysail and carefully plotted out our course, knowing these were treacherous waters. What a wild sight. Off our starboard, blind rollers foaming with fury created waves with curling white tops. Looking off the port bow, we saw green water and spray as the seas collided with the reef extending off the point. Despite lurking dangers, it was an outstandingly beautiful day of wall to wall blue skies!

It was Sunday. We drove our two dinghies toward the beach at Naluwaki Village on Waya. A group of children charged out into the shallow water eager to land our dinghies for us. The entire village was expecting us as we'd told them the previous day that we'd like to attend the church service.

A very attractive young woman named Ullamulla, from the Lau group, acted as our hostess, escorting us to the village. She is married to a fisherman from this village. They lived in Suva but were visiting his family.

Once in the village we were invited to the preacher's *bure* to wait until time for church. The preacher sat against one wall. He was finely clad in a pressed dark blue suit coat, white shirt and tie. Around his waist he wore a nicely tailored *sulu*. Proudly he showed us his two Bibles: one in Fijian, one in American English. Church was announced first by the ringing of the bell and then by drumming on the *lali*—a hollowed out section of log. We were escorted into the new building, not yet completed, and seated on the platform at the front of the church along with the preacher and several elders. The entire congregation sat on the floor, as did we. In front were the

147

children, youngest first. In the middle were the women singers and on the other side the male choir members. Toward the back were a scattering of women with infants, breast feeding them when deemed necessary. And, finally, at the very back, the young men. At the conclusion of the service, George and Jan were invited to the preacher's for Sunday feast while Joy and I went to the home of a young couple with a newborn baby. We were seated in their *bure* and served fish soup made with coconut cream, boiled fish and boiled cassava root—the usual fare in Fijian villages.

We had the large Pickmere charts of the Yasawas. These are the most recent charts of the area; even so they are out of date. This is cause for concern in coral waters. If the sun is at your back, no problem, because reefs are quite visible then. Unfortunately, in August the sun is in the northern quarter so sailing north in the Yasawas meant poor or restricted visibility for reef spotting.

Our closest call was going from Natuvale Bay on Naviti Island to Nanuva-Sewa Island (the Blue Lagoon). As we discovered, this area contains countless uncharted reefs and shallow patches. The winds, cooking at 25 knots, moved us along at a good clip. Even on the western side where we were somewhat protected from the wind, white caps heaped up, carried atop moderate swells. Most of the terrain was dry and barren, but occasional green spots flourished where the hillside had not been ravaged by the national sport of "flaming the land."

Suddenly, looking over the side, I saw the bottom! The depth sounder dropped to 24 feet and steadily continued to drop. Where to steer? I couldn't distinguish the water's color. I alerted Joy who ran to the bow to watch. We survived several such episodes with accelerated heartbeats. George and Jan had the advantage of being behind us. We could tell them when not to follow us. Looking astern, we could easily distinguish color and tell them what course to steer.

As we rounded the northern tip of the island into a very brisk wind, *Banshee* heeled over smartly and the water hissed past our bow. Funnelled between the two islands, the wind roared into the narrow reef-strewn pass. We began short tacking in 30 knots through a pass bounded by reefs on every side! So as to be able to point a little higher and have more punch, we turned on the engine and motor sailed through the windswept passage. Once in the lee of Nanuya-Sewa, conditions moderated. We wanted to anchor in the Blue Lagoon, next to Turtle Island. We were coming to visit our Fijian friend Vilise and his family. We had met Vilise in Tonga. He was cruising with some friends of ours for several months. He invited us to visit him when we came to Fiji

The lagoon was studded with fingers of reef almost impossible to see since we were facing directly into the sun. Slowly we crept along, one eye looking down into the water, the other on the depth sounder. Finally we selected a place and put down the hook. Unfortunately we had positioned ourselves directly opposite the slot between Nanuya-Sewa and Turtle Island. Later we reanchored in a more protected place.

We had barely anchored when a kayak we had spotted earlier coming in from the other side of the island came along side us. We were surprised when we realized the occupant was a young woman. She looked rather bedraggled, windblown and her eyes—unprotected by sunglasses—were very red.

Her first words after a greeting were, "When you go back to the mainland, can you mail some postcards for me?" We explained we had just arrived and had no intention of returning to Lautoka for some time. I sensed that she was very tired and could use a rest. "Would you like to come aboard and have a cup of coffee or tea and relax?"

"Coffee! Oh, I'd really love some coffee." We soon learned Lynne Davies, an Australian, had kayaked from Lautoka to the Yasawas! Her ambition was to circumnavigate the Yasawas in her kayak. No wonder she was bedraggled and windblown. That day she had come almost the same distance as we, but she was on the windward side of the island, paddling against a 25 knot tradewind! She had lost her sunglasses and the glare was bothering her eyes. I dug out my spare sunglasses and insisted she take them. There was no place in the Yasawas to buy sunglasses.

We sent a note to Vilise with a Fijian who paddled up to talk with us. An hour or so later Vilise came out in his long boat, all smiles and extremely surprised to see us. We had arrived at a perfect time, he said, as there was to be a feast in his village that night. It was a celebration for a baby that was ten days old. They would be having turtle, the food eaten at such a celebration. Lynne had been camping out every night on the beach. Vilise invited her to stay with his family in their *bure.*

Close to sundown Vilise came to pick us up. We would tow our dinghy and he would show us where to anchor it. Now was high tide and small boats could pass between the two islands, but the tide would be low when we wanted to come back to *Banshee* later that night.

Normally there was no chief in Vilise's village, only his extended family. But tonight the chief had come from another island to attend the festivities. So we brought *kava*. Lynne, Joy and I were taken to the *bure* where the chief was drinking *kava* with other men. Vilise introduced us to the chief. We sat down and had *sevu sevu*—three women with 20 or 30 men! The *bure* was jam packed. And what an unusual experience for these Fijian men and for us. They were astounded to hear Lynne had kayaked alone to the Yasawas from Lautoka and was paddling around the entire chain. They were further astounded to learn Joy and I had sailed across the Pacific from L.A.! We were inundating this small gathering with more than its share of independent women. They handled it well, with grace and unhidden respect. Fijians have a habit of clicking their tongues when amazed. There was a lot of tongue clicking that night.

After two rounds of *kava* and much animated conversation, Vilise escorted us outside to his wife Salome, who thought we might be ready to eat. We followed her to the other end of the village to a *bure* where everyone sat in two long rows facing each other with the cassava spread out on banana leaves between them. We were given a shallow bowl and told to eat. Soon a tin dish filled with broth and pieces of turtle was passed down to us. I noticed others dunking cassava into the broth and eating with their hands. I followed suit but very soon a large spoon was respectfully handed to me with a broad smile. The light was too dim to see what I was eating, but my mouth detected pieces of varying consistency. Some were rather chewy, others of grainier quality of say a piece of canned beef, and then the soft unresisting pieces of fat. I saw something in my bowl with strange spongelike extrusions. It was whitish. I asked Lynne if she knew what it was. She shook her head no. Did she feel adventurous? I didn't want to eat it. Yes. So, I slipped it into her bowl. Later she said it was delicious. It was turtle throat!

After dinner Salome dropped us off at another *bure* for a cup of tea. Present were women and children and only one man. No one spoke much English but we managed and enjoyed the hot tea served, as it is everywhere in the South Pacific, in a bowl rather than a cup.

The evening ended with us returning to the original *bure* for more *kava* drinking. Again, we were the only women present. We were guests of honor and this was how they acknowledged it.

The following day Lynne left to continue her cicumnavigation of the islands. She promised to stay with us for a few days upon her return. She returned several days later, and we enjoyed her novel stories of adventure, including her days as crew member on the Australian tall ship, *Eye of the Wind*.

Toward the end of August another special celebration occurred. We took *Banshee* across the bay and anchored with many Fijian boats that had come from all over Fiji to attend the fiftieth anniversary of the Catholic Mission School where Vilise's father went when the school opened as a single *bure*.

This was no event whipped up for tourists. It was a native celebration, a strange blend of Christian and old Fijian customs. We arrived about half an hour before the outdoor mass was completed. Crowds of people sat on woven mats spread over the ground in the shade of palm thatch. Only the archbishop, priests and other men of the cloth were seated on chairs in an area where the posts were decorated with fresh flowers.

At the conclusion of the mass, school children danced and sang. The singers and musicians who pounded bamboo sticks for rhythm sat in a circle. They provided music for the dancing children—all girls.

After that bit of entertainment, the feast, which had been in preparation since the previous day, was ready to serve. The Fijian men had constructed very ingenious earth ovens. The fire was built in the ground where holes had been carved out and huge cast iron pots sat on top of the ground over the fires. The style in which people were fed testified to the Fijian idea of social rank. The dignitaries—mostly priests and nuns and village chiefs—were seated at their own mat. Their menu differed considerably from that eaten by us commoners. They had an array of special foods, including salads, fresh fruit and meat. The masses ate from the common pot. We lined up—adults after the children—for roots such as tapioca and various kinds of yams that were spread out on a table on top of banana leaves. Another line ended at big pots of beef stew, curried beef and curried fish. At another table one could obtain slices of roast pig. They had slaughtered two cows and two pigs for the event.

Following the noon meal, we were treated to more entertainment. This time women danced. Once again the musicians sat in a circle. The harmony was dissonant, sung in interesting rhythmic patterns that set-up a pull between male and female voices. It was certainly Fijian music, not western music. What got the most applause was comic dancing done by men. They imitated the women's dancing. Not to be outdone, once the men finished, two women got up and imitated the men! The crowd was ecstatic.

It was too late to return to the Blue Lagoon that evening. In the morning the sun was in our eyes. Vilise came on board with his family to guide us back to our anchorage. I could hardly believe his appearance. He had a black eye and a nasty cut above his eye. He was very subdued, not at all characteristic of his vibrant and playful personality. Salome told us he had gotten in a fight the previous night while drinking *kava*. It was his second night on *kava* with no sleep.

We stayed five weeks at the Blue Lagoon, breaking it up by sailing north after the third week and returning after about a week for another two-week stay. We made almost daily visits to Enedala, Vilise's village. Often we brought our laundry to wash in their well water. An eight-month drought in western Fiji meant fresh water was at a premium. Our drinking water came from the Blue Lagoon tourist boats. They also brought water to villagers. We bathed strictly in salt water, using just a little fresh water to rinse our hair. We also brought our oars to the village to sand and paint.

Vilise and Salome were easy to be with. Sometimes we brought items of food and spare pieces of line or other odds and ends that Vilise or Salome could use. Often they would serve us a meal or tea. Vilise built a very attractive main *bure* where he and Salome and their son and daughter sleep and where they served us wonderfully delicious meals. Salome once made a gourmet meal of two kinds of fish, each cooked in a delicate sauce. This was served with a tasty salad made from *nama*, a berrylike seaweed. In addition to their main *bure,* they have a small one where they usually eat breakfast, a cooking *bure*, a storage *bure* and a *bure* outhouse as well as a very small enclosed area where one can bathe in a wash tub. Sometimes we had them on board for a meal. Nothing put a smile on Salome's face faster than being served chicken or pork—she's tired of fish, having it every day. They both like curry, but Vilise's favorite food is spaghetti.

So often where Hollywood steps in to film spells the ruin of a beautiful place. No so the Blue Lagoon—at least not yet. And like all settings it can have different faces. I can do no better than describe it as I saw it on two occasions. As we walked along the beach one afternoon all was still. A very low tide exposed mounds of yellow sandbars and a zigzagged shoreline. No one was in sight and no human sounds. If I didn't know better, I would have thought the area uninhabited. I could see the village across the lagoon but no sign of life. And around the point lies Enedala, not at all visible from this vantage point. I thought of Enedala with its neat *bures* blending with the vegetation, all sitting silently facing the broad reefs that break the sea as it rolls shoreward on the windward side of the island.

The only sounds were bird calls or the sudden rush of wings. I looked out over the famous Blue Lagoon. Today it could be called the Gray Lagoon. The still, silent Gray Lagoon. Water and sky blended; a monochromatic world. Silence is the color of gray on gray on gray. The coconut trees hung listless in the humid air like limp appendages of a sleeping giant. The Blue Lagoon at rest. On another day it would come alive with brilliant sapphire water, hard edged against the light green that laps the golden tongues of sand. Now all was grayness dissolving into silence.

On another day, it was very different. Our trips to the village were determined by the tide. Usually we preferred high tide. About an hour before and after high water we could easily get through the narrow pass between the two islands by dinghy. At the narrowest point the islands are about 50 feet apart. A deep channel zigzags over the sandbar at the entrance from the Blue Lagoon side. At low water the whole area dries, allowing one to walk over the wet sand past lines of mangroves on each side. The channel leads to a much larger area separating the two islands. Going through about an hour and a half before high tide one morning was a challenge. The 20 plus knot wind swept right down the channel, ruffling the water. Areas were still too shallow for the outboard, so we poled or paddled or walked the dinghy through the shallows. Once through the channel the water deepened enough for the outboard. We were beam to the wavelets coming at us from the open sea. The scene looking back to the Blue Lagoon was outstanding. Rows of rounded mountains in the background, an array of gray tones and earth colors, set off by patches of green waving palms. The foreground vibrated with bright green mangroves bobbing furiously atop their reddish branches. The sea was a sparkling moss green with golden patches flashing amidst forest green where grass covered the bottom. And seaward, brilliant stripes of cobalt blue alternating with deep blue ribbons. Here and there slivers of sandbar in bas relief looked like prehistoric lizards.

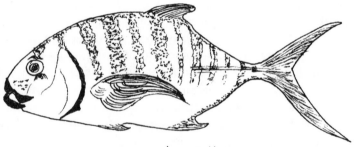

golden trevally

Chapter 18

Beware of False Tuis!

Maria, Vilise's mother, loved hearing about our adventures for the two weeks we temporarily left the Blue Lagoon. Our first stop was at Nacula Island, Maria's birth place. She knew all the people we met there and the events—which I'll soon describe—brought gales of laughter from her. For once because of our connections with Vilise's family, the Fijian "con game" eventually backfired and left some members of Nacula village embarrassed. They'll not forget the two American women on *Banshee* for some time.

On September 3, we dropped our hook in Nakerelevu Bay, a lovely spot on the west side of Nacula Island. Here we were securely tucked in behind a deserted island named Yaromo. I could hardly wait to dinghy over and explore the miniature paradise. Neither of us wanted at that moment to deal with the hassle of a dinghy trip into Nacula village for *sevu sevu*. This was a mistake! After all we knew the protocol.

No more than half a mile long, Yaromo nonetheless presents a variety of landscapes. One end is steep volcanic rock of elaborate patterns where the sea has carved for eons. On the ridge where volcanic soil has collected, a stand of ironwood trees sway and sigh as the wind sweeps over them. The remaining half of the island is smooth sand beach planted in coconut palms and pandanas.

Extending from one side of the island out into clear aquamarine water is an extensive sandspit where opposing seas meet head on. At this point incoming seas are divided and redirected, causing the wavelets to come from two different directions as they lap the smooth golden sand.

We landed near the sandspit in shallow water and immediately sank down in the soft sand. Dragging the dinghy above the water line, we pressed the anchor firmly into the sand. Right above the high watermark was a collection of broken shells and coral pieces left behind from a higher tide, perhaps a past storm. Soon we walked across the sandy interior to the seaward side of the island. Here long flows of black lava rock were flattened and intricately sculpted. On this side the reef extended out a good half mile. The sea pounded on the reef, sending cascades of white foam over numerous coral outcroppings. Enjoying the warmth, seabirds sat on the exposed reef, their breasts facing the sun. Interesting tidepools lay in between the rugged lava forms. On the surface they were quiet, but in their shallow depths, a tiny world, a microcosm, existed, thriving, reproducing. Erosion had worked an amazing variety of lacelike designs into the rock.

For close to half an hour we leisurely walked among the lava formations and then on the smooth beach, taking some photos and finding an occasional shell. Feeling relaxed, we sat on the beach to talk and enjoy the incredible scene.

It was then, after sitting so for perhaps fifteen minutes, that we noticed a native boat approaching *Banshee*. It disappeared from sight as it moved to the far side of the boat. We weren't terribly concerned because we had locked the boat. Quickly the native boat shot back into view and we could see two men sitting in the boat. Spotting our dinghy, the driver turned the boat towards us. As they approached the shore we walked towards them. A handsome young man, the driver, told us he was Pio and the thin gray haired man with him was the *tui*, the high chief of Nacula Island. Pio rather sternly told us we should not have come to Yaromo without first clearing it with the *tui* in Nacula village. We apologized and said we would gladly come in the morning—it was then about 4:30. Pio was most polite but insisted we should have *sevu sevu* immediately—that was what the *tui* wanted.

With this development, we invited them to come aboard *Banshee* so we could present our papers and our bundle of *Kava*. I had a few twinges. Something just didn't seem quite right. But I said nothing. Joy presented the *kava*, placing it in front of the *tui*. He touched the roots; then he and Pio began clapping and chanting. The only words we understood were "Los Angeles," "America" and "Fiji."

We then served them coffee and cookies. Pio's English was good. Periodically he translated for the *tui* who spoke no English. Pio expressed interest in some of our electronic equipment and asked intelligent questions about their operation. He was especially fascinated by the SatNav when we explained how it worked.

Before leaving, Pio asked if we would like some fruit. We said that would be very nice and asked if we could perhaps have some fresh water from their village. He assured us that would be no problem. In fact, if we gave him our jugs he would bring the water to us himself. We asked if we could visit the village in the morning and he said we could.

The next morning, we left about two hours after high tide. We had to cross about three-quarters of a mile of reef between our anchorage and the village. With the tide falling, crossing was difficult at times. Occasionally we had to tip the outboard up, turn it off and momentarily row. But it was a spectacular run over the coral with numerous shapes and colors spreading out only three to four feet below us and scads of fish darting in and out of their hiding places.

Coming into the shore, who should we see but Pio and the *tui* carrying our water jugs out to load into Pio's boat which floated in the shallows. Now, seeing the *tui* carrying our water jug, I knew something was amiss. I looked at Joy. Her expression told me that the same suspicion was going through her mind! But we said nothing. We both know that *tuis* don't go out in long boats chasing down yachties and they don't deliver water! Pio pointed to a large basket filled with papayas. These were for us he said.

Pio offered to take us around his village. After anchoring our dinghy we followed him. A very attractive village, Nacula is also the largest on the island. Most dwellings were thatch, but a few of cement block with corrugated iron roofs stood out, being ill-fitting and ugly. Growing everywhere were tremendous sized breadfruit trees whose big boughs of hand-shaped leaves provided large areas of shade. I commented on them and Pio said they were known throughout the Yasawas for their breadfruit. Finally reaching the end of the village, we stopped where a group of people were gathered around an older man who was carving a stick, making a spear for catching fish bait. He signalled us over and introduced himself, extending his hand for a shake. He was Pio's older brother.

After a few minutes we were invited inside the brother's *bure* where we were joined by about ten family members who crowed around the mat where a feast was spread. The menu consisted of boiled tapioca, boiled fish, octopus cooked in coconut cream, fish soup and canned sardines in tomato sauce with onions. Quite a spread for lunch. Hundreds of flies, it seemed, had come too. Some of the younger children fanned with one hand, eating with the other. At the end of the meal we were served a bowl of tea.

So, here we were. The man who had deceived us about the *tui* now brought us here for a large meal. For the duration of our stay Pio brought us fresh fruit every day! Obviously Pio did not want to cheat us—he merely wanted the *kava* and just went about getting it in a surreptitious way!

Maria laughed and laughed about this episode. I know the next time she saw Pio she shamed him about his actions. She knews what he didn't, that we would have given him some *kava*!

Our next stop in the Yasawa chain was Sawa-i-lau, a place very famous for its wonderful caves. We anchored next to a high island marvelously chiseled by time and erosion into fantastic shapes. Our first stop ashore was at the village, located on another island, for *sevu sevu*. Here we paid our one dollar each to visit the cave.

The cave's entrance lies but a short climb up cement stairs added to make the ascent easier for the large number of visitors coming on the Blue Lagoon Cruises. We waited until the boat and its tourists had gone so we had the cave to ourselves. After entering, more steps led us down into the cave to a large pool. We changed into our swim suits and diving masks and jumped in for a swim to explore the cave's natural wonders. The underwater part is as spectacular as the portion above water. We knew there was an underwater entrance to another cave but were unsuccessful in our attempts to find it. Never mind, there was enough to see right in the cave where we were. Certain underwater areas were spotlighted by shafts of sunlight falling through openings in the wall and ceiling. What a sensation to swim in this mysterious realm. The only sign of humankind was some graffiti.

Later, at low tide, we walked around the back side of this island, admiring incredible rock formations that extended to the top of the tall mountain. It was here, just a bit inland, that we discovered an ancient sanctuary laid out with stones in a fashion similar to some we had seen in the Society Islands. The existence of the sanctuary was astounding because I have never seen any mention of such areas in Fiji. I took pictures so I could later compare it with sites we have visited all across the Pacific.

We knew that very few cruisers sail to the northernmost village of the Yasawas. But, after reading a description of the area, we wanted to sail there. What sold me on it was the sand. Vilise said it was like walking in flour. To me that recalled the soft sandy beaches on Florida's Gulf of Mexico. I would probably go anywhere to find sand that squeaks when you walk on it.

It was a place neither Joy nor I will ever forget—not all for positive reasons, unfortunately. The day was perfect; blue skies and pleasant trade winds made for a fine sail. We sailed right up into the very broad bay in front of the most picturesque Fijian village we've seen anywhere. The village, Yasawairara, faces a wide, curved beach with sand that *was* soft as flour. When we arrived, there was a strong offshore breeze creating very large rollers that crashed on shore, making a landing untenable. A worse problem soon made itself apparent. The hillside behind this picture postcard village was ablaze! Smoke and ash followed a direct path to us. Giant pieces of ash rained down upon our decks. Ash, along with tons of smoke, poured down our hatches and through our open ports. We had just anchored and wanted to have a late lunch and relax, and we needed some time to decide what to do. We closed the hatches and ports and, in the stifling heat, ate a hurriedly put together lunch.

After carefully looking around the large harbor and consulting our chart, we decided it was safe to anchor on the other side of the harbor which had the additional advantage of a non-surfy beach.

It was 3:30 in the afternoon by the time we had resettled ourselves, gathered our bundle of *kava* for the chief and put on our shore togs—*sulus*. We rowed ashore and made a nice landing in silky sand. It felt so good on our feet! Two men approached and the introductions went around as we shook hands. After a brief conversation with a well spoken young man, Katty or Kitti, we told him we would like to see the chief of the village for *sevu sevu*. He said, "Right over here," and escorted us toward a *bure* just off the beach. A man sat on the ground husking coconuts. Katti said this was the man whom we should present *kava*.

Again, we were so trusting when we should have been skeptical. But it was a little while before we realized we had been conned again! There followed a clapping, chanting ceremony without *kava* drinking—there was none available there. After a brief conversation, we asked if we could go to the village. Permission was granted, but when we started off down the beach walking toward the village a half mile away, someone called out excitedly to us and began motioning that we should walk in another direction. But we responded that we wanted to go to the village along the beach. No further objection was raised.

Shortly after we entered the village, however, a man hurried over to us and said we had to have *sevu sevu* with the mayor of the village! We were shocked and responded that we had just had *sevu sevu*. No, he insisted, we had not. Follow him. On the way we told him our story. He said we should tell it to the mayor. We did, after signing in his visitor's book. He was visibly upset. He wanted the obligatory *kava*. We said we had no more *kava* because we had given it to the other man. We learned that this was a common occurrence. Nonetheless, the mayor seemed upset at us. I was upset with him and suggested that they should police their own people. How could they expect us, strangers, to know who was the correct person to see? We trusted the honesty of their villagers. My argument fell on deaf ears, but I suspect because it was a case of loosing face. The mayor also questioned why we had moved our boat. We should be anchored in front of their village, he insisted. I tried to explain we had moved because of the smoke. It was impossible to breathe and we didn't want ash all over the outside and inside of our boat. My explanation went unheard. He kept insisting we reanchor in front of the village. We could bring *kava* the next time we came in.

We left the village, went straight to our dinghy and back to *Banshee*. Joy and I discussed what had happened. Both of us felt very put off by the deceit and the mayor's lack of understanding. We decided we would leave early the next morning and return to the Blue Lagoon and our friends.

I think, in retrospect, that this was an instance of very different customs coming into conflict. According to our sense of justice, the mayor should have understood our plight. We were visitors. But I think Fijian custom is that there are no extenuating circumstances. A visitor should/must go to the mayor with *kava* and must anchor in front of the village. Nothing, absolutely nothing, changes these requirements.

The next morning we left Yasawairara, which I dubbed "Ash Hole," and had a beautiful and very fast passage back home—to Vilise's family and the Blue Lagoon.

Joy and I talked about whether to tell Vilise and Salome what had happened in Nacula and "Ash Hole." Joy thought we should not but I thought no harm would be done and I wanted to know what we should have done. Vilise and Salome were appalled by the deceptions. They also assured us we had done nothing wrong. Vilise explained that some Fijians just want the *kava* and whatever gifts may be forthcoming. Such Fijians think that passing yachties know no one so their actions will go unnoticed. This time, there will be reverberations all the way up to Yasawairara because Vilise personally knows the characters involved.

Sooner or later all good things must end. On September 13, with a lot of sadness, we said our goodbyes to Vilise's family and left the Blue Lagoon. We wanted to sail to Malololailai, a resort area where many yachts were congregating in preparation for the Malololailai-Port Vila race. Although we weren't going to Vanuatu and would not be racing, many of our friends were. This would be the last time we'd see some of them. Also, we wanted to participate in the prerace week activities.

Daniel, Vilise's brother, offered to go with us as a guide back to Lautoka. With him along we could cut through the reef—something too hazardous to do without local knowledge—and make the passage in one day instead of two. We had a lovely sail, dragging two fishing lines astern. Daniel caught two beautiful fish—a large walu and a travali. We had no strikes on our line. To ease our disappointment, Daniel kindly presented the travali to us in Lautoka.

When the racers left on September 27 for Port Vila, it was a gray and windless day. It was a depressing day, partly because we were one of only five yachts left anchored at Malololailai. An even more serious reason for our low spirits was the second coup which had occurred the day before. This time, the new leader, Rabuka's, approach was more militant. Curfews were imposed on Suva and Lautoka from 8 P.M. to 5 P.M. Despite the fact that Fiji is a multi-religious country, Rabuka was trying to make everyone uphold Sunday as a Christian sacred day. Taxi and bus service on Sunday were banned. The tourist industry, already severely depressed from the first coup, would experience more setbacks with the new regulations. The Indian population was almost in tears. A few days later Rabuka declared Fiji a Republic.

Emotionally we were ready to leave, but we were waiting for the right weather. In the meantime, after one more sail to Lautoka to provision, we were simply hanging out at Malololailai doing various jobs on *Banshee* while we waited. After the awful beating going to New Zealand the previous year we were closely monitoring the weather. We could pick up weather reports generated out of Wellington or New Caledonia on our ham radio. These are given in what is called "fleet code," groups of five digits, and you must know the code to determine the meaning. The report is sent in Morse code at about 23 words per minute. Joy and I have both studied Morse code for our radio licenses but we learned code at 13 words per minute. To deal with this problem, we purchased a decoder. It plugs into the ham radio and the five digit number group comes out on the screen. After writing these down and having learned what they mean, Joy is able to take the information and plot it, thus making her own weather map. What we were looking for was a nice high, one that would settle in for about a week. That would get us most of the way back to New Zealand.

As we waited, a few yachts came in with friends we'd not seen for a year or more. With summer coming on, the weather was becoming quite hot. Going over the side to clean the bottom of the boat proved to be a refreshing dip. While scrubbing underwater, we encountered three remoras who had started living on *Banshee's* keel. One was quite large, the other two small. They were keeping one side of the keel clean! The big one was especially shy, moving around to keep its distance from us. The small ones swam right up to us, presumably eating things we knocked loose from the hull.

Finally, the high we wanted came. On October 30 at 1 P.M., we cleared the Malolo Pass and zing—a large *walu* hit our fishing line. A good omen for the beginning of our passage to the Bay of Islands! We called Brian, Jan and BJ on *Foxy Lady II* on the VHF to tell them about the *walu* and bid them farewell.

Killer whale
(Orcinus orca)

Chapter 19

Waterfalls and Whales

Our careful monitoring of the weather paid off. Overall the weather for our thirteen-day return passage to New Zealand made this our best passage to date. If anything, the wind was too light. The second day out, a wayward small front brought torrential rains and wind enough that we reefed both the main and staysail. But it was of short duration; before dawn, conditions were back to normal and we pushed forward under full sail.

Several unusual things occurred. On the third day out I became shakey with chills and fever and muscle cramps. I also noticed I was very thirsty and had been consuming great quantities of water which didn't relieve my thirst. Suddenly it occurred to me that perhaps I was dehydrated. I drank one glass of Gatorade and instantly felt one hundred percent better! If one glass was good, why not a second? I downed a second and most of my symptoms disappeared. At sea it's easy to become dehydrated and not even realize it. Since leaving L.A., we've carried Gatorade with us, knowing that it restores the body's electrolytic balance. We have also found it very effective for overexposure to the sun and becoming overheated.

People who have not made an ocean passage probably don't know how unusual it is to encounter another vessel at sea, especially another sailboat. We had been talking by ham radio with Tom and Trudy on *Kings Ransom* for several days. They had left Lautoka about two days after us. Before they left, we asked them if they would pick up some delicious Fijian salami we had discovered only days before leaving. They said they would. Since then Tom had joked with us about having a rendezvous at sea to deliver the "goods." Strangely enough we did have an unplanned and unexpected meeting. On the fifth day out around 10:30 P.M. I sighted a light. Joy called on Channel 16 and an English yacht, *Mustang*, responded. After our short exchange with them, Tom also responded to our call. We exchanged our dead reckoned position and the course each of us was steering. *Kings Ransom* was about five miles astern!

We had been beating since early evening under a full main and genny, but squalls came and we dropped the genny and hoisted the staysail. With the squally conditions, the wind varied from 4 to 20 knots and consequently our speed fluctuated from one to four knots. With all these variables, our course and speed were most irregular. At midnight Joy came on watch and I went below. At the same time Tom, on *Kings Ransom,* went below and Trudy took her watch.

I had just dropped off to sleep when Joy excitedly called me on deck saying a boat was running us down. I bounded topside, and no more than 100 yards off our starboard beam a boat was directly pointing at us and rapidly closing the distance. It was dark, but I was sure the charging boat was *Kings Ransom.* I called them on the radio. They saw us. Joy wanted me to take the wheel. She was then hand steering, having disengaged the windvane. She went to talk on the radio and standby to tack if need be. Just as we were about to tack, *Kings Ransom's* bow fell away as they tacked.

Once everything was under control, Tom explained on the radio what had happened. Trudy was on watch. She saw our light and realized we were getting closer, but in the darkness it wasn't until they were very close that she could see we were on a collision course. Their boat was being steered by a windvane too, and she tried to get it to change course. When it didn't respond as quickly as she wanted it to, she tried to change it again and again. By then the windvane was confused and the boat out of control. She called Tom who disengaged the vane and hand steered the boat through the tack. Being a larger boat than *Banshee* and with a longer waterline, *Kings Ransom* was faster and gradually crept past us in the night. By late morning they slipped over the horizon, out of sight. After coming that close we never got our salami, not until we made Opua.

By November 4, lighter winds were setting in and becoming easterly. We put up the genny and full main. Over a 24-hour period even with the light winds we still clocked 80 sea miles. With even lighter winds the following day, we hoisted our newly cut drifter. It had been a spinnaker, but we had found so little use for it at sea that we'd had a sailmaker recut it for us. We added hanks to the tack and now had a perfectly good sea-going drifter.

On the seventh day with light winds to no wind, our mileage fell to 50.36 miles from noon to noon fix. In the light winds with the drifter, the Aires didn't like to steer so it became necessary to use the autopilot. We had the good fortune to catch a 20-pound albacore, a beautiful fat tuna with a jet black back, silver body and long graceful fins. Its delicious white meat fed us four generous meals. Over the three years we have discovered many new ways to prepare fish. Two of our favorites are herb butter fish and fish curry.

For three days we alternated between flying the drifter and running the engine. On November 9, we were only 150 miles off the Bay of Islands and eager to make port before any nasty weather brewed up. Fortunately the wind picked up after going SW and then S. Mostly now, the days were overcast with occasional bursts of heavy rain. We landed another albacore, a 15-pounder, which Joy cleaned, filleted and froze for future use.

Finally on November 11 at 4 A.M. we passed the Cape Brett light under power as the wind had died. In no time the sun was popping up from behind a jagged row of misty mountains, casting a fanlike glow on the glassy water. Off to the right side of the bay was another panoramic scene, thick wisps of fog curling down the hillsides, filling the valley. I felt excited and warm, like I was coming home! Stretching out on all sides were green carpeted hills, English country buildings scattered amongst elegant tall poplars. Everywhere rolling velvety hillsides were topped with uniformly shaped trees. Pastoral serenity, a setting that intensified the sense of some ancient past.

The early morning chill cut through my three layers of clothing. But I didn't care. The scene was special. I had left the tropics and entered another zone, not only geographically but culturally. Here was a land whose inhabitants speak my language. More than that, we share an age-old culture consisting of thousands upon thousands of details, many unspoken things existing only at a subconscious level. Perhaps this very reason creates such a strong bond, as if of inborn kinship. Normally I reject such notions as pure chauvinism, but I have learned during my three years with South Pacific peoples that the differences between us, though culturally based, are profound. I would be glad to embrace some Anglo-Saxon ways for a change.

To some these remarks may seem racist. Nonetheless I can't deny that I was really looking forward to listening to a classical music radio station, intellectual discussions on art, politics, literature and so on, being able to go to concerts, museums, libraries.

Even the landscape and the climate offered me a deep sense of joy and peacefulness. So many intangibles.

We spent a couple of weeks in Opua, relaxing, picking up mail, making phone calls to friends in Auckland, and putting the boat straight. Then, at the invitation of Don and Jill Cottle, we made our way up the Kerikeri River to visit them at their lovely home tucked amidst citrus, apple, plum and peach trees and a kiwi fruit orchard.

With a heavy flowing tide and light wind, we had to power up the river. We started out in a light drizzle about an hour before high tide. The depth sounder never showed less than seven feet, proving that we could only transit the river at high water. It was a scenic trip with houses scattered along the banks and an number of yachts and launches moored along the shore or close to the channel itself. Here was more idyllic countryside wrapped in mist. Sleek, blanketed horses grazed and gazed across soft rolling paddocks. As we continued up the river, it narrowed and twisted past muddy banks and towering gum trees. Just before the final turn to the Kerikeri town basin, we spotted *Operculum*, belonging to our friends Henry and Janik Wakelam, moored close to the river's edge. We were looking forward to speaking with Janik again, a strong very capable French woman who had singlehandedly circumnavigated before marrying Henry. She seems not to have made much of her feat, a low-keyed, leisurely voyage lasting from 1975-1983.

Someone had offered us a pile mooring upon arrival, so we eased ourselves over and picked up the tag line without any trauma and secured ourselves facing the Stone Store with lush forested area off to port. The Stone Store, over 100 years old, is one of the historic buildings in Kerikeri. The town prides itself on being the cradle of New Zealand's European settlement

We had called Don and Jill through Kerikeri radio, so they knew approximately when we would arrive. Thanks to their generous hospitality, we enjoyed several days visiting with them. A highlight for me was being able to play a fine piano again and have a go at the harpsichord. Jill and I had good fun reading through some four-handed piano music. Her circular music room has splendid acoustics. It was like hearing music in a concert hall.

Don, who is both dairyman and kiwi fruit grower, told us many interesting things about kiwi fruit. The plant, originally from China, is grown in a fashion much like wine grapes, except that the runners are overhead at a distance suitable to pruning and picking. In order to produce perfect fruit for export, Don hires beehives for several days so that there will be sufficient bees to repeatedly pollinate the blossoms. The plants have no nectar, only pollen. Late November is the proper time to pollinate the plants. Only it had been raining too much. Honeybees will not go out to work in inclement weather. Ideally, according to Don, would be bumblebees that work in any kind of weather. Unfortunately they are not available commercially.

One of the delightful things about Kerikeri is its natural environment. Thick vegetation grows along the river within the town basin. Giant eucalyptus trees with their smooth silvery bark crowd the shores. From our mooring we could hear the roar of the cascading river upstream. Early morning, the forest rang with a chorus of song from bell birds and *tuis*. The *tui*, a native, is a small black bird with a fancy ring of curling white feathers that encircle the bird's upper body. Their calls, differing from area to area, are tuneful phrases, impossible to describe but the most spectacular calls of any bird. Daily, two duck families visited, begging bread. From one day to the next we could observe their growth! Not only by the change in their size, but by the change in their feathers which were taking on juvenile coloration.

One afternoon, we walked the track up the Kerikeri River. Scarcely any sun penetrated the densely overgrown native forest thick with multitudinous ferns, tree ferns and even some *kauri* trees. Bird calls and the flutter of wings sounded a natural symphony that mixed pleasantly with the smells of dampened earth. Our destination was the Wharepoke Falls, a broad wall of water that crashed, swirled and shot over smooth boulders, suddenly becoming still and silent as it flowed over masses of seaweed and sand on the river bed.

On the day of our departure, Don and Jill came around to give us a royal send off, bringing two large boxes of tangelos and grapefruit and a large bag of avocados. Our plan was to sail a few miles north along the coast for Whangaroa, a deep fjordlike all-weather harbor. Shortly after leaving Kerikeri, I got too negligent with my steering—I was gazing at the river scenery—and went aground in deep, mucky mud! The depth sounder read three feet. I couldn't get us off. No more than five minutes later a large yacht,

Zepher V, came up the river and seeing our plight offered to tow us off. We must have been living right, it was the only vessel we saw all the way down the river.

With New Zealand weather being changeable and often blowing a gale, we made two attempts to sail to Whangaroa. On the first attempt, we got to the Cavalli Islands when the wind picked up in gale force squalls right on the nose. There is a very narrow, unmarked passage between the islands and the mainland. In the blinding squalls that developed, it was impossible to try to claw our way through those hazardous waters. Visibility shrank to zero and the seas slammed across the bow, throwing spray over *Banshee's* deck. Even back in the cockpit we got periodic saltwater dousings.

We opted to go outside the Cavallis, thus passing them to seaward since the squalls were hugging the shore. Of course, true to the diabolic nature of things on such occasions, once we'd sailed out and set a course around the islands, the squall line had engulfed the islands. We were now being thrashed again by turbulent sharp seas and wind that shook the rigging with a loud whine. Sometimes you have to change plans. We jibed and with the wind and seas astern, *Banshee* began surfing along at 6-8 knots, her bow surfing over steel gray seas as we flew back to the shelter of Opua.

It took a week for the weather to settle down. Still the winds were NW, right on the nose. But what a glorious day we set out on. The sun skipped over the seas creating a dazzling sparkle while big fluffy cumulus clouds chased each other across a deep azure sky. This wondrous domed panorama arched over bright green hills and bays outlined in craggy brown rocks. Escorting us over turquoise waves were endless flocks of terns, gulls, ganets and sooty shearwaters. Their assorted cries and screeches could compete with a bright Vivaldi concerto.

Rather than sail all the way to Whangaroa that day, we decided to stop off for the night in Mahinepua Bay. It is a wide-mouth bay with a shallow bottom. Even anchored a good half mile off shore, we found the bottom fell to about 15 feet at low water. Tired, we made an early dinner and went to bed just after dark. Around midnight a terrific thunderstorm broke overhead. Lightning flashed and big claps of thunder rumbled right down the alpine hills surrounding us. And rain—rain so heavy and the drops so large we thought it was a hail storm! Shining the flashlight into the cockpit, we ascertained

Motoring in *Nessie* across the Tamaki River to the Panmure Yacht and Boating Club dock. *Banshee* is moored beyond the line of boats in the distance.

Banshee's belaying pins on the starboard side.

Joy and Jan Hoffman at a *kava* ceremony with the men of Lalati village on Mbengga Island, Fiji.

Salome and her nephew in front of her *bure* at Eneldala village, Fiji.

The meeting house in Dravuni village at the Astrolabe Reef, Fiji.

A view of the interior. Unfortunately this building was being replaced by one of concrete block with a corrugated iron roof.

Lynne Davis, the Australian woman who solo kayaked around the Yasawas in Fiji.

Joy photographed this killer whale as it approached *Banshee* just offshore in New Zealand waters.

Having dinner with our good friends Jim and Joyce Irving at their home in Auckland.

Chatting with Enid Emtage in her wonderful garden.

At the chart table in *Banshee*.

Joy rests during our hike to Muller Glacier on New Zealand's South Island.

that it was rain, not hail. In the midst of this clatter I smelled a very strong odor of ozone, released by the storm! I had never before encountered this strange phenomenon. Once the rain ceased, gale force winds rocketed through, churning up the shallow bay, setting *Banshee* into a rapid bobbing motion.

Clear air and bright sun greeted us at sunrise. After a quick breakfast, we hoisted anchor and raised sail. A brisk wind pushed us rapidly past Flat Island, then past Stephanson Island and into the narrow entrance of Whangaroa Harbor. Suddenly there was no wind. Inside the protected fjordlike harbor, the water was glassy and the sails went limp. Down they came and we entered a fairyland under power. Steep, rugged mountains, very reminiscent of the Marquesas, jutted up into the clouds. In awe we powered around the labyrinth into little fingers cutting narrowly into green clad, boulder encrusted mountains.

We selected Lane's Cove as our first anchorage. At the head of the little cove was a small cabin snuggled in the midst of greenery and tall gums. Bird calls echoed across the water with the sweetness of a flute in duet with an oboe. Natural music in the stillness, and the rain softly falling. Is this not the way we were meant to live?

The following day we took the dinghy up a creek at high tide. After rounding the first bend, we spotted a thin waterfall shining like a silver thread as it cascaded from the highest peak, vanishing hundreds of feet down in a verdant mass of foliage. The creek narrowed to a needle. We tied the dinghy to a tree and jumped ashore by way of a fallen branch. Wild yellow daisies and lavender thistles shot up over the tall grass, swaying in the morning breeze. Ferns, ferns and more ferns, everywhere. It was a primeval landscape.

So our days in Whangaroa passed exploring rugged landscape, hiking along streams and waterfalls, viewing wild flowers and sitting out a gale before we could depart. When we left, we sailed once more through the Cavallis. It was back to Opua for a quick miniprovisioning before making a leisurely passage south to Auckland.

The day before Christmas we anchored in the lovely little harbor Whangamumu. The previous year we had intended to stay here but we missed it. The entrance is obscured and commonly sailors miss it, as we did. This time we navigated very carefully and found it. We celebrated Christmas Eve with homemade eggnog

Christmas Day we woke to a screaming gale and found ourselves boat bound for the day. We opened Christmas packages from
family and made pancakes topped with Vermont maple syrup, a gift
from my aunt and uncle in Lexington, Massachusetts. It was a day
for reading, writing and Scrabble, safe and cozy while the elements
raged outside. Of course, we rolled around inside.

The next day dawned perfectly. Off we went into the deep hills,
following a stream into a dark interior shaded by masses of *pangas*
(tree ferns) and *casaurinas*—commonly called tea trees because the
early settlers did brew tea with their leaves. The highlight was a
rock climb off the beach by the old whaling station. Most of the trail
was a steep go over rocks and boulders beside a stream which
offered numerous waterfalls. The rock walls behind the falls housed
several varieties of mosses and a lovely segmented plant with saw-
toothed edges. Here and there in the mossy dampness, hiding
amongst leaves and twigs were mushrooms.

New Year's Day, 1988, found us at Kawau Island, anchored in
Mansion House Bay. Few boats were anchored here when we
arrived, but a change in wind direction brought a steady stream of
boats into the small bay. Soon one could almost walk boat to boat.
With anchor lines wrapped and hopelessly tangled, no one could
have made a quick getaway. Still the ferry managed to weave its
way through the mad flotilla of happy boaters all toasting in the
New Year with a bang. Noticing our American flag waving off the
stern, some Kiwis invited us to their boat for some New Year's cheer.
It's the only time I've heard a New Year celebrated with the playing
of bagpipes! What a nice sound coming across the water at midnight, punctuated with the bang of fireworks.

Before going to Kawau, we had set off early one morning from
Tutukaka on the mainland to go back to the Hen and Chickens
Islands. I was in the cockpit steering and as usual looking out over
the water, enjoying the sight of land and sea. I thought I saw
something at a distance—a fin. I kept looking and then it appeared
again. Too big for a dolphin. Could it be a whale? Suddenly I saw
more than one fin and the creatures were coming toward us. I told
Joy and suggested she grab a camera.

There were four of them and they were definitely coming
straight at us. As they came, they detoured to our stern, swimming

with their heads only inches from our stern. There was no mistaking them. They were killer whales. Orcas. Since they have a reputation for attacking boats, both of us were a mite concerned. We had already pulled in the trailing log so it wouldn't get swallowed. It lay in a tangled heap on the stern. Then they moved from our stern to our beam, swimming along at the same speed as us, periodically diving, resurfacing and spouting. They were magnificent! Apparently they weren't going to attack. This was a friendly curious visit. We began to relax and enjoy having them close by where we could watch them and their amazingly graceful movements. Joy began snapping pictures of them. I was tempted to reach over the side and touch them, but restrained myself. After all, they have teeth and I didn't want to spook them. If they hit us that would be the end of *Banshee*.

They left, but a bit later we were visited by a second group, only two this time. They behaved exactly like the first group, swimming right beside us for ten or fifteen minutes.

Several hours later, when we anchored at the Southern Cove of Lady Alice Island, a group of Orcas swam past. Word went around the anchorage and everyone came on deck to watch.

Coming to Auckland, you must have a mooring or take a slip in the marina. There is no place for boats to anchor. We had called ahead from the Bay of Islands to make reservations for a few days' stay in Westhaven. From Kawau we had tried calling but had no answer. New Zealand has the strange habit of everyone—every business—closing from about mid-December to mid-January! You might say the whole country closes down for almost a month! A few things are open. The fire station, hospitals, gas stations. We thought an urban marina the size of West Haven with several thousand slips would have at least one person in the office. They didn't. We had not been told where to go for a slip, so we pulled temporarily into a fuel dock and Joy went to phone the marina. No answer. But, we were in luck. The man at the fuel dock knew of an empty slip right there in a private marina. He said we could stay overnight. He furnished us with a key to the showers and the laundry.

No cruiser can ask for more. A lovely hot shower and a way to wash that mounting heap of laundry. Welcome back to Auckland!

Chapter 20

Rainbows in the Wilderness

After living three years on the water in the confines of a 34-foot boat, we were eager to embark on an overland voyage! Our old 1967 Hillman, purchased in Auckland, stood up to the rigors of close to 6,000 miles in seven weeks pulling behind it a Scamper Camper— a tent on wheels that collapses into a compact trailer.

Although only two islands, this nation, Aotearoa, "the land of the long white cloud," contains every type of landscape to be found in the world: desert, glaciers, rain forest, seacoast, alpine mountains, rivers, waterfalls, rolling paddocks, plains and fjords. All are there waiting to be discovered.

Even though the Europeans have only been in New Zealand since around 1840, in that time, sadly, much of the natural environment has been destroyed. In less than one century, the native forest of New Zealand has been reduced to sixteen percent of the original. Settlement activities have bought on the erosion of 15 1/4 million acres, almost one sixth of the land mass! As a result of this destruction of habitat, thousands of native birds, plants and fertile soil have been lost. Fortunately, New Zealanders, better informed today about ecology, are making valiant efforts to preserve natural habitats and prevent further catastrophic disruption of the natural balance. Because of its small population—under five million—New Zealand is largely rural. The majority of the population resides in the North Island. Consequently the South Island retains sizeable uninhabited land masses. Even more astounding, some portions, especially the southwestern area of impenetrable rain forest, is unexplored.

Biologically speaking, because of its isolation and geographic location, New Zealand offers opportunities to study plants and animals found nowhere else in the world. Some of its plants raise interesting puzzles and perhaps offer some geological clues reaching back to a period before continental drift. Take the tree fuchsia, a plant with greenish-purple flowers. In the north of New Zealand, it is an evergreen but in the south, it is deciduous. These trees also occur as natives in South America but not elsewhere—apart from one species in Tahiti. From this evidence some scientists have surmised that there once was a land bridge between New Zealand and South America before the ice cap covered Antarctica.

Another interesting and unusual feature about New Zealand is the number of flightless birds found here. Biologists have suggested that the lack of mammals to prey upon birds encouraged the evolution of birds without wings. Strangely, the only native mammals are seals and two species of bats.

Apart from its fascinating natural features, New Zealand is renown for its social progressiveness. Foremost in its liberal legislation was giving women the vote in 1893—earlier than Australia or the United States—and establishing an old-age pension in 1898. By far the most engaging social issue has been the interactions between Maoris and Europeans, an ongoing question still actively debated today.

The Maoris themselves pose yet another subject of great interest. Archaeologists and anthropologists are attempting to reconstruct early history in an effort to reveal more about the Maoris transoceanic voyages to New Zealand and their subsequent settlement. Coming to a temperate climate, the Maoris had to change many of their traditional ways, their food, dress and shelter in order to adapt to a harsher climate. This change sets them apart from all other Polynesian peoples.

Maori legends relate that Maui, a cultural hero, fished up the North Island by using the jawbone of his grandmother, smeared with his own blood. The Maori name, *Te Ika a Maui*, "the Fish of Maui," reflects this legendary origin. Maori legends also speak of the arrival of their ancestors in oceangoing canoes that sailed from Hawaiki. Even today Maoris can tell you which tribe they are descended from, which canoe brought their ancestors to these shores.

But where is Hawaiki? This appears to be the name of the original homeland that was carried by the Polynesians across the Pacific and given to various places where they settled. We can trace this linguistically: Hawaiki becomes *Hawaii* among the Hawaiians, *Savaii* among Samoans, *Avaiki* among Cook Islanders and *Havai'i* the original name of Raiatea in the Society Islands.

Archaeological finding and carbon dating have established that peoples of east Polynesian origin settled at sites along the thousand-mile length of New Zealand at least by the eighth century. Usually these early settlers are referred to as *moa*-hunters because the bones and eggs of the *moa*, a very large flightless bird, have been found in their graves and at village sites. *Moa* is the Polynesian word for domestic fowl, but the *moa*, sizewise, was no domestic fowl. This squat and massive bird, standing higher than a person provided an enormous amount of food. The birds ranged over both North and South Islands. By the time the Europeans came, the *moa* was extinct and all but forgotten.

The first European to discover New Zealand was the Dutch navigator, Abel Janszoon Tasman, on December 13, 1642. On this day two Dutch ships, *Heemskerck* and *Zeehaen* landed on the west coast of the South Island. A few days later, anchored in Golden Bay—named Murderer's Bay by Tasman—they were visited by Maoris. Tasman dubbed the newly discovered land Staten Landt, but it was soon renamed Nieuw Zeeland after the Dutch province.

A little more than a century later, James Cook was the next European to land in New Zealand. Like Tasman, Cook was searching for a southern continent believed to lie between South Africa and South America. In 1769 Cook circumnavigated New Zealand, proving that it was not the hoped for continent. Two distinguished botanists with Cook, Joseph Banks and Daniel Solander, contributed much to European knowledge of the South Pacific. Today it is known that three-quarters of New Zealand's flora is unique.

Cook's geographical observations revealed that New Zealand's two islands extend over a thousand miles long, over 13 degrees of latitude, comprising a landmass about the size of Great Britain or Italy. Moreover, New Zealand lies in the midst of ocean quite remote from any continent. Its nearest continental neighbor, Australia, is almost 1300 miles distant across the Tasman Sea. It is 6,000 miles from Asia and America.

The first inroads of European settlement began as an extension of the Australian frontier. In 1792 a ship from Sydney left a few settlers at Dusky Sound, a fjord on the southwest coast of the South Island. A few whaling vessels began fishing these waters. By 1800, British, American and French whalers regularly fished the coast, calling at the Bay of Islands or other harbors to reprovision or trade with the Maoris.

British emigrants began arriving around 1840. Most of these pioneers were from the upper working class or lower middle class. They came to a settlement different in concept from earlier colonies. And, New Zealand became a colony under unusual circumstances. The Treaty of Waitangi, signed by Maori chiefs, was intended to establish a just society in which two different races could live together peacefully. In the treaty, the chiefs ceded their sovereignty to the Queen. In return, the Queen guaranteed the Maoris possession of the lands, forest, fisheries and other properties they possessed individually or collectively. From the beginning the character of New Zealand society was different and it has continued to be so even today, having led the western world in some of the most progressive social policies.

Perhaps more than any other place settled by Anglo-Saxons, New Zealand has tended to retain many native words, especially place names and plants. Today the Maoris are a people with one foot in each culture, sometimes causing them confusion and dissatisfaction. While Maoris have adopted *pakeha* (European) dress, housing, occupations and language, many still retain large parts of their older culture, still meet in the *Maerae* (their meeting house) and teach their traditions and language to their children.

While necessity forced the Maoris to use different materials in the making of clothing and shelter and this change helped to develop new techniques, it does not necessarily account for the rich assortment of musical instruments nor for the most ornate carvings and artistic designs of any of the Polynesians. Their musical instruments are of four kinds: membranophones (drums with vibrating cover), autophones (percussion such as wooden gongs), aerophones (wind instruments) and cordophones (string instruments). Other Polynesians may have instruments from two of these groups but not from all four groups.

Moreover, the Maoris have invented several instruments. One impressive invention is a long trumpet. In Polynesia, Triton shells and Cassis shells were natural trumpets and the only kind used. In New Zealand Triton shells were quite limited. Maoris made long trumpets from resonant wood such as matai. They split a length of wood longitudinally, grooved the split surfaces, then lashed the two lengths together. Such trumpets range in size from four and a half feet to six feet, but may be as short as two feet.

Carving as an art form in New Zealand was no doubt greatly stimulated by the woodwork of houses and their elaborate decoration. Consequently the Maoris reached the peak in wood carving among the Polynesians. The conventional human figure became the chief motif found in meeting houses, on wall posts, as well as a popular breast ornament know as the *hei tiki*.

Curvilinear motifs, a progression of loops and curves so popular on Maori carvings, is absent in the rest of Polynesia. Likewise, painting, while present to a limited extent in parts of Polynesia, assumed a very important place in New Zealand. The rafters of the meeting houses were painted with designs in red, black and white. In New Zealand the development of more solid houses with massive woodwork spurred artistic development to a degree found nowhere else in Polynesia. In this manner, art and craft reacted on each other, resulting in a peak of artistic achievement extraordinary for a stone age culture.

****

Having already spent some months upon arrival in the North Island, we were eager to get to the South Island to begin our camping. Leaving from Auckland, we stopped the first night in Taupo as guests of Olivia and Jeff Marchant and their sons Peter and Steven, five and eight. Eager to show us as much of their community as they could in an overnight visit, they drove us down to Lake Taupo, a huge inland fresh water lake that has made Taupo one of New Zealand's most popular resorts. Even though it was a breezy day, we went for a short walk along the lake. After dinner Olivia took us up to the thermal baths for a very relaxing dip that aided in sinking us into a very sound sleep.

Following Highway 1, we continued south through the center of the North Island. Finally the road came out to the Tasman Sea where we found a campsite on the coast at Foxton. I was unprepared for the luxurious amenities found at many caravan/camping sites: communal kitchen with stainless steel sinks, hot and cold running water, showers, flush toilets, often TV/game rooms. Not only are these places higher priced than the more natural areas, they also tend to be crowded. We tried to utilize such accommodations only several times a week when we wanted a shower, preferring to spend most of our time in wilderness areas.

Cook Strait has a reputation for its gales. Amazingly we hit it during a calm period. The ferry left Wellington midafternoon, arriving in Picton before dark. A stiff breeze ruffled the greenish waters of the strait but we stayed on deck for the crossing and the spectacular entrance through the Marlborough Sounds, finally landing in Queen Charlotte Sound. High wooded mountains rose up steeply from the many fingered waterways of the sounds. Once off the ferry, we quickly left the colorful little town of Picton behind as we slowly drove up the narrow winding road to Waikawa Maritime Park. We pitched our tent on a grassy paddock facing a protected inlet. Even at 9 P.M. it was still light. I sat outside watching the haze settle over the distant hills on the opposite side of the inlet and beyond. As the sky darkened, a chill wind nipped at my arms and shoulders, encouraging me to retreat inside the tent. Bird calls rang out in the stillness and some sheep came by, bleating mournfully.

Our second primitive campsite in the Sounds was at Puketea Bay. It was reached by an unsealed (unpaved) road covered with gravel. The drive was hot, windy and dusty, mostly through foothills. Winding around and bumping over the rutted road, we had occasional splashes of color from the fjord fingers as they cut through the green clad mountains.

After setting up camp, we took a short walk uphill to the Portage Hotel, but finding nothing of particular interest other than the scenery, we returned to camp. Had there been any spectators watching us earlier as we pulled the trailer in, they would have thought us most peculiar. We detached the trailer from the car and hand pushed it into position. I still had not mastered the art of backing with a trailer and this spot was especially tricky. It required negotiating deep ruts and bumps and several sharp curves.

Again, we were serenaded by birds and, from sunup to sundown, the ubiquitous sound of the cicadas buzzing. The next morning a strenuous hike, straight uphill it seemed, rewarded us with a glorious view: three inlets in sight at once with their waters sparkling silver, turquoise and emerald in the morning sun as the breeze swept down ruffling the surface into millions of whitecaps.

Two days later, we drove out of the bush back over the metalled road of graded gravel. Coming out of the mountains, we saw a flat plain below, subdivided into paddocks cut through by lakes and rivers. In the midst of this patchwork lay the little town of Havelock. Here we found a simple but charming motor camp that had everything we needed—a place to wash the car, a hot shower to scrub the dust from our pores, and an automatic washing machine. Camped next to us was an American couple from Porterville, California, who were biking and tenting around the South Island. In the same camp we met a solo biker from Alaska.

After a day to clean up, we set off for the bush again, this time taking a one lane road—dirt of course—to the top of Mt. Riley. I thought it would be a wonderful place to pitch the tent, on the top of the world, but Joy said a resounding *no*. I should have known that would be her answer; she detests heights—although she thinks nothing of going to the top of *Banshee's* mast in a bosun's chair! I tried to use this argument with her, but, as I suspected when voicing it, she steadfastly refused to camp "at the top of the world." Disappointed, I acquiesced. We descended again to sea level and splashed over a low concrete bridge that was flooded.

Following signs, we eventually located another primitive camp. Onamalutu, situated on a river by the same name, lies on the edge of a broad grassy field. It is backed by an area of native trees and bush now tended by the forest service. In some respects this was one of the most beautiful places we stayed. Shortly after our arrival some day picnickers departed, leaving us alone. The bush walks here are kept clear by the caretaker. Rather than building nuclear weapons, New Zealand tends forest areas such as this. It was like a natural botanical garden as the trees were labeled with their common and botanical names.

We took several of the trails. Each led to a river filled with rounded stones smoothed by the water. Wild blackberries climbed over shoreside bush. We picked a pail full and ate them with fresh milk. At night Onamalutu came alive with echoing songs of *tuis*, bell birds and the *pukeko* (sounding like its name), a striking blue and black bird with bright red beak. Among the birds we saw were California quail, *pukeko* and wood pigeons.

A scenic drive from the highlands and forest of Onamalutu brought us into wine country where we made several stops at cellars to learn more about the New Zealand wine industry. This area, past Richmond Forest, became high desert covered with golden brown grass that stood brittle in the summer heat. We could have been in California wine country. Heading east toward the Pacific coast, we eventually came to hilly sand dunes and soon we began to feel a cooling of the temperature as the welcome ocean air laden with soothing moistness circulated through the car. The coast stretched on and on, a light gray sand beach making a striking contrast with the light greens and blues of the shallow ocean. For miles the scene continued with no one on the beach and no signs of civilization except for a railroad track that paralleled the coast.

Still several miles north of Kaikoura appeared an outcrop of brown rocks where the sea threw foam into the air. Long trails of bull kelp waved rhythmically back and forth in the surge. We parked and eagerly rushed to the shore to watch the multitude of seals congregated on the rocks. Our first seals since leaving Mexico! True to character, some were snoozing contentedly drying out on the heated rocks. Others slid into the water for a swim and several young males sounded off at each other making territorial assertions.

We decided to take a side road off to Blue Duck Reserve. Unpaved, the road wound up through alpine mountains and velvet meadows. Pines and tree ferns crowded in toward the road. A deep azure sky, cloudless, crowned the drowsy summer day as the sound of invisible cicadas droned over the stillness.

Without ever seeing a blue duck, we turned the car around and descended once more to the coast and on to a campsite just south of Kaikoura. Here we made friends with a ram who came to the fence, making strange noises of greeting. In return for pats on the nose, he licked our hands. He kept an eye out for a ewe who also wanted a pet and some of the greenery available on our side of the fence. When she approached, he rudely chased her away, sometimes nipping at her hind quarters. We learned that Freckles had become a pet lamb when his mother died and he was raised on a bottle.

On a beautiful day with wispy mares tails fanning across the sky, we walked out to the point of Kaikoura Peninsula. It was low tide. The sea had retreated a good half mile from the shore exposing exotic shapes in the limestone. Here stunning patterns stood out, some slanting and sharp, others flat, scoured smooth by countless tides. Out toward the point, a series of channels have been carved and lovely tidepools have developed. Around the rocky edge, an almost imperceptible pulse of the sea periodically raised the water, and long streamers of golden brown kelp rippled like heavy braids of hair. The rocks were almost entirely covered in some areas by colonies of limpets, most of them an inch or more in diameter. Alongside, but less numerous, were soft black mollusks. A bright purple starfish inhabited one pool.

Around the point of the peninsula, we came upon fur seals sunning and frolicking, some rolling lazily from side to side, some stretching their necks, others cavorting in the surf, and one show-off did a porpoise leap and dive—surging through the air like a torpedo.

We drove on to Christchurch with the hope of visiting the botanic gardens, but a soggy rainy day squelched that. Instead we visited the museum and enjoyed a great exhibit of Maori arts and crafts and a very fine geological display. Momentarily we poked our heads out in the rain long enough for a short walk to the edge of the botanical garden. With its large trees and fancy flower beds, the scene there beside the Avon River looked entirely English. Toward the end of the day we made our way back to the center of town for the Evensong service at Christchurch Cathedral, a program of music sung by a male choir.

From Christchurch we headed south along the coast to Banks Peninsula. After a steep, winding road we reached the summit. Below lay blue fingered bays, reminiscent of Marlborough Sounds, where the sea varied from flat and glassy to white capped. We made the long descent, driving to Akaroa, a seaside village originally settled by the French. Today the streets are all still called *rue*. After visiting the bakery, we lunched on the bay where a stiff, cold breeze threatened to blow away our lunch. Standing nearby to make off with any stray morsels were a group of fussing gulls. Here we purchased a few provisions and ice for our ice chest before driving to another area of the peninsula, Pigeon Bay.

Pigeon Bay was another wilderness camp. We no more than parked the car, having decided where to pitch our tent, when a very pleasant man in the caravan beside us came out and invited us in for a cup of coffee. Bill Dekker, a Dutchman who came to New Zealand about 30 years ago and stayed, readily extended friendship and kindness in a manner we've encountered so frequently in this country. In the course of our conversation, he offered to take us out in his launch a few days hence to hunt for abalone, called *paua* here. He was leaving for the weekend to return to home and wife and offered us his spring water in his absence and the use of his heating pot. It was an interesting affair, looking much like a thermos bottle, but, unlike a thermos, the center was space. Water filled in around the hollow area. It sits on a small frame about an inch above the ground and a fire is built underneath, then small twigs are fed down through the center. In about five minutes the water is boiling. The device is a Kiwi invention, I believe.

At this camp we met another friendly neighbor who was camping in a one-person tent, Hugh Wilson, an engaging botanist from a family of "mountaineers" as he calls them. Hugh had biked to this area from Christchurch and was doing a survey of plants in the area. He was a mine of information not only about plants but about Maori history and traditions. Following his advice, we visited a nearby area of protected native vegetation. In addition to tall native podocarps—a relative of pine trees—was the jumble of native ferns, lianas, climbers and creepers. Upon entering the sanctuary, we were greeted by a small bird, a fantail so-called because of its oversized fan-shaped tail. It and several others flew right up almost into our faces. Characteristically the birds manifest a nervous kind of behavior, constantly in motion even when they have alighted. Several followed us, continuously darting in front of us.

Before driving into the interior to visit Mount Cook, we stayed several days with Win and John White in Timaru. We had met them some months earlier in Fiji at Saveni Beach and they had graciously invited us to stay with them. It was a real treat to eat fresh vegetables out of Win's garden and to look at her fantastic shell collection, the result of years of avid searching.

The drive through the interior was dramatic. The road twisted, roughly following the Tasman River. Winding back and forth permitted changing views of the snow-capped Mount Cook. Much of the time clouds obscured the 3,764 meter peak. But clearing occasionally, we caught glimpses of its blue and mauve shadowed face. After climbing several thousand feet, we attained a gray alluvial plain, the wide swath left behind the glacier's retreat. Steep mountains rise up, exposing miles of barren rock. Our wilderness camp lay in the midst of this flattened plain facing Muller Glacier.

Day and night it emitted a thundering roar as tons of ice and snow cascaded down several thousand feet.

On a sunny day we hiked as close as we could to Muller Glacier, up to Kea Point. A narrow track cut through a thick assortment of scrub, ranging from alpine plants to succulents and cacti. Having reached the summit, we could look down the steep precipice to the glacier's path with its dirty gray icy walls. On the floor were several sink holes and an ice cave beckoned from the opposite wall. Being thirsty on the way down, we enjoyed drinking fresh rain water trapped in broad, cupped leaves. Halfway down the trail we met four California tourists who asked if they would find a coffee shop at the top. We had to report that the trail became even more rugged. Before coming to the top, they would have to push through shoulder-high vegetation as we had done. No coffee shop, we informed them, no bottled Coke, but they should sample the rain water captured in the leaves. This brought a very disgusted expression to their faces. As they would learn—sooner or later—New Zealand is not commercial like California.

Before leaving this area and returning to the coast, we decided to drive over to the Tasman Glacier, the largest in the world. It was a cold day with heavy mist when we started out. After about 15 miles on a rough unpaved road across flat land, the road narrowed to one lane and began its steep ascent. The higher we went, the thicker the fog. Finally we arrived at the end of the road. We parked the car—having left the trailer back where the road narrowed—and began walking up a steep trail. By the time we reached the summit, the fog had completely closed in. Where we should be able to view the glacier was only an opaque fogbank! At this altitude, after climbing, we were panting. Breathing in the cold air was painful. Here we stood in the midst of fog. Thanks to the forest service, a plaque showed the glacier and all visible peaks. From where we stood 180 years ago one could step onto the glacier! Now the glacier is 500 feet below! All glaciers are receding at an astounding rate giving credence, some believe, to be the "green house" effect.

In Dunedin just a few blocks from the city's center, we found a wonderful camp on a stream. It had lovely showers and a lounge with a piano that was in tune! I had been playing for perhaps ten minutes when a man walked up to me. We started talking and I learned Garvin was a flutist with the Christchurch Orchestra. For the next three days we had regular sessions in the evening, sight reading music we found there.

Rain plagued us—from drizzle to downpour—so much rain in fact that we could actually see the stream rise. Fortunately Dunedin has attractions suitable for soggy weather. Its museum houses a top-notch collection of South Pacific artifacts. A break in the weather the second day permitted us time to visit the botanical gardens and aviary. The garden truly had something for everyone: native New Zealand bush, Australian plants, trees from all over the world, an herb garden with every plant mentioned in Shakespeare, a rose garden, a glass house cactus garden, an indoor fern garden, an alpine garden. We had lunch at the garden restaurant overlooking scads of ducks and sea gulls busily swimming, screeching and quacking in the pool and on the grass.

After three days in these environs we said our farewells to Garvin and Marion. In the morning rain, we collapsed our tent and in lingering fog, we drove to Otago Peninsula where we had made reservations to visit the royal albatross colony. These birds at Taiaroa Colony are the only albatrosses breeding on the New Zealand mainland. Their location has made it necessary to protect the birds from a host of threats including outright vandalism (the theft of eggs, stonings of nest, birds and eggs) and predators such as cats, dogs and ferrets. Protection has continued since 1937. Today there are 11 or 12 albatross pairs in residence each year. Since albatrosses breed in alternate years, this means that over 20 pairs have adopted Taiaroa Head as their breeding grounds. It is an informative visit with the guide and a good video revealing many interesting facts about these magnificent birds. We saw four adult birds and one chick. The birds mate for life, but not until they are eight or ten years old. The oldest known albatross is 60 plus years old. A mature bird weights between 14 to 18 pounds, has a wing span of 9 to 10 feet, and can fly up to speeds of 120 kilometers per hour!

While on the Otago Peninsula, we also went to another area to visit a seal and a yellow-eyed penguin colony. This entailed playing a minimal fee to the farmer on whose land these creatures live and obtaining a key from him so we could enter his property. After driving uphill and across sheep and goat paddocks, we came to the other side of the peninsula to two bays. In one, with pounding seas crashing over an outcrop of rocks and ledges on a tiny island just off shore, 10 or 15 fur seals were basking.

In the next cove, a wide, white beach with tall sand dunes lay totally inaccessible 400 or 500 feet below us. Looking carefully through binoculars, I finally spotted some strange tracks leading up the sand dunes. At the end of one set stood a yellow-eyed penguin, an endangered species. Slowly my eyes picked up other specks dotting the hillside. Even through the binoculars they were difficult to see. It was disappointing.

After a very noisy night camped on the "village green" at Portobello, (noisy because the young males met here for a rugby match but spent more time in the meeting house boasting and drinking beer) we drove for half a day to Curio Beach. The attraction here is a petrified forest on the beach in the surf. We arrived at the ideal time, low tide, so we could view the logs and whole trees that had fallen here 160 million years ago.

Nearby we found an extraordinarily beautiful primitive campground. To add protection from the wind, the forest service has cut places out of the native flax, a plant that grows quite tall. Inside these places, a tent is well protected from the wind. Our site had ocean on two sides. To the front, on a ridge, we overlooked the petrified forest and fantastically formed rocks around which swirled masses of bull kelp.

On an after dinner walk on the rocks, Joy spotted a lone penguin. I got within about ten feet of it and could see that it was moulting. At first I thought it was a yellow-eyed penguin, but after studying it, I decided it was a yellow-crested penguin. The bird remained in the same spot on the rocks for the two days we were there. We looked for but never saw another of its kind here.

Our next destination was Bluff, the southernmost point of land on the South Island. Just a few miles south of Foveaux Strait lies Stewart Island. With only a few more weeks left to see the west coast of the South Island, cross Cook Strait and drive back to Auckland, we had to forego a ferry trip to Stewart Island.

It was summer when we came to Buff, nonetheless it was raining and very cold. During the night, hard, gusty winds rattled the tent with fury. When the weather showed no improvement the next day, we packed up the tent and drove northward to Fjordland. We drove most of the day, and as we came inland and into the foothills, the weather improved. In sunshine, sparkling rivers and streams gurgled through forested valleys. Toward the end of the day about halfway on the road to Milford Sound, we camped in a lovely wilderness area, Deer Flat, right on the river under graceful, silver beeches.

A curious and friendly little South Island robin flew right up to us as soon as we got out of the car. Once the tent was up, it flew inside and landed beside me on the bed, having no fear. It became our constant companion. Before dinner we took a short walk along the river and were fortunate to see four paradise ducks only 100 yards away. We built a fire outside, but periodic, misty clouds and sprinkles caused us to abandon the fire, having left some potatoes to bake in the coals. When the sun slipped behind the towering mountains, a penetrating chill drove us inside the tent where we made a vegetable dish on the indoor propane stove. Into this extravaganza we put fresh field mushrooms, fresh pea pods, broccoli, onions, garlic and fresh ginger root. Our kerosene lantern not only provided light but gave off enough heat to keep the tent cozy on chill evenings.

A medium heavy rain continued through the night. By morning the world of green trees and cottony clouds drifting across a blue sky was only a memory. The monotonous plop, plop of rain on the tent and in the trees was disconcerting. We had wanted to push on to Milford Sound today. I stuck my head outside to have a look. The distant mountains were wrapped in a silver curtain of rain, haze, fog. The little robin called out and even flew over to me. On the ground around the tent stood three or four inches of water, puddling where it ran off the tent. It was cold. I told the robin I wouldn't be out to play. Naturally we had to cook something for breakfast and then run the lantern for light and warmth. That was our downfall. It was only a matter of time before the heat caused condensation on the metal tent poles. These wetted the roof of the tent, in time causing it to become saturated and leak.

As the day progressed, more and more drips appeared. We spent the day trying to read amidst all our pans scattered over both beds to catch steady streams of rain. It was a losing battle. Both beds and bedding were becoming waterlogged! We kept hoping the rain would let up. It didn't. Our tempers had flared and then smoldering anger settled in my bones with the dampness. Milford Sound gets in excess of 300 inches of rain a year. I grumbled that it was getting 100 that day!

By four in the afternoon we had had enough wet and cold. We collapsed the tent. Soaked through, despite rain gear, we drove back down to Te Anau, and with hoards of other wet tenters took a room for the night. We got the last available room.

It was still raining the next day. We abandoned the plan to go to Milford Sound. Instead we drove on to Queenstown for a look. Too tourist oriented for us, we continued on to Arrowtown. In earlier days, it had been a gold mining center. We found a camp and rented a hut because our tent beds were soaked. A very considerate manager offered his boiler room to dry out our foam pads. It took two days. In the meantime it snowed. The freshly covered mountains provided a spectacular view from our door.

From Arrowtown we began our ascent through mountainous terrain thick with beech and waterfalls streaking down through dark green forests. Often in clearings we saw rainbows, sometime double ones. We discovered a wonderful camp, Cameron Flat, again by the side of a rapidly flowing river. Not long after settling in, two bikers set up camp nearby. We talked with the woman from Montana who mostly biked alone on an 18-speed mountain bike.

By morning the rain was steady and the air was wintery. Reluctantly we packed up the tent. It was the end of February and we were running out of time. We drove away heading for Haast Pass through steep, rugged country. What splendor! Every few miles high waterfalls rushed down sheer walls of rain forest. Several times we stopped to walk and admire, listen to roaring falls, feel the gentle rain and absorb some of the energy of rapidly running rivers. Often little fantails rushed out to greet us.

Reaching the west coast, we drove on to Fox Glacier Camp. The rain got heavier as the day progressed. Not wanting to get our recently dried beds soggy again, we rented a hut at Fox Glacier. From our window we had a full view of the ice cap shining golden in the setting sun.

Amazingly the day dawned clear and bright. We were eager to drive to the glacier, but our car wouldn't start. A couple of hours later after being towed to the town garage for a quick fix, it was going again. We drove to the end of the road, passing waterfalls. After parking, we walked along the glacial river toward the base of Fox

Glacier. Its foot was dirty gray but higher up, patches of blue and green tinted the glistening ice and snow. Tributary streams rushed over boulders, eventually joining the river. We turned back only when a sign forbade going closer to the glacier because of danger from slides.

Our next stop was a camp in view of Franz Joseph Glacier. A narrow road through thick bush ended at a flat basin facing the glacier. Having exerted our energies on the former giant Fox Glacier, we sat in the car admiring this one and watching a *kea*, a native parrot, begging from anyone who came by.

The last of February found us at an almost new camp built and maintained by the National Park Service. It lies in a valley bordered on one side by tall cliffs and on the other by the Tasman Sea. Running along the edge of the camp is a fairly large river. Here the vegetation appears very tropical because of an abundance of nikau palms. The only palm native to New Zealand, it is shorter than a coconut palm. The crown, just under the fronds, is shiny green like a royal palm. The blossom of small berries starts out a bright yellowish-orange that eventually turns bright red. At Punakeiki, the nikau palms populate the hillsides along with thousands of tree ferns, both highly visible in the heavy rain forest. The tropical atmosphere with steep, jagged mountains looks much like Moorea. The big attraction here are the curiously formed rocks called "pancake" rocks. Punakaiki means "place of good eating," referring not to the rocks but to the abundance of shellfish.

The next two weeks were a collage of images and impressions. We visited Hokitika, the source of greenstone (nephrite) used extensively by the Maoris for making jewelry and ceremonial adzes, then on to Murchinson where we enjoyed the forest setting at Riverview Park and found an injured baby finch. Here early morning fog formed wisps that clung to the tops of cedars. The damp air smelled earthy, fertile. Bird songs spun out slowly, echoing in the damp interiors. At night strange forest sounds pierced the quiet. These sounds were palpable like the sharp edge of a knife pulled across velvet.

Along the road a visual feast of distant hills purple and blue, cream-colored sheep nonchalantly grazing, blackberry brambles heavy, buzzed by circling bees. Morning air that sparkled, its transparency cool, hinting of autumn. More native forests, thick and dark, delicately shaped silver beech poised like Japanese bonsai. Here and there streams frothing in song.

Waking in the morning, I noticed the warm temperature as the sun struck the tent and the smell of canvas. Bird songs, a symphony vibrating through pine needles in harmony with the rushing stream. Sparkling dew diamonds in the grass trod by drowsy sheep. Large farmsteads cradled by mountains, spreading into the distance an array of greens. Rows and rows of pines, evenly shaped, conforming to slanty hillsides. Alive, green, fluttering poplars in straight lines converging on the horizon, slightest yellowing, turning gold from frosty nights. Fall, creeping up.

Stops along the roadside to purchase farm fresh fruits and vegetables. Wonderful fresh corn, carrots, squash, peppers, cucumbers. On to fields of tobacco, corn and hops reaching skyward on trellises. Past sheep, cows, regal horses, their heads graceful and elegant. Intelligent eyes.

Racing ever onward at last to the sea again. A spectacular gold beach, a crescent bay of deep blue, gentle seas lapping the golden sands, sandstone boulders topped with trees. Hot summer days tempered by cool sea breezes. Then inland to Pelorus River, to wilderness tracks and waterfalls. A primeval forest of ferns, podocarps, mosses, liverworts.

Finally we were back in Picton, having completed our circle. Too late for the ferry, we camped for the night and withstood high winds that threatened to blow the tent away or rip it to shreds. After waiting in line most of the morning, we got on the afternoon ferry for Wellington. This passage was rough. Visibility was limited.

It was raining on the North Island when we pitched our tent in Lower Hutt alongside the river. Bad weather continuing and our time running out, we decided to drive straight from Wellington to Auckland. We called Joyce to tell her we'd be arriving late. Late became later when we blew a tire on the trailer and then the car started cutting out. We found a mechanic after hours. He discovered a loose wire from the distributor to the coil. Finally around 10 P.M. we pulled into Joyce and Jim's driveway. Joyce had our beds made and dinner ready. Though richer for many experiences in the South Island, we were very happy to be home again, back with good friends on familiar turf.

Chapter 21

Song of the Oyster Catcher

The plan we developed while still in Fiji was to spend a year in Auckland so Joy could find a teaching position to earn some money. This lengthy break would also give me time to write.

For once we had decided to play first and work later. After returning to Auckland from the South Island, Joy and I had a week to repack our bags and fly back to the States for a month to visit family and friends. By mid-April we were back in Auckland living aboard *Banshee* on the hard at Half Moon Bay boatyard.

Since the second week in January, *Banshee* had been sitting there in a cradle looking a bit forlorn stripped of her mast and most of her gear. Although the security at Half Moon Bay is good, we didn't want to take unnecessary chances. Prior to leaving for the South Island, our Kiwi friends Hilton and Melva had helped us load sails, lines, radios, navigation gear—virtually anything that could be unfastened—into their truck. For five months they stored our valuables in their home.

Now the hard work lay before us. We scraped and sanded the spars day after day. Then we began the prep work for painting with a two-part epoxy paint. Just the time the spars were ready for paint, the lovely summerlike weather—which had continued for an unprecedented two weeks—was a thing of the past. Huge black clouds covered the sky, bringing rain and gales. Each day the painter we hired to spray the spars grumpily reported that the weather ruled out painting.

This holdup did not mean that Joy and I could sit back and twiddle our thumbs. We had another important job to do—replace all the rigging wire. The wire was only eight years old, but the roller swages are the parts most likely to give way, long before the wire. There are several problems with swages. Salt accumulates between the swage and the wire. Eventually the swage develops hairline cracks—almost impossible to detect—which can cause a rigging failure. Before leaving Fiji, Joy had gone aloft to examine the swages. We also checked out the deck ends as well. We found no damage but after eight years—three of which were heavy ocean sailing—we were wary. Many dismastings result from a swage failure. In fact, our suspicions were well founded. Once we had the rigging off, we found three cracked swages.

We had decided to do away with swages altogether since they have a relatively short lifetime. Additionally, if they do fail at sea, there's no way to replace them until you reach a boatyard that has a roller swaging machine. Finding one in most of the ports we visit is about as likely as finding a mink fur hanging on a coconut tree. Considering all of these problems, we chose to use an English-made fitting called Sta-Lok. These fittings are designed so that one can readily monitor what is happening and with simple hand tools one can easily make repairs even at sea.

We also went to a larger size rigging wire. We asked the riggers at the yard to teach us how to connect the Sta-Loks, assuring them we would pay for the time it took. They expressed shock that we would consider doing the rigging ourselves but agreed to show us what to do. The instruction took all of ten minutes! But the real boon was that they offered to let us make up the stays in their shed. This made life more pleasant, giving us a clean, dry place inside in which to work.

In the midst of all this, Joy was going out on job interviews. Before leaving for the South Island, she had made preliminary efforts, contacting school principals and writing letters to them enclosing copies of her academic credentials. Additionally she sent transcripts, degree certificates and letters of reference from former principals to the Department of Education in Wellington so they could evaluate her experience.

Of course she needed to have a work permit before she could be hired—and herein lies a Catch 22. No one can get a work permit without first having a job. Joy was able to overcome this formality by having a principal who wanted to hire her and who went to bat for her. Because of his efforts, they plowed through the bureaucratic quagmire. It was a frantic time with Joy washing off the boatyard grime and spiffing up for interviews. Meanwhile I plodded along doing various jobs and falling into bed exhausted each night.

One day Joe, the painter, actually sprayed the final coat of paint on the spars. Before he had finished, the wind came up from the wrong direction blowing hundreds of fluffy tufts of pampas grass all over the wet paint. This meant resanding and preparing the surface again.

By now the wet weather had set in. Again the two riggers came to our rescue by arranging with their company to let us use one of their sheds for painting. Since the shed was not on the premises, it meant they had to transport our spars the ten miles to the shed on a specially articulated trailer that was meant to carry masts. So away they went and away we went following the mast down the road.

Then there was sanding down the bottom of the boat before applying new antifoul paint. Being about fifty percent copper, this paint is extremely poisonous. In order to minimize the hazard, one should sand the bottom wet, continuously hosing water over the surface. Joy volunteered for this distasteful job. Once completed I wanted to begin painting but the rain persisted. Finally all our jobs were done except the bottom. Totally frustrated I started applying paint—between rain squalls.

Eventually, everything completed, *Banshee* was launched. Her mast had been restepped and the damage to our dining table when the mast came below decks too fast had been repaired. We were ready to go up the Tamaki River to the pile mooring we had rented for a year. Joy had to go to work on the day we were ready to go. John Neave, a New Zealand friend, offered to come with me. I was very happy he came. I didn't know the river beyond Half Moon Bay at all. Although the channel is marked, it narrows in many places. My biggest concern, however, was mooring between two piles—something I had done only once in a flat calm. With the strong tidal current in the Tamaki—three to four knots—and the wind blowing 15 knots, I was overjoyed to have John's help. His wife, Nita, also took the morning off, driving her car up the Tamaki to meet us at our destination.

It was nothing short of miraculous that Joy and I had access to the Tamaki mooring. Six months before, while still in the Bay of Islands, we had met the owners of the mooring. We told them our plan to remain in Auckland for a year. They asked if we'd be interested in renting their mooring. Technically the Auckland Habour Board does not allow liveaboards except in the Tamaki, so their offer was good. For two to three months, marinas will overlook liveaboards, but this means moving frequently. Marina slips are expensive and our aim was to save money. So the Hall's offer to rent us their mooring was music to our ears. What we didn't know then was that Joy would end up getting a teaching position at Tamaki College, only a five-minute drive from our mooring!

The mooring was directly opposite the Panmure Yacht and Boating Club. Thanks to their policy of welcoming cruising boats, we were able to become members of the club for a small monthly fee and use the club's facilities which include hot and cold showers, restaurant/bar, dock with water and diesel.

Even though in the last three or four decades Auckland and other towns have grown up around the Tamaki River, it remains an attractive area. Tragically the river itself is polluted. To the east the river empties into the Tamaki Strait and to the west into the Waitemata Harbour. Going south, the river winds its way past rolling hills, gradually narrowing at its upper end. Except for a small sliver of land blocking its exit, it would flow into the Tasman sea. This spot is the shortest distance on earth between two oceans.

To both Maoris and early European settlers, the Tamaki Estuary played an important role. Before there were any roads, the river was a major artery, affording access in a few hours from the mainland to any of the many islands and harbors in the Hauraki Gulf. Apart from a narrow channel running the length of the river, much of it dries at low tide. In former times these mud flats provided an abundance of shellfish. In earlier days the rich land to the west of the river was heavily farmed. Today the communities of Panmure, Tamaki, Glen Innes and Bucklands Beach continue to sprawl over the land bordering the river.

The river itself has become a popular area for mooring yachts and launches. Several yacht clubs established along the shore serve several thousand boats clustered along the Tamaki. Despite human encroachment, there is still much open space and a pastoral atmosphere. Grassy shores and trees stretch for miles along its banks and the region attracts a host of birds that live, feed and breed here. The estuary has been declared a bird sanctuary.

For us it is these inhabitants that make the Tamaki such an interesting place to live. I have seen ducks—both the indigenous New Zealand grey duck and mallards, who may be migratory or permanent settlers—several gulls (the large black back, the smaller red billed, the grey billed species), white faced herons, pied stilts, pied shags (cormorants), kingfishers, terns and oyster catchers.

On a still day you can wake to a concert of bird chatter, the noises of feeding, mating and fighting. Over it all rings the high cheep, cheep trill of the oyster catcher.

From the beginning, Bernard, the owner of the Lane Motor Boat Company who manages our mooring, warned us against parking our car overnight in the yacht club parking lot. He assured us it would be stolen. He offered us a place at his yard behind a wall snugged away in a jungle of ginger plants. He thought the car would not be seen here from the street. But it was. About two weeks later we ascended the steep hill early one morning to find someone had broken into our car. The ignition wires were hanging like a mass of dead worms. Fortunately the attempt at hot wiring had failed because we had a kill switch and a battery isolator switch that foiled the would-be thief. Trevor, the mechanic at Lane's, a sort of self-appointed gnome who looked out for the two American yachts-women, took Joy to school and called an auto electrician to fix our car.

The attempted theft made us feel very vulnerable.

Unexpectedly our situation changed not too long after that. One day someone rowed up to our boat to say hello. What a surprise. It was Ian Carline. Three years previously we had met Ian and his wife, Ngaire, in Papeete. After a ten-year circumnavigation they had come back to New Zealand, their home. Their boat was moored just up the river from ours. Their house was just up the road from the yacht club. In the course of our conversation, we mentioned the problem with our car. Ian said he had a solution. We could park in his neighbor's yard.

Ian introduced us to Enid and Bert Emtage, two wonderful New Zealanders in their seventies. This was the beginning of a very special relationship that blossomed into a warm and comfortable friendship. From the beginning Enid and Bert seemed to like us, probably because they too have a strong love of the sea. Bert comes from a family of fishermen. He grew up on a tiny island next to Kawau Island. As a boy he learned about ships and the sea. When he married Enid, a farm girl, he taught her boat handling. Together they spent many years fishing—to augment his income from a regular job—and pleasure boating in the Hauraki Gulf. They had four children and their son George built a trimaran in their yard. He was the first New Zealander to qualify to race a trimaran offshore. He sailed to New Caledonia, the Solomons and Australia.

Still living in the same house for over fifty years, Enid and Bert farm almost the entire portion of their property and thus supply most of their own food. An inventor at heart, Bert can take anybody's cast-off junk and make something useful of it. There's nothing he can't repair or improve. Enid's ingenuity extends to beautiful flower arrangements she creates from the inexhaustible variety she grows to creating acrylic paintings of landscapes and seascapes. As we've learned, she always has time in her busy schedule to help solve even the most mundane problem, to chat and to serve a cup of tea with homemade bickies.

About two weeks after we came up the Tamaki, winter began. Our New Zealand "chip stove" is a kind of miniature fireplace which burns wood or coal. Though an antique, it proved its merit daily. Without its heat, our bodies, so acclimated to a tropical climate, would not have survived the Antarctic airs. Some mornings we could have ice skated on our decks!

By burning 50 to 70 pounds of coal every ten days we combated the bone-aching coldness. But it was messy. After a month or so our white bulkhead had grayed.

With Joy's work schedule, we arose around 6 A.M. The first one up on cold mornings, amidst vigorous protestations and loud expletives, piled up the coal and lit the fire. Most days I stayed aboard writing, only leaving the boat on *Nessie* to drop Joy off at the dock in the morning and pick her up in the evening. During the day I kept the fire burning.

The worst of the New Zealand winter on the Tamaki is not the cold. It is the gales, a steady procession of lows that sweep across the country one after the other. The Tamaki is a corridor. Gales coming across the Tasman funnel right up the river. A cold wind of 50 knots cuts deep and quick. As the gales charged through, they beat the shallow river into sharp peaks. To get *Nessie* to the dock, we had to slam through this mass of steep seas for half a mile.

Crossing in 50-knot gusts one day, Joy seriously thought she wouldn't see the other side. One afternoon I crossed in a steady 45-knot wind. In a full set of foul-weather gear, I sat in the bottom of the dinghy to achieve the greatest amount of stability. As the seas were abeam, I could not always steer a straight course. I watched for the biggest seas, then steered directly into them. In this zigzagged fashion, I finally reached the dock where Joy stood with her feet firmly planted, defying the horrendous winds. I handed up her foul-weather gear and got a wry smile. I fully expected her to say she would stay ashore or suggest that we both stay ashore. She didn't. Determined, she got in and we slogged our way back, spray flying everywhere.

The weather greatly curtailed our ability and our desire to socialize. Sometimes, on weekends when a gale or storm hit, we were boat bound. Crossing the channel for any reason didn't seem worth the risk. Theft or the threat of it also dampened our desire to leave the boat after dark. Only a few days after coming onto our mooring, eight boats nearby were broken into. For several months we declined all invitations that would keep us out past dark.

I began to feel like a prisoner and to resent my servitude. Gradually we met several other liveaboards. They advised that it was reasonably safe to go away on nights when the yacht club bar was open, if you returned around 10 P.M. when it closed. We tried it, leaving a light on inside and the radio playing.

While the yacht club was only five minutes from Joy's school, our procedure for getting ashore and fetching the car took considerably longer. First, there was the dinghy ride ashore. In good weather with absolutely perfect conditions and a healthy outboard, the half-mile crossing from our boat to the dock would take ten minutes. But this was New Zealand winter. Seldom were the conditions optimum. Usually the wind was whistling up rough water, allowing us to creep along at a wet snail's pace to avoid drenching ourselves. Sometimes, especially after continuous rain, the outboard would only run at very low RPMs. It would cough and sputter, a sure sign that it had water in its carburetor. Cleaning the carburetor required 30 minutes or longer. Even at its worst, though, the little two-horsepower Suzuki never let us down completely. (It certainly has proved far superior to the outboard it replaced, the Tohatsu that came to an ignominious end in Huahine where it burst into flames and self-destructed within five minutes.)

Once ashore, we then had to walk two long blocks to Enid's house. Often we were laden down with jugs, books and packages of one sort or another. Pushing against the wind and splashing through puddles, we usually arrived after about a ten-minute walk.

Now we had to dig the garage key out of a container hidden the flower bed. Before starting the car, we opened the hood and switched on the battery isolator switch. The routine inside the car was to reach down and under the dashboard to flick on that switch. Next, pull out the choke and hope it would start. On cold mornings it usually required three or four attempts before the old engine coughed noisily and then came to life. Once backed out of the garage with the engine off, we'd raise the bonnet and check the water and oil. In this old car, checking the fluids was absolutely essential as it seemed to guzzle everything put into it. Now at last, after 20 to 30 minutes we were ready for the five minute drive to Tamaki College.

For the most part once Joy started teaching we became basically land-based although we lived aboard. By May, most of our friends who had come to New Zealand had left, heading for new horizons. Before that we had said good-bye to many of our friends in Fiji who were not returning to New Zealand. It was kind of lonely with no cruisers around.

One day I decided to drive into Auckland and visit Bob and Sally on *Sylvia*. As I was walking down the dock to their boat, who should I see but Margaret, *La Dam de Mer!* I had heard she was in Auckland but had not seen her. We spotted each other at about the same time. With a loud squeal, she half-danced, half-flew toward me. And she was talking non-stop, a hundred questions at once. She came aboard *Sylvia* with me and filled me in on the events of her life.

She had been in New Zealand for two years freelance writing, mostly for a local boating magazine. Shortly after arriving in this country, she had found a boat builder who would build a 30-foot steel yacht for her at a price she could afford. But alas, another tragic setback; before completing the boat, the chap had gone bankrupt. So, for some time her boat had remained uncompleted. Meanwhile Margaret was looking for a sponsor to finish the boat and support her while she continued her circumnavigation.

In May we saw George and Jan from *Io* on their brief layover between Australia and the States. A month later George returned for a two-day stop in transit to Brisbane. Jan was not with him. The split came as no surprise to anyone. George had always said their 27 years of marriage had been a continuous battle. He will continue cruising and Jan will make a new life ashore.

We also lost another cruising friend. A few months into the new year we were surprised to have a letter from Marie telling us Milt had died unexpectedly in Brisbane in the hospital. *Moonchild* was shipped back to the States, and Marie, having found a compatible friend, was continuing to sail westward.

In July, I was invited to speak to an audience of 350 to 400 women at the Auckland Travel Club, telling them about our Pacific meanderings. How very English they looked decked out in hat and gloves! As Enid expressed it, they are "toffy" women. Dressed to the teeth as they were, they treated me graciously, totally accepting me in my typical winter attire—a pair of cords and plaid wool shirt.

Their enthusiasm and intelligent questions at the conclusion of my talk thrilled me. I realized that in an audience of American women in the age range of 50 to 75, few would give a tinker's damn about our Pacific voyage. Why was this group different?

I thought about it and concluded that it is because New Zealand is really a seafaring nation. One out of every five persons owns a boat. Being an island nation means that almost everyone lives in sight of the ocean. Everyone here has had some experience in a boat—be it a row boat or an interisland ferry. Everyone has close friends or family who have sailed locally or offshore. So, sailing or "yachting" as they call it here, is commonplace and something everyone knows enough about to carry on an intelligent conversation.

Perhaps there is another factor, too. New Zealand is still a young country and the older generation is very much in touch with their pioneer past. Instilled in these women is a strong sense of independence and self-sufficiency. Many of them raise their own vegetables and plant outstanding flower gardens even though they live in the midst of a cosmopolitan city. For this reason they are interested in other women whose experiences require independence.

In the midst of winter gales, it seemed the cold, short days would never end. Most of my days were spent aboard, but for diversion I had joined Joyce Irving in going to a watercolor painting class once a week. On the phone I told Ernestine Maddox, the art teacher—a petite woman probably in her seventies, that I was a "rank beginner." Even so, she accepted me in her class. All my life I have yearned to be able to draw natural things and have felt watercolors to be the most delicate and expressive form of graphic art. But I felt I had no talent. I appreciated Ernestine's patience. Under her guidance my eyes and hands were being trained.

In class Ernestine placed flowers and leaves in vases or around the table for the students—never more than eight in her studio—to paint. My early assignments were painting leaves and stems, exercises to acquaint me with color and to learn brush control. Outside of class I tried to spend some time each day drawing and sketching. The weather prohibited most attempts to do anything outside in winter.

Then spring burst upon New Zealand. Everywhere life was budding, sprouting. Poplar trees and willows began showing fringes of green; apple trees lining the streets became masses of pink flowers. Out of the ground came such a rich variety of forms and colors. I told Enid about my art classes and she often gave me bunches of flowers to paint and turned her sunporch over to me as a studio. On good days I could sit in her garden where there were endless vistas to paint and sketch. A painter herself, Enid seemed to take pleasure in critiquing my attempts. She always gave solid, sound suggestions and I enjoyed the exchange when we talked about color, perspective, shadow, shade and so on.

As I write this, our New Zealand experience is coming to an end, but our cruising will continue. In our final months in New Zealand we'll be directing our energies primarily toward finishing all the projects on *Banshee* to prepare for our next passage. Sometime between mid-April and mid-May we'll leave for New Caledonia. From there we'll cruise Vanuatu and the Solomon Islands, for the first time getting off the set track—the milk run. Vanuatu and the Solomons, being less developed than other island nations we have visited, promise new insights, different tradition, art and customs. Basically we'll be leaving behind the Polynesian peoples as we enter into a predominantly Melanesian world.

Four years afloat have whetted our appetites. Cruising is a viable lifestyle and for me at this point in my life far more motivating and invigorating than being tied down to one place. I look forward to the newness and challenges of each day. As our friend George on *Io* is fond of saying: "When I get up each morning, I have no idea what the day holds in store for me. That's what I like about cruising."

George's words epitomize this lifestyle. There are so many variables and so many unknowns because of people, places, events.

One of the most appealing aspects to me about cruising is the kind of friendship and camaraderie that develops. Even though our contacts may be rare and limited, the bond of friendship persists. Our tracks may cross and crisscross many times in many places and then one day we separate, going different directions. We may never see each other again, but, we'll never forget what we've shared, and just maybe one day as we come into a little secluded cove, some place at the far reaches of the world, we will find them again, anchored at our destination.

Editor's Note

Women at the helm crossing oceans or sailing around the world are becoming less unusual every day. Many of the most celebrated sailors since the 1950s have been women. Here are some of the record breakers and pioneers.

Ann Davison, the first woman to sail alone across the Atlantic in 1952 in her 23-foot *Felicity Ann.* (The boat that was bought and rebuilt by Jeannine's friends Margie Anderson and Mary Thompson from Alaska, who visited *Banshee* in Moorea. Chapter 9.)

Ingeborg von Heister crossed the Atlantic alone in her trimaran *Ultima Ratio* in 1969 and again in 1970. **Nicolette Milnes-Walker** sailed solo across the Atlantic in her 30-foot sloop *Aziz* in 1971.

In 1969, **Sharon Sites Adams** became the first woman to cross the Pacific alone, from Yokohama to San Diego, in her 31-foot ketch *Sea Sharp II.*

Clare Francis made an outstanding Atlantic crossing in 1973, and when she entered the 1976 OSTAR race, she set a record for the fastest crossing by a woman, just less than 29 days. She was a remarkable 13th out of 121 starters.

Marie-Claude Fauroux, Teresa Remiszewska, Anne Michailof and **Ida Castigliani** have all completed single handed OSTAR races across the Atlantic in recent years. Although **Judy Lawson** and **Rachel Hayward** failed to finish their OSTARS, both were very close to the finish line when forced to abandon the attempt.

Other women who have crossed the Atlantic alone are **Florence Arthaud, Amy Boyer, Brigette Aubry, Anne Miller** and **Margaret Hicks**. (Margaret Hicks is the *La Dame de Mer* in Chapter 9 whom Jeannine and Joy met in Cook's Bay, Moorea.)

Annette Wilde sailed the Tasman Sea, and **Noriko Kobay-ashi** and **Linda Weber-Retti** sailed alone across the Pacific.

The first woman to circle the globe singlehanded was **Krystyna Chojnowska-Liskiewicz** from Poland. She sailed her 31-foot boat *Mazurek* east to west via the Panama Canal in 1976-78.

The first lone woman to circumnavigate by way of Cape Horn was New Zealand-born **Naomi James** who finished the voyage in 1978. She sailed the 53-foot *Express Crusader*. **Brigitte Oudry** also circumnavigated alone later that same year, taking the same eastward route as James in her 34-foot sloop *Gea*.

Also remarkable are the voyages of two Australian women who sailed mostly solo but occasionally had others with them. **Ann Gash** (whom Jeannine and Joy met in Opua, New Zealand) sailed nearly around the world in 1977; she sustained severe damage from a collision and had to ship her 26-foot *Ilimo* back to England. Ann has made numerous other long-distance passages, including a two-way Pacific crossing, and may possibly have spent more time sailing offshore alone than any other woman.

The other Australian, **Julia Hazel**, has been cruising the world for more than 10 years in her 28-foot steel sloop *Jeshan*, which she built herself.

A French woman, **Janik Wakelam** singlehandedly circum-navigated from 1975-1983. She leisurely meandered around the world in *Jonathan* rounding the Cape of Good Hope in her small boat. (Joy and Jeannine met Janik and her husband Henry on their boat *Operculum*. Chapter 19.)

Tania Aebi, an 18-year-old American who set out from New York in 1985 and who finished her circumnavigation in her 26-foot *Varuna* in 1987, is the most recently celebrated circumnavigator and the youngest. (Tania was the good Samaritan who helped Jeannine and Joy find their dingy in a Pago Pago harbor when they all returned one night to find *Nessie*, the dingy, and Tania's oars missing. Chapter 10.)

In 1988, **Kay Cottee,** an Australian shipbuilder, became the first woman to circumnavigate non-stop. She sailed her 36-foot sloop *Blackmore's First Lady* around the world in 189 days.

Mother Courage Press salutes these women—and Jeannine Talley and Joy Smith—for their courage and their spirit of adventure.